Praise for
Digital Transformation Champions

"The key to successful digital transformation is disciplined execution and a structured path forward. *Digital Transformation Champions* delivers precisely that—a clear, actionable guide to upskilling a workforce equipped for the demands of digital evolution. With strategic insights and a step-by-step approach, this book ensures that every element is aligned for predictable and sustainable outcomes. For leaders committed to mastering the complexities of digital training, this is your playbook."

—TONY SALDANHA, global thought leader in digital transformation and author of *Why Digital Transformations Fail: The Surprising Disciplines of How to Take Off and Stay Ahead*

"Missy's holistic approach to training includes not just knowledge transfer but the multiple essential components that drive lasting business adoption. I've had the privilege of partnering with her in the trenches at Green Mountain/Keurig, where I saw firsthand how her grit, resilience, and deep understanding of the full learning ecosystem translate into this structured playbook. She strikes a rare balance between IQ—the right tools, technology, content, and measurement—and EQ—selecting and developing the right trainers, demonstrating authentic leadership, and cultivating strong stakeholder relationships. And she brings it all to life with stories and real-world examples that add color and credibility to every topic. It's a read that is both engaging and essential for anyone navigating the complex and multidimensional journey of digital transformation!"

—JENNIFER ENGELHARDT, digital transformation change expert

How to Design and Deliver a Training
Program That Achieves Business Results

DIGITAL TRANSFORMATION CHAMPIONS

MISSY PARKS

RIVER GROVE
BOOKS

Published by River Grove Books
Austin, TX
www.rivergrovebooks.com

Distributed by River Grove Books

Design and composition by Greenleaf Book Group
Cover design by Greenleaf Book Group
Cover image © Adobe Stock/Elaine

Publisher's Cataloging-in-Publication data is available.

Print ISBN: 978-1-63299-918-4

eBook ISBN: 978-1-63299-919-1

First Edition

To Cooper Miller and Lillie Miller, who have taught me most about joy and living life to its fullest, and to business learners, who determine the success of any digital transformation.

Contents

Introduction

"If you understand something you're passionate
about, you have an obligation to share it."
—Twyla Tharp, Choreographer

Training programs that support a digital transformation seem like they should be straightforward: People learn new tools to carry out redesigned processes to change how a business delivers customer value. Yet training success is not a given with digital transformations, where much can and will go wrong along the way. Unfortunately, this results in people ill-prepared to change. This book seeks to minimize the damage by giving digital transformation training leaders a holistic overview of planning and carrying out a learning program based on universal deliverables. My own and others' experiences, informed by research, show that training leaders who apply the set of concepts in this book see better learning results and lasting adoption of transformative business change. Those who focus on just a few elements of the whole experience mixed results. The goal is seeing a critical mass of people demonstrate their ability to use new systems and their knowledge of new processes. Designing and implementing a successful digital training program to achieve this goal is often challenging, but it is doable—and it's essential for realizing the promise of a digital transformation. It's about the people.

WHY DIGITAL TRANSFORMATION TRAINING PROGRAMS FALL SHORT

Digital transformations involving business system implementations and reengineered business processes are commonplace. Even so, consistent, successful learning outcomes continue to elude many project and business teams. This results in prolonged, painful hypercare periods after launch, or lack of adoption at worst, when there is no change. According to one recent report, 70% of implementations for over 900 applications faced challenges in seeing people use new tools and follow redesigned business processes (Whatfix, 2022). Research highlights that many digital implementations involve training gaps that become a root cause of failed business transformations (Phelan, 2012a; Duplaga and Astani, 2003; Wheatley, 2007). These data points make sense. When people don't feel ready for new ways of working or don't know how to use a new system to do their jobs, change remains inaccessible.

Part of what makes leading training for digital transformation challenging are the variables in every project and the training work itself.

- Off-the-shelf training materials usually don't exist for digital transformations. Customized training must be produced for processes, activities, and problem-solving *specific to a business*.

- A time crunch commonly occurs between training, system build, configuration, and testing milestones, especially for a first implementation.

- Project leaders may undervalue training, consider training as a late-stage activity, or think that having videos and job aids alone will see people adequately learn what they need to know.

- Business leaders may choose to outsource training to a vendor without understanding the implications or the scope of what success requires and who will do what.

- The training effort may be overemphasized and microscopically managed, often following a disastrous major deployment. This presents its own set of challenges.

- Managers, supervisors, and even learners may see training as an annoyance when there's a lack of leadership support or people are not given time away from their day-to-day work to learn.

- Business teams may insist on approaches for training or materials, schedules, and timing that inadvertently create difficulties for employees instead of bolstering their learning.

- Issues within a project, across the business function, and even with the company culture can change the ways in which a digital transformation training strategy gets carried out, despite agreed-upon plans.

All these elements show up in different ways with every program stage, and there's always something new. It's never the same. The business goals for the digital transformation, the technical solution, the business processes, the project team, the business leaders, the training team structure and skills, along with the variety of end users combine to create a unique set of circumstances. Yet despite all these variables, an effective digital transformation training effort must support the program and help realize the business return on investment. Achieving this requires a structured, holistic approach for the training plans, deliverables, work across multiple teams, and management of the interdependencies. *Digital Transformation Champions* helps with this by introducing the activities, the best practices, and the most effective techniques for how to navigate what gets in the way.

IS THIS BOOK FOR YOU?

Digital Transformation Champions is written for those tasked with training lead responsibilities and for business and project leaders vested in the people aspects of a digital transformation. Of course, ultimately, it is for the learners in digital transformations, as they are the ones who will benefit the most from a framework that helps the training team partner across the transformation and business teams. But before they learn from this framework, it needs to be built. Different project team members play the following roles in a digital transformation training program:

- *Digital transformation training leads* have responsibility and accountability for the training program. Those new to training lead roles will find in these pages a proven approach, useful models, and helpful guidance. Experienced training leads will find new ideas and tactics.

- *Digital transformation program and business leaders*, especially those taking on their roles for the first time, will benefit from recognizing the details required for digital transformation training success. These criteria are *especially* important to understand when the decision gets made to outsource the training effort to a third-party vendor or the solution provider.

- *Change management leaders* will learn to recognize how work with today-to-morrow changes, and stakeholder management can be coordinated to positively impact learner success. *Digital Transformation Champions* presents opportunities and ideas for partnering effectively with change, communications, and training efforts for best outcomes.

Each digital transformation team member has specific roles and responsibilities. *Digital Transformation Champions* organizes the related activities and the details about inputs and the work from others that is necessary for building materials, planning training, and helping to realize the intended outcomes a digital transformation promises.

WHAT EXACTLY IS THIS BOOK ABOUT AND HOW WILL IT HELP?

I chose the title *Digital Transformation Champions* for this guide because it focuses on the activities and teamwork to realize the winning outcome envisioned at the start of a business transformation. *Digital Transformation Champions* provides a model for leading a digital transformation training program in any industry, whether the tool being introduced is AI-based, a single-task solution, or a full-scale ERP. Upskilling a company's employees involves many moving parts and pieces that must come together at the right time. This book shows training leads and others how to realize more effective outcomes for their business learners, whatever the digital transformation—and how to track, measure, and predict learner success early on, before it's too late to change tactics.

Championing Digital Transformation Success

A fundamental tenet underscores *Digital Transformation Champions*: What's most important is *getting* things right, not being right. I believe most people start their day planning to achieve, not fail. Knowing this, training leaders are best served operating from the perspective that everyone's doing their best, all wish to succeed, and others on the program and from business teams will want to step up to help realize shared goals. Maintaining this outlook becomes difficult when timelines get compressed, when delays in design and build emerge, and when there's low accountability for on-time deliverables that the training team depends upon. However, a structured approach, knowledge about best practices, and recognizing ways to navigate the pitfalls will help training leads and others complete the work that sees people prepared for new ways of working.

HOW TO USE *DIGITAL TRANSFORMATION CHAMPIONS*

This book has twenty-one chapters; the first twenty are organized into three parts, with eleven samples to help you get started. The chapters are grouped into sections tied to the five essential digital transformation training deliverables.

Content

Each chapter begins with an overview about a topic and why it matters. Details follow in three parts: "Basics," "Best Practices," and then "What Gets in the Way" (and how to work smarter). Sample one-page dashboards and other tools illustrate the concepts and show ways to share the information with others. This handbook draws upon articles, books, videos, and studies about digital transformation training, including a comprehensive review of digital training and learner research findings in research I conducted (Parks, 2012). I also include examples and stories from my own training program experiences and those that colleagues have shared with me. What makes *Digital Transformation Champions* unique is how it ties all these resources together. By design, there's just enough information—data and stories—to explain why. You'll also benefit from DONAs, which stands for things Done Once and Never Again. Together, the chapters of *Digital Transformation Champions* present a structured approach for *planning and carrying out* a digital transformation training program that sees learners prepared for a go live—and the digital future beyond.

Section Groupings

The chapters in *Digital Transformation Champions* are organized by five universal training delivery milestones necessary for successful outcomes. Find these five sections of the book summarized in the following table.

Section Groupings

Delivery Milestone	Chapters	Samples
1. Project, business, and training leaders align on the digital transformation training strategy, activities, tools, and resources.	Ch. 1—Training Strategy for a Winning Digital Transformation Ch. 2—Learning Topics and Audience Insights for a Strong Foundation Ch. 3—Responsibility and Decision-Making Clarity Drive Success Ch. 4—Training Leadership for Lasting Impact Ch. 5—Equipping Project Teams with Core Knowledge Ch. 6—Funding Support for the Digital Transformation Training Program Ch. 7—Stakeholder Presentations That Make an Impact	*Sample 1*—Digital Transformation Training Program Checklist *Sample 2*—Milestone Map and Training Timeline *Sample 3*—Vendor Checklist for Training Success *Sample 4*—Learner Audience Snapshot *Sample 5*—Stakeholder Connection Map *Sample 6*—Digital Transformation Training Status at a Glance *Sample 7*—Responsibility and Decision-Making Matrix
2. Training, practice, and learning materials are approved and ready for end user learning.	Ch. 8—Tools and Technologies to Power Training Ch. 9—Frameworks for Quality Content and Fast-Track Development Ch. 10—Blueprint for Developing Training Materials Ch. 11—Information Gathering with Subject Matter Experts Ch. 12—Quality Assurance Through Material Reviews and Approvals Ch. 13—Final Material Production with Editing, Translation, and Printing Ch. 14—Games to Engage Learners Ch. 15—Metrics for Learner Knowledge and Confidence	*Sample 8*—Training Material Development Tracker *Sample 9*—Learner Insights Survey

Delivery Milestone	Chapters	Samples
3. Risks are anticipated, reported, and managed.	*Ch. 16*—Training Dependencies as Boosters, Not Barriers	*Sample 10*—Training Preparation and Learner Readiness Dashboard
4. Training facilitators are onboarded and prepared to facilitate training and practice sessions, then support post-launch needs.	*Ch. 17*—Business Trainers as the Essential Factor for Transformation Success	*Sample 11*—Business Trainer Overview at a Glance
5. Training program execution, completion, and learner feedback are tracked and reported with regular dashboards, gaps actioned, and learned lessons captured.	*Ch. 18*—Progress Updates That Keep Leadership Informed *Ch. 19*—Learner Readiness Tracking and Reporting for Day One and Beyond *Ch. 20*—Training Closeout for Reflection and Celebration	*Updates to the earlier samples*

WHERE TO BEGIN

Training leaders have accountability for what the digital training program must deliver. The work involves much more than training materials created a month or so before going live. Building and maintaining our professional toolbox is ongoing, and *Digital Transformation Champions* is designed to help, wherever you are in your career and whichever phase of the digital transformation project.

- If you're new in a digital transformation training lead role, start with a chapter at a time. If the project is just launching, start with strategy and audience analyses. Build out the training plan on a page for your program.

- If you have a vendor coordinating your digital transformation training, start with the vendor checklist and review the relevant chapters. Think beyond the launch.

- If your digital training program is underway, refer to the section matching your next major milestone, perhaps tracking material development or working with functional trainers.

- If you're an experienced digital transformation training lead, reflect back on your last training project. Refer to the relevant chapters and review the best practices and ideas for working smarter to handle what can get in the way. You may confirm your own knowledge and perhaps recognize your own experiences.

A NOTE ABOUT WORDS AND TERMS

When working in this field, you'll run across a diverse set of terms that describe concepts related to digital transformation and training. Each program or business will label the same idea differently. For example, people pulled from the business and tasked with teaching and supporting their peers may be called *super users*, *power users*, *lead users*, *ambassadors*, *change agents*, *business trainers*, *functional trainers*, and so on. Similarly, the date when a business and people begin using new systems and working differently may be called a *go live*, a *launch*, an *implementation*, or a *deployment date*. To help readers use *Digital Transformation Champions*, there is intentionally descriptive text to explain terms and avoid confusion.

Project and *program* are used throughout to denote focused activities that have a beginning and end. Programs are larger, multi-project undertakings. Digital transformation training initiatives can be programs on larger transformations or projects for smaller implementations.

The phrase *digital transformation* itself deserves comment. For many, the words describe the implementation of large-scale software solutions to automate business operations. For industry visionaries, the phrase describes a multi-component, customer-focused ecosystem comprising the operational backbone and data structures, which *Digital Transformation Champions* addresses (MIT, 2022). It's taken decades to see acronyms like EMR and ERP replaced with a single phrase that has widespread meaning, so I embrace the broader understanding of *digital transformation* throughout this book.

WHY I WROTE *DIGITAL TRANSFORMATION CHAMPIONS*

Teaching people to use new systems to carry out their jobs differently is both my profession and passion. I've led a variety of technical transformations in my career and worked with just about 100 instructional designers (IDs), 1,000-plus functional trainers, and, indirectly, tens of thousands of learners. My journey has been rich in experience, and I've found greatest successes through partnerships with others. In my twenty-five-plus years of leading digital transformation training programs, I count myself very fortunate to have worked with exceptionally talented training colleagues and inspiring business leaders. Other significant learnings have come from the literature and testing leading practices in my own work. The challenges, constructive feedback, and exciting accomplishments have made mine an ongoing journey of continuous improvement. Along the way, mentors and industry thought leaders have generously shared their ideas with me. *Digital Transformation Champions* consolidates this collective wisdom. Others' experiences, and my own, are what I'm bringing to this book to help you benefit from knowledge about how to succeed with your own digital transformation training programs.

Above all else, what my career has taught me is that the true art of an effective digital training program involves pulling together what's known, identifying what's missing, and anticipating and course correcting around what comes up. *Digital Transformation Champions* presents commonsense, proven methods for organizing and advancing what matters and navigating the rest. Despite the variability and challenges of digital transformations, *Digital Transformation Champions* promotes a simple vision: Learning new business technology and processes can be effective, efficient, and even enjoyable for learners. After using the principles in this book in my own training programs, I've heard from people delighted with their digital training experience and excited to use a new system and work differently. Wouldn't it be great if this were the norm?

—Missy Parks

2025

Training Strategy for a Winning Digital Transformation

"Technology is nothing. What's important is that you have a faith in people, that they're basically good and smart, and if you give them tools, they'll do wonderful things with them."

—**Steve Jobs,** Apple Co-Founder and Visionary Technologist

The strategy provides a summary and overview of the digital transformation training program. A training strategy features two things: a compelling business-based vision for learning and enough specifics about the learners, the activities, and the key interdependencies to illustrate how all the parts of the training program enable the digital transformation. The training strategy is a shared story about building new process and system knowledge among the different people who make the transformation a reality. All leaders retell parts of this throughout the phases of the digital transformation program and all the related implementations. Repeated messaging about the ways that groups of people will learn about and be able to adopt new ways of working unites program and business teams behind a common cause so the transformation can succeed.

BASICS

A great strategy is a learner and business success map that gets repurposed and referenced continuously. The strategy starts with a training vision about preparing people to follow new processes and correctly use new tools. A digital transformation training strategy is a long-range plan that sets forth the philosophy and the major milestones needed to deliver the expected outcomes within a particular time frame. The training lead compiles the strategy, gathers the overall requirements, drafts the document, coordinates reviews, collects inputs, and, finally, secures approval to move forward from the appropriate stakeholders so planning and work get underway.

If you are the lead, often you will need to create this strategy. In some cases, a strategy may already exist, or an implementation partner may provide a model that gets tailored for the business, the culture, or the learner needs for one or a series of transformation launches. Whatever the starting point, this chapter covers how to describe the comprehensive learning program and the mechanics required to achieve the business transformation goals, one learner at a time.

In all cases, the training strategy includes key topics. The following checklist serves as an outline for thinking and information gathering. Details in the next chapters of *Digital Transformation Champions* delve even deeper so you can refine the strategy for *your* digital transformation training program.

Essentials for Your Strong Strategy

The following are general guidelines.

- *Purpose and audience for the training strategy.* The digital transformation leaders, all project colleagues, business stakeholders, and executives need to understand the big picture of transformation training and the partnership required to succeed. The training team members need to recognize the role each plays in the bigger picture of the whole program.

- *Vision for the training effort.* The training program fundamentally enables the business outcomes set forth in the digital transformation through effective, even enjoyable, learning experiences that have measurable outcomes.

- *Description of the learner audiences.* Explain the systematic process to identify groups of learners, their needs, and their training experience to help others see the scope of the transformation project in terms of the people.

- *Philosophy about adult learning relative to the digital transformation training program.* Let the project and business teams know about the documented needs adults have as they learn and practice new topics. The instructional designers (IDs) will keep these in mind as they design and create training materials. Those leading training and hands-on practice will prepare to meet these needs.

- *Training plans, deliverables, and the major milestones.* As the rest of the transformation program teams complete their tasks, what are the key training activities at a high level? Typically these might include material creation, reviews, and approvals; training schedule creation and approvals; pre-training communications; and post-training feedback and knowledge verification.

- *Training delivery options.* The strategy should note how end users will be trained. Will there be one mode or a blend of self-paced, instructor-led, virtual, in-person, or hybrid models? Who will lead any instructor-led training sessions? If functional business trainers, call out their selection, onboarding, and preparation in the major activities list. If consultant or professional trainers, this will incur a cost. In either case, the strategy must note it.

- *Measures of success that use business- and learner-focused language.* How should the project assess the training program? How will the training team measure its success? What are the measurable outcomes expected for training and demonstration of learning?

- *Expected catalog of the training content.* Identify the types and descriptions of the materials that will support learning during and after the transformation go live.

- *Tools and technologies.* Document the toolsets the training team will use to create, deliver, and track learning.

- *Key interdependencies.* Call out the deliverables that others provide that the training team and learners will need to learn to carry out their work. Activities and deliverables not produced by the team training directly affect end user learning. Examples include system and process changes during later stages of the launch, security role design, and security mapping of roles to people, among others.

- *Examples of summary plans on a page that will be produced.* These may include a sample of the learner groups or tracking and completion reporting to illustrate a commitment to communicate about the training work and its progress.

- *Risk management.* Note whether any unmet training needs will appear first in status or will be posted in the risks, actions, issues, and decisions (RAID) log. Escalating risks, highlighting issues, and noting decisions consistently will help ensure training is never a reason for a delay in the go live date.

- *Training team.* Use a tabular view or structured layout to illustrate workstream alignment with names, pictures, and callouts about how the team members will work together and with the project and business teams to generate the expected results.

- *Out-of-scope work.* Specify what the training lead and team are not expected or planning to do.

- *Sustainability considerations.* Address new learning needs and material updates. How will the training materials help people who are changing jobs and new hires who need to know business processes and how to use work systems? As systems or process changes occur, how will updates to the materials get made and what communications about these changes can be expected?

- *Optional: action plan and/or a work breakdown structure, if needed.* A high-level project plan of the major milestones, activities, and deliverables may need to be provided to the training team.

- *Optional: a responsibilities matrix.* Details about responsibility and decision-making for the training work may be helpful on some projects. Alternately, include a sample structure to communicate a willingness to use the tool to clarify roles and responsibilities.

The training leader designs and documents a holistic training program within the strategy, secures its sign-off, and then promotes the vision and teaches the network of digital transformation stakeholders about the plan, the activities, and how to work together to succeed.

BEST PRACTICES

Considerations and specific steps will aid training leads and others who develop a comprehensive digital transformation strategy draft in a week's time.

Clarify the Format and Review Process

Seek input from project and business leaders who will approve the strategy about the purpose and the finished format of the digital transformation training strategy. Will there be a formal review with a small or very large audience? Is a document or a slide deck expected, or possibly both? A fellow training lead sees value in having both because the slides are presentation-ready and reference the longer text where the details live. While I've done this, I see that detailed slides get the most views and others can repurpose the information more easily. Other training lead colleagues confirm a preference for strategy decks over documents.

Whether document or slide deck, do maintain a change control log and plan for updates annually or semiannually, and after major implementations.

Link Training to Business Results

Focus the training vision and strategy on achieving business results through effective learning experiences that see processes and systems used as designed. Cross-reference specifics in the digital transformation business case. For example, if the purpose of the transformation targets enhanced agility, speed, and data-driven decision-making, or improving customer experience or elevating profitability, note the topics and relevant activities as components of the training program. Ask the leaders of the digital transformation program for their goals as a starting point.

Focus on Learner Proficiency

Describe the purpose of the training strategy in terms of the activities that will prepare people to learn how to use new tools and processes. Emphasize that they will have time to practice—*before* the launch, while carrying out their regular jobs. Illustrate the multiple learning activities that see ability and confidence develop. Identify the support available during and after training. Learning involves more than a single training event.

Apply Adult Learning Principles

Describe how the digital transformation training program incorporates and meets the needs that adult learners have for acquiring new information and building knowledge in the workplace. Address how the design of materials, training delivery, practice, and certification activities support these goals.

- Hands-on practice develops learner ability and confidence and is a necessary component of a digital transformation training.
- Post-training tests and certification effectively demonstrate learner knowledge and ability, and thus function as quantitative demonstrations of progress toward the overall business expectations for go live readiness.

Drive Continuous Improvement

Document the milestones for structured reviews, feedback, and lessons-learned cycles within each training program phase. These inputs that lead to better ways of working and changes include project partners, subject matter experts (SMEs), business leaders, functional business trainers, and, especially valuable, the learners.

Customize the Strategy When Called For

A strategy is the starting point for the first few deployments of a digital transformation program and for subsequent implementation projects. Digital transformations continue for years and a lighter, tailored *approach* may provide a better overview for subsequent launches. An approach references the strategy, repurposes its elements, and explains benefits that the training program will deliver for a smaller implementation or different technology solution.

The approach is typically a deck that repurposes components of the strategy and updates other details about the people, business processes, and transformation adoption for a *specific transformation implementation*. As the training program repeatedly executes plans aligned with the strategy, the highlights are enough to remind business leaders of key aspects while focusing on the specific elements of training for an implementation.

Done well, an approach takes less time to create than a strategy. A tailored approach versus a general strategy will resonate with business executives and their teams so they understand training activities, timelines, and learner experiences specific to their functions. To illustrate the value, a Corporate 500 supply chain VP announced after a thirty-minute run-through of the overall training approach with specific emphasis on the transformation deployment for his organization, "Best training approach I've ever seen." This was a stakeholder who went on to relay the transformation training story to his leaders, and we secured broad support.

The following pages include a basic recipe for creating a digital deployment training approach by reusing or *recycling* from the strategy to support the implementation. Find notes about each component for the additional or *specific* details needed to tailor an effective digital transformation training program approach.

Training Overview and Planning

- *Recycle*—Digital Training Vision, Purpose, and Highlights

- *Recycle*—Digital Training Strategy Highlights and Lessons Learned from Previous Deployments

- *Specific*—Project Scope and Business Considerations Affecting Training Approach and Curriculum

- *Tailor*—Stages of Training by Learner Audience

- *Recycle*—Training Activity by Deployment Timeline

- *Specific*—High-Level Role-Based and/or Process-Based Curriculum Listing

- *Specific*—Audience Analysis

- *Recycle*—Training Material Components and Tools

- *Recycle*—A Role-Based Curriculum Example

Training Execution

- *Specific*—Timeline and Activities by Learners
- *Specific*—Training Team and Contacts by Process
- *Recycle*—Business Support and Functional Trainers
- *Recycle*—Training Technology—User-Facing Screenshots (e.g., learning management system and library of training how-to resources)
- *Recycle*—Training Metrics
- *Recycle*—Material Development Process and Milestones, Including Reviews and Approvals
- *Tailor*—Key Enablers, Dependencies, and Success Factors for End User Learning That Apply to the Launch

The Appendix When the Strategy Is Customized

- *Specific*—Deployment(s)—Detailed Audience Analysis (Process/Workstream/ Value Stream/Site or other logical organization for training planning)
- *Specific*—Curriculum Plan Detail
- *Tailor*—Training Roles and Responsibility Matrix, if needed

Summarize the Strategy with Dashboards

Two samples help provide high-level summaries about the digital transformation training program. Sample 1, Digital Transformation Training Program Checklist, details all of the key elements of a training program. Sample 2, Milestone Map and Training Timeline, describes major groups of work over the program timeline.

With a comprehensive strategy or tailored approach, there are some things that can challenge the training team. Recognize these as possibilities up front and design workarounds, or lean into them when they occur throughout the project.

WHAT GETS IN THE WAY

Some things come up regularly, and because every digital transformation project and combination of business functions and training team members are unique, some things come up regularly and other distinct issues will challenge the training team's ability to carry out its work. Knowing these and determining whether they could apply allow you to address them in your training strategy. The following are some of the most common situations you'll face. For each, I've included suggestions for getting around them by "working smarter."

Dealing with a "Training Comes Last" Mindset

"Training comes last" is what a few program leaders said when I requested information about solution decisions or worked to advance training activities when dates slipped. These words aren't a surprise since a focus on the system and testing can occur at the expense of people preparation. More than one book describes digital transformation training as a last-phase consideration (Cameron, 2009; Kapp, Latham, and Ford-Latham, 2001). However, the exact opposite is true.

Working Smarter: Training activities need to come earlier in the transformation process. Ask anyone who has had to develop materials while processes and technology are being defined about the value of early engagement *before* all the decisions get made. An ID explains, "It's so much more effective to be involved up front. Otherwise, there's never enough time with SMEs to answer all the questions about how the processes and system will work so I can design training and create materials." The strongest digital transformation training leader I've worked with repeated a mantra: "Training goes live first."

Training development work should parallel the late system build and solution confirmation or "fit gap" phases of the project timelines. For best outcomes, role- and process-based training material drafts get created and reviewed early while the business process teams are making decisions about the configuration and who will do what. ID questions are often especially helpful at this stage of the project, and it avoids duplicative meetings later on. To enable more effective collaboration that saves time and money, onboard and engage IDs with the work team members who are designing business processes and the solution. The goal is to avoid a tsunami of work later, when process team members lack the time to help, especially during a first implementation of a major transformation. As a Gartner best practice, training should have an early seat at the project table alongside the other technical and process team leads (Phelan, 2012a).

Lacking Cross-Functional Collaboration

Training work crosses multiple team and business areas. Close collaboration among all of them is required to get things done and see issues addressed to avoid delays. Gaps in cross-functional partnerships emerge early and may highlight differences in the way IDs carry out their work. In other cases, the process team and leads may be frustrated with solution design, build, or configuration, and even process decision-making, so they are unable to provide answers. These issues in working together slow material creation and can negatively impact the learners' experience and preparation to do their jobs.

Working Smarter: The training strategy should set forth a dependency for consistent, early engagement between business teams, process team experts, local contacts, and the training team. This dependency applies to specific activities, notably material development and training plans. Establishing a dependency from the start helps progress advance as far and as early as possible, without rework. Additionally, when delays occur, they need to be communicated, escalated, and managed in the interest of ensuring an on-time start of end user training.

Skipping Feedback on the Strategy

When you're presenting the training strategy to busy people who had a meeting before and will have another one after yours, it's important to be specific. Make it clear you're asking for feedback and suggestions, always. One program leader notably failed to help make the training strategy more relevant for others with a few simple word changes early on. While business leaders appreciated the strategy, it did not fully resonate with them. Eventually, the language changed based on later feedback.

The small details do matter when telling a story about the transformation and the activities that will pull people away from their jobs for hours at a time.

Working Smarter: While the drafting of a training strategy should take less than a week, plan to spend several more weeks discussing sections and collecting and incorporating feedback. Ask, "Do we understand the needs?" or "Does the strategy feel right?" Use the audience analysis and a stakeholder map to ensure you have feedback from all key stakeholders. Make it clear in your presentations that you're looking to enhance the strategy *draft* and count on feedback from others who know the business and the people—even when you do too. Factor into the strategy all concerns that business and program leaders raise. Soliciting, welcoming, acknowledging, and incorporating broad input into the strategy help set a foundation for the collaboration required for a successful training program.

Failing to Recognize Expectations and Concerns

This obstacle is the hardest to manage, in my experience. Even with direct requests for feedback and a broadly reviewed and approved strategy, gaps in understanding and support can occur. Thinking may change, and new stakeholders may reach incorrect conclusions about training scope or responsibility. Behind the scenes, decisions about training may get made in meetings without input from the training lead. I've seen supervisors pull out sections of approved training materials to decrease the length of a course for work schedules, which unsurprisingly resulted in notable hypercare issues due to gaps in the expected learning. Program leaders may make decisions about testing timelines without consulting the training leader, even though the work directly overlaps with end user training and often involves the same resources. In another example, a business division brought in its own training lead because of a perceived gap.

Working Smarter: In an introductory conversation, secure a commitment from all program leads and business stakeholders to provide direct, honest, and transparent feedback, at any point, about what is and is not working with the digital transformation training program. I use a phrase from usability testing: "Anything you dislike won't hurt my feelings." Reinforce the importance of direct feedback with leaders. Again, it's about getting things right for the learners and business, not *being* right.

Prioritizing Materials Over Everything Else

A strategy that focuses exclusively on training materials will not produce the expected learning outcomes because there are even more critical planning and preparatory activities that determine whether people are prepared or not. Having many hours of training materials can still see a yearlong hypercare period. Similarly, having high-quality training materials and a well-configured and fully tested system can fail to see people prepared for new ways of working when those who facilitate end user training are unskilled or have not demonstrated their own abilities as teachers of the new system and effective coaches.

Working Smarter: Digital transformation training requires a holistic approach for attending to all the training success factors, for managing the myriad activities, and for coordinating execution of training. While there are many such factors to oversee, learning outcomes are always better when the training materials are high quality, so this remains an essential goal along with the others detailed in the digital transformation training strategy.

Ignoring Training Interdependencies

Failure to receive handoffs from others that the training program requires can create issues for the training program. Examples include timely material reviews and approvals, information about system changes, security role design, or data structures. Without these handoffs and effective communication about their status, training materials may be incomplete or incorrect. In some cases, the IDs provide a visual placeholder when the materials have to be produced and a key decision remains outstanding. In other cases where decisions do not get made, the start of training has had to be delayed so those leading the sessions can have time to prepare once the training materials are updated and final reviews are completed.

Working Smarter: Identify the critical dependencies for the digital training program in your training strategy. Make sure that your work breakdown and the project plan include these key handoffs as milestones for ongoing visibility. Also include them on relevant dashboards, with status indicators to communicate progress, risk, and completion. You'll see ideas in the *Digital Transformation Champions* samples at the end of the book.

Relying Too Much on Vendors

When I ask leaders about training for digital transformation programs and hear the reply, "We have a vendor doing all of that," I can anticipate and unfortunately see gaps emerge. In these cases, training is an expensive add-on to an implementation statement of work that is usually not reviewed by a learner or leader experienced with technology implementations.

Working Smarter: Use the Vendor Checklist for Training Success provided as sample 3 to discuss and document who will handle which aspects of the training. Clarify what has not yet been considered and what is out of scope. The goal is avoiding any surprises for the business and the learners.

Overlooking Long-Term Sustainability

The business expects to use digital transformation training materials much like any other business asset—for the duration, not just a single go live. Training materials must help new hires and people changing jobs learn the work and support subsequent implementations.

Working Smarter: Explicitly note the durability of the products beyond go live and identify where responsibility lies for keeping materials and tools updated on an ongoing basis. Explain that today-tomorrow change highlights are detailed not in the training courses, but in separate communications, typically produced by the change management team. After the go live, no one has a previous reference for old ways of working. People need to understand the business process and how to correctly use tools, solve problems, and get support. Note any handoffs for material updates and the decisions about long-term tool and technology maintenance. Introduce the concept of *localization* to explain updates to the materials for subsequent implementations or for specific audiences.

Assuming Everyone Is Already on Board

Never assume you're building upon previous implementation successes and knowledge about the digital transformation training program. You're always starting over with every deployment or launch and with each new group of stakeholders.

Working Smarter: Refine, re-review, and make the training strategy or approach story relevant for every stakeholder audience. Share drafts in advance and seek input on specific components to understand and meet the expectations for the digital transformation training. Speak to the "what's in it for me" in a manner that respects ways of working and what's already known about the learners, business teams, and culture. Add notes about specific wants, needs, and expectations key stakeholders have about the training program so they can support and promote it with their teams.

Final Note

A business- and people-focused training strategy or tailored approach, strengthened with *ongoing* input from key stakeholders and learned lessons, provides a compelling training vision. The best strategy or approach sees the project team and stakeholders actively supporting it because it strives to accomplish, in equal measure, both the business results and the people readiness necessary for realizing the overarching digital transformation business goals. Identifying the distinct groups of learners and what they need to know is the topic of the next chapter.

---

(2)

Learning Topics and Audience Insights for a Strong Foundation

"When you know your audience, your audience knows."
—Unknown

An audience analysis provides a structured view of the transformation in terms of the business lines and the people who will learn new ways of doing their jobs. Describing what these groups of people need to know and do is the foundation for the training team's work. For example, learner needs determine the structure of the courses, modules, lessons, and actual training materials that will be produced. Counts of learners by job and department, the locations, and the work hours decide the time-lines, logistics, plans, and structure of end user training. Finally, an audience analysis should also identify the key stakeholders for each group of learners who will help or possibly challenge the success of the training program.

BASICS

Finding the intersection between the curricula and the audience—the *what* that needs to be learned and the *who* that needs to know it—is a digital transformation training leader's very important task. The following explains how to identify the curricula, detail the learner and stakeholder audiences for the topics, and summarize the information to use internally and to share with others.

What Learners Need to Know and Do

A learning program provides instruction and information so people can develop skills and gain knowledge about how to do their job differently. Curricula describes the training topics, based on needs. A traditional learning needs analysis starts with desired behavior changes that define the learning objectives (Friedman & Yarbrough, 1985). For example, if business metrics reveal a problem in how customer service or shipping clerks are performing a task, a business representative communicates the behavior changes needed to an instructional designer (ID), who then creates materials and a training lesson appropriate to the need. The learning outcome can be measured. Digital transformation initiatives involve redefined work processes and an enabling system, usually across multiple areas of a business, all at once. The training opportunity is how to effectively see many people ready to carry out the variety of jobs in profoundly different ways. The grouping of courses, topics, and job-based activities that people will perform is directly tied to the processes and activities that the system enables. In other words, business processes, subprocesses, and activities along with security roles, when they exist, provide a start for the curriculum plan. The curricula get refined over the phases of the digital transformation program and its launches.

Consider a generic sales process detailed from an APQC process listing (2024) as an example of how the process models transfer to curriculum planning.

Process and Role Starts

Information for Curriculum Planning

Business Area	Process	Subprocesses & Activities	Security Role(s) Involved
The functional work area	What is being reengineered, optimized, and transformed	Task-oriented process and procedural activities	Who is involved in the work tasks—who will learn new ways of working

Course Grouping	Module	Activities	Target Learners with Job-Specific Lessons
Sales	Order management and execution	Order receipt, entry, and validation Demand fulfillment management Retail activities monitoring Financial accruals calculation Accrual vs. plan tracking	Sales rep Customer support rep Sales finance analyst Sales manager Customer support manager Finance analyst

The business teams in a digital transformation produce listings of business-relevant processes and activities and then identify the jobs or security roles of the people who will do the work. IDs consolidate technical and functional resources and work in the system to craft training that provides a relevant overview of the process, what happens within and independent of the system, and, importantly, the specific activities each person in a job will perform to successfully complete their daily tasks.

Typically, the curriculum gets folded into the learner audience analysis. If it's a first launch, it will be very high-level, which also helps inform the audience analysis.

Key Learner Groups

The business areas that are in scope and specifically the people who will do the work after the transformation are the starting point for a training audience analysis. This thorough understanding about the groups of learners is the foundation of a successful digital transformation training program. Consider the following prompts to help identify and describe all the learner audiences.

- What are the company or business lines that the program team identifies as in scope for the transformation overall? For a specific implementation phase, group, or wave?

- What are the geographies and physical locations where people work within each business?

- What are the departments, teams, and jobs that carry out the in-scope process activities?

- What are the counts of people within each discrete group of learners, by process or job function, and by geography?

- What days and hours do each of the audience groups work?

- Are there any regular months, weeks, or days that people are *unavailable* for training?

- Will the training for these groups need to take place during working hours, or off-shift with overtime pay? Are there regulations to consider? For example, breaks needed every so many hours?

- By location and business function, how is training developed and delivered today?

- When does training normally occur and how does this vary? By what means?

- Is training delivered virtually or in person?

- Are there training rooms?

- Does everyone have an assigned computer or work with a shared computer? What other considerations about hands-on practice can be noted?

- What sample training materials used on the job could be provided for reference? (Note: There may be no structured training beyond a show-and-tell model, using the live system.)

- What languages do the learners speak? Are there requirements for multiple-language materials?

- What accommodations must be considered to meet any special needs the learners have for the transformation?

- What needs do the learners have that the business accommodates in other training programs? Are there already structures in place to assist learners with sight, hearing, or other needs?

- Who coordinates the scheduling, logistics, and training reporting at each location or within each team?

- Relative to the launch date, when will digital transformation training likely occur for each audience?

- Will business leaders expect knowledge certification, beyond a post-training test, for select group of learners who perform business-critical work to formally demonstrate their readiness for the go live?

- What is the experience and perception of work and system training today?

A comprehensive picture about the learners and training topics in a summarized view at the early stages of the transformation can help the program and business teams understand the scope of training. It helps the training team move forward with planning for material development, tools, and delivery. The learner summary blends together all the key inputs and becomes part of the strategy or approach to help explain the digital transformation training program and all of the supporting training activities for project leads, business teams, and stakeholders. See sample 4, Learner Audience Snapshot.

Collaboration with Business Partners

Who are the stakeholders for the digital transformation training program? Identify these leaders and individuals across the relevant business divisions, functions, and physical locations from the audience analysis. Stakeholders include digital transformation project team leaders, business-training team members, functional trainers from the business, and others impacted by whether people can learn new processes and know how to transact in a new system. While organizing stakeholder data is often a change management deliverable, training leads benefit from a list focused on the training needs that includes training managers and others not typically captured in an executive-level analysis. See sample 5, Stakeholder Connection Map.

Identifying the training topics, the learners, their needs, and the partners for the training program sets a strong foundation for all the work that follows.

BEST PRACTICES

A few steps will accelerate preparation of the curriculum plan, as well as the learner and training stakeholder analyses.

Use the Existing Information Sources

Kickoff decks and functional design documents describe the digital transformation in terms of the business lines, processes, and functions. These resources help draft a plan of the training topics and courses and a start of the audience analysis. Summaries about the people or end users impacted by the digital transformation may be a change management deliverable. On one project, a rock-star role mapper on the change management team maintained a constant eye on the HR data for impacted business areas. She became the go-to for all questions about people counts. Most often the training lead requests an HR export and pivots the data to identify the business lines of the digital transformation, work locations, jobs, and counts of people within each group of learners. This information is the core of the learner audience analysis, which then gets supplemented with additional inputs.

Identify Key Training Contacts to Coordinate Learning and Offer Support to Learners

Local business contacts are essential. They develop and coordinate decisions about training schedules and support the business trainers. When creating the audience analysis, identify these people, often in HR or business-training roles, who can provide the necessary input about how training occurs today and details about learner schedules and needs. They are also the likely people who will help with the plans, preparations, and successful execution of the digital transformation training for their site or team.

Validate Preliminary Curricula and Audience Summaries for Accuracy

Once you have a summary learner analysis on a page, review it with others. Gather feedback from the business and project leads. Do the high-level course topics and learner groups align with the overall scope of the digital transformation? Once there's project-level validation and alignment, begin reviewing it with key business stakeholders.

Meet with site leaders, senior VPs, training executives, and others who lead the functions whose people will receive digital transformation training. Ask, "Here's what I'm seeing; what resonates with you and what might be missing?" Inquire about experiences with other training initiatives: "What worked? What didn't? What should be started, stopped, or continued? Is there someone else I need to speak with?"

These reviews are an investment and worth the weeks of effort they'll require. As the details develop about the training strategy, engage all the relevant functional leaders and influencers for their feedback about the training topics and audience analysis. This is a necessary step because these stakeholders can be essential supporters or notable detractors. A ten-minute conversation can yield valuable information in the moment and cultivate a key partner for the training initiative.

Make "Good Enough" Early Estimates of Learner Counts

The purpose of getting early counts is to distinguish whether there are, for example, a total of five, or fifty, or five hundred, or five thousand learners who need to learn the same thing. These numbers affect training material development plans and logistics for how training gets carried out. Do expect variation in the granularity. Counts conducted up to a year or more in advance of a go live are preliminary at best. People change jobs or leave the company, and others get hired. In some businesses, you'll need to consider annual or semiannual reorganizations as well.

Role-to-position mapping that occurs later on—matching jobs and then people to the system security roles months ahead of the launch—provides the best, most accurate counts of learners, which the training team matches to assigned courses and learning activities.

Establish Clear Roles for Managing People and Security Role Mapping

Because it's the best source of the actual work people will carry out and also the counts of learners for each specific training track, the training team needs to know two things about the digital transformation security roles early on.

- Where is the master listing of security roles and the activities they enable stored, and how often is it updated? Ongoing information about the security roles and their design ensures that the training content will help people carry out their jobs, and then that the right people receive the training they need.

- Who has responsibility on the project team to coordinate, track, and report on the mapping of people-to-system security roles? To ensure all business learners get identified, role-mapping counts must be updated monthly and more frequently as the starts for testing and training approach.

The role design and people count snapshots inform work that multiple project teams must complete. The counts also allow business leaders and training contacts to prepare for the overall transformation.

A few things will make it difficult to plan learning topics and identify the learner audiences.

WHAT GETS IN THE WAY

The challenges that come up are rooted in how and which information is gathered and then shared.

Gathering Inputs Inefficiently About the Learner Audiences

I've seen training leads start by scheduling one-on-one hour-long meetings with thirty-plus business contacts to talk about learner counts and transformation training. Not surprisingly, many of these meetings were declined and had to be rescheduled, if they took place at all. While the intent is to connect with business teams, the time (one-hour meetings) is excessive, stretching audience analysis into months instead of several weeks.

Working Smarter: Strive for efficiency and respect your own and others' time. Use existing information, combine efforts, and conduct surveys to make smart use of time. I've found this approach works best, and my training lead colleagues confirm it.

1. Ask the program leaders to identify all key contacts, ideally in the training or HR function, who can provide input about current training, logistics planning, and other needed inputs across the in-scope business areas.

2. The training lead holds a single, short kickoff call with this group and records it for those who cannot attend. Use this time to provide a single, comprehensive overview about the audience analysis work. Introduce what information is being sought and briefly note why it matters to the business teams and the learners. Clearly state what is being asked of those on the call and the time frame to complete the work. Communicate willingness to answer any questions during and after the call.

3. Create a survey or provide a file to collect all the detailed inputs about the learner groups each contact supports. Schedule short calls only with those who fail to respond or when additional information is needed.

4. Report in your status about the progress or any delays by function. Close any outstanding gaps by asking business leaders to help obtain needed inputs or complete tasks.

5. Finally, determine whether the information gathering could be combined with other activities for change and communication.

Providing Estimates Too Early About Training Time or Learning Complexity

Some business leaders may require estimates about total learning time by course or group of learners at the start of the transformation program, before any formal review of processes and systems takes place by the IDs. This estimation exercise can be carried out with roughly estimated assumptions and explanations. Even so, on some projects the ID may be held to the initial durations, even when those were very poorly aligned with the time needed to learn the content as it developed. Further, subject matter expert and business team inputs during training development can increase the length of final training time if there is demand for additional detail or more hands-on activities than initially anticipated. Know, too, that inflated and incorrect estimates can stress the business teams with what's coming down the road.

Working Smarter: Recognize how the data you're collecting will get used. Is it to justify training resources and effort? Does an estimated learning time for each process area help the business understand the impact of the change? Workstream leads can help provide estimates and the extent of process change based on their experiences with earlier projects. Preliminary timing estimates can be helpful for early training schedule planning. The actual timing is always updated once the materials are developed, reviewed, and approved ahead of training schedule creation. Until then, if necessary, compile data-based estimates that are the best sets of information available *at that time*. It's important to call out the preliminary nature of the estimates and always date the summary plan on a page. Later, further into the material development cycle, use the verified timing information. Recalculate and communicate the change by always adding an "updated as of" date notation on the plan on a page.

Not Recognizing the Broad Value of the Learner Personas

When asked about not providing an audience analysis on my first major digital transformation program, I explained to the system implementor that I and the training team knew the learners. What I failed to appreciate is the importance of summarizing the detail for the rest of the project team and the business stakeholders. Eventually counts of learners emerged from the role-mapping activities and the training plans illustrated the delivery and execution approach. An up-front summary would have been helpful to the implementation partners and business leaders to appreciate the scope of the digital transformation and the importance of training activities across the business functions.

Working Smarter: Draft and maintain the Learner Audience Snapshot, sample 4, and include it with the training strategy or tailored approach presentations. When counts of learners or role-mapping counts change, these signal updates for who will need and participate in which training course. These details and ongoing updates also feature in the Digital Transformation Training Status at a Glance—sample 6.

Final Note

Maintain a learner-focused perspective by highlighting who will learn what across all the business lines affected by the digital transformation. It's a success factor for best training material design and selecting the right tools to deliver a training program that works well for the business. Roles, responsibilities, and decision-making for all the training activities is the topic of the next chapter.

3

Responsibility and Decision-Making Clarity Drive Success

"People want to know what's expected of them.
When roles are ambiguous, frustration follows."

—Brené Brown, Author and Social Scientist

Knowing who does what is fundamental to any group effort and a necessity for digital transformations. A responsibility matrix—a structure that maps work, specifies who does what, and identifies the person or role with accountability and authority—can help business and training teams avoid confusion that arises with informal agreements or, worse, assumptions. Having clarity about work ownership also helps minimize conflict and prevent delay. The skillful construct of a responsibility matrix lies in making it as simply useful as it needs to be. It should contain just enough detail, in a format that works for all the people involved and for the situations at hand.

BASICS

A responsibility matrix matches key training-related activities to the people involved by name or job and the role they have. It includes descriptions about how each person or role is involved in each aspect of the training work. Tasks, milestones, or work categories for digital training typically appear as a list down the page. Listed across the top of the table are the roles, functions, or teams involved in the work. In detailed models, individual names may be used. The intersection of each task and role contains a description about their involvement with the work.

Mastering Clarity with the RACI Model

A RACI (pronounced "ray-see") is the term for this structure about responsibility for training activities and work output. The plan of digital transformation training activities, sometimes called a work breakdown structure (WBS), is a useful starting point. The corresponding RACI matrix includes some of the same items, without timing or dates, and identifies who produces, reviews, and approves an item. A RACI matrix can be structured around tasks, deliverables, or a blend of the two. The intersection of who and what includes a designation about involvement in the task, which can be summarized with the RACI-D acronym.

- **R**esponsible for doing or getting the work done
- **A**ccountable for ensuring outcomes and addressing failures
- **C**onsulted about the work, the deliverable, or requirements
- **I**nformed or communicated with about status, outcomes, issues, and decisions
- **D**ecision-making authority, when it's someone other than the person who is accountable

See sample 7 for two models of a RACI-D matrix.

Decoding Decision-Making Dynamics

With the addition of a "D," the model becomes a RACI-D model. The RACI-D matrix can be helpful when it makes sense to clarify the decision-maker. For example, training leads typically require approval from business owners on many things such as the training schedule or final approval for training materials. When questions arise requiring business sign-off and validation or approval, who has this responsibility? When the training lead needs to navigate conversations with business teams new to digital transformation training, showing the agreed-upon expectations about project team, business, and stakeholder involvement with specific work tasks helps reinforce the important fact that *many people* are involved in learner readiness and lasting adoption.

The partnerships that see digital transformations succeed benefit from clarity about who does what and who makes important decisions and will drive the use of a RACI chart.

BEST PRACTICES

The RACI structure is a common business tool, and there are a few things to keep in mind that help see it contribute to the best outcomes for digital training.

Build Your RACI with the Essentials in Mind

The following are general guidelines.

- Use verb statements aligned with the WBS to describe the work or an item being produced: develop materials, review materials, approve materials, develop the schedule, approve the schedule.

- Recognize that multiple people can be tasked with responsibility, informed, or consulted. For example, in *developing* training materials, an instructional designer (ID) is *responsible* for the work and the business teams and subject matter experts are both *consulted*.

- Appreciate that only one person is ever accountable. For instance, the training lead would be accountable for the many training deliverables and activities related to developing and planning the training. A business owner can be accountable for training completion, while the local training contact would be responsible for seeing that training gets carried out as planned.

These standard RACI concepts are summarized well in an online resource (Morgan, 2022).

Clarify the Difference Between Responsible and Accountable

Accountability can be seen as the strategic ownership for overall completion of an activity or deliverable. *Responsibility* is tactical and involves doing the work. As an example, consider how accountability works in training material development. The digital transformation training lead is *accountable* for seeing that all materials get finished on time across the instructional design team. This is not the role of a business owner or project manager. IDs do the work, so they have *responsibility* for creating training materials.

Similarly, consider training execution. A local business contact from HR or training has *responsibility* for planning the training session schedule and coordinating logistics for in-person sessions. This responsibility could also be shared with the learning management system administrator who loads the schedule and manages invitations. The training lead in this case gets consulted. Ultimately, a senior business leader is *accountable* for employees taking time from their work to attend and complete training and for acquiring and demonstrating their new knowledge.

Assemble Your RACI Approach with These Steps

With much trial and error in this space, these are the steps I've found most helpful to create a useful RACI model for a training program.

1. Start simply. List your *key* training tasks and work deliverables, not all of them. Focus on those that involve multiple people in various roles and functional areas. Try a few different RACI headings and information layouts. Do you use an R/A/C/I/D column structure and place names in the cell, or list names/ roles and place letters in the cell? Map responsibility and accountability for a few of the entries and then get feedback.

2. Confirm the value, need, and approach for the RACI. Talk with the people you'll work with who have ultimate responsibility and decision-making authority for the transformation program about the proposed RACI and structure. Get their input. The purpose of this key step is to confirm the value of the matrix and the way it is laid out before you build out the rest of it.

3. Identify one decision-maker or approver. Having more than one person listed as the accountable approver or decision-maker increases effort and overall risk to the task getting completed on time. Instead, designate one person to streamline the process. This person may choose to involve or consult others before making the decision or issuing approval.

4. Find efficiency. Once everything is mapped onto the matrix, assess the work and look for opportunities to add efficiency. For example, can anyone with "Consulted" be moved to "Informed" instead?

5. Assess workload. Identify any people whose workloads may be over-allocated. Perhaps you need to request additional resources or redistribute the work.

6. Cross-reference the RACI chart with the stakeholder chart. Ensure that both lists reflect *all* key stakeholders—if not by name, then by role or functional business area. The goal is to include all of the involved parties in the roles listing.

7. Use a RACI when training work gets outsourced. See the Vendor Checklist for Training Success, sample 3, to understand the vendor's planned deliverables and expectations for how business teams remain involved.

8. Always include a legend. Remind reviewers what each letter of the RACI and D mean in *your* responsibility matrix to avoid confusion with other models where terms and their use may have been different.

Add Deliverables the Training Team Needs to Succeed

Chapter 16 details the seven critical activities that others outside the training team complete, one of which is security role design and role mapping. The system or environment learners will use for practice and communications about the digital transformation are two others. About these, the training team typically gets consulted. The training team may not build the training environment though must weigh in about the structure and timing for its availability, as well as its ongoing support. Likewise, the training team must be consulted for program communications. Listing these interdependent activities where others are responsible and accountable and training is consulted helps ensure that the training team is involved where needed.

Overall, the details about responsibility help drive high-performing teamwork and illustrate how the training work will get carried out across the digital transformation program and business teams.

WHAT GETS IN THE WAY

There are a few watch items to know about developing a RACI for your training program.

Being Overly Rigid

Some people have specific preferences about using responsibility matrices. Some say only one person can be responsible, or a responsible person cannot also be accountable. Others insist on combining "Consulted" and "Informed" categories. One executive I worked with even directed that the definitions of the R and the A be swapped. I've also worked with people who dislike the idea of a responsibility matrix altogether and refuse to use it, despite evident conflicts and confusion about who does what.

Working Smarter: Overcome biases that get in the way of making a structured model work. As you would with any good data visualization, make the framework simple, clear, and relevant. Remember the legend when you use abbreviations. Provide a prototype to those you work with and ask them for their reactions and preferences. Agree on what will best support those involved with the training program. Ask them, "How can we map tasks and responsibilities to see us work together well?" Remember that even responsibility matrices have approvers.

Lacking a Clear Decision-Maker

While the accountable person may have decision-making authority, in some cases—usually reflecting business culture—a business leader may have the "D" for decisions about training tools, types of images and illustrations, and the instructional formats, not just approval of content accuracy and relevance for the learner audience. When these expectations come to light later in the project timeline, it can be hard to unwind and rework things to accommodate late requirements when decision-making is presumed or, even worse, assumed.

Working Smarter: Neutralize potential conflicts and avoid confusion by clarifying decision-making in your matrix. A RACI is suggested as a component of the training strategy. Your audience analysis surfaces the key stakeholders so you can determine and document their involvement early in the process. Clearly call out who makes decisions for key training work and deliverables so everyone is prepared.

Skipping Dialogue About Roles and Responsibilities

On one project, instead of having a conversation about the work and who does what, a painful back-and-forth occurred while updating a training RACI at the request of one functional business lead. There were multiple rounds of out-of-context updates and a sense that something was missing. When the key business leader finally felt confident work wouldn't fall to his team, it was "done."

Working Smarter: In this example, delays happened because something about the business still needed to be known and clarified. Taking the time to build a thorough RACI-D is just one tool that helps establish who will do what. Asking about and delving into specific concerns to understand business leader agendas is an important training lead responsibility. To navigate these situations as elegantly as possible, keep in mind the principle of getting things right by working together.

Using an Ineffective RACI Structure

Creating a RACI takes time, even with a simple framework. Building out a detailed RACI that gets shelved and not used because it's not helpful means the effort is wasted.

Working Smarter: Start with a very simple RACI with some of the key tasks that both training and business teams work together on. If there's a request for a very detailed RACI model for all training tasks for large-scale transformations, clarify the purpose, reviewers, and the RACI user audiences. Build RACI incrementally, targeting anticipated or known areas of confusion. Always seek feedback about the usefulness from those whose names and roles are included.

Final Note

Remember, the best responsibility model contains just enough detail about who does what, in a format that works for all the people involved and for the work in your digital transformation training program. Typically, the overall business sponsor and program manager are among those to approve the training RACI. The training lead ensures the framework is relevant and that it's kept up to date as the work and responsibility shift and as feedback gets offered. This work is a component of digital training program leadership, the topic of the next chapter.

4

Training Leadership for Lasting Impact

"Power is the ability to get things done."
—**Rosabeth Moss Kanter,** Strategy, Innovation, and Change Leadership Professor

Business leadership involves establishing and promoting a compelling vision, then inspiring others to work together to achieve it. What distinguishes digital transformation training leadership from other forms is two things: a relative lack of direct control for a broad set of critical activities along with limited decision-making power, despite high accountability for the outcomes. To see tasks and training deliverables met on time, the training lead must flex exceptional influence, communication, and management skills. The ability to connect, collaborate, and establish partnerships is essential too. Yet even with these necessary skills and using a structured approach for training program management, results are not a guarantee. Digital training leads must also attend to and work well with a large network of people involved in the business's digital transformation.

BASICS

This chapter, arguably the most important one in the book for training leads, focuses on leadership. While tens of thousands of resources exist about leadership, I call out three key categories because they best help digital transformation program training leads in their work:

- Training team management

- Project and business team management

- Self-management

Colleagues experienced with even larger teams and more deployments validate the importance of these three areas of digital transformation training leadership. I acknowledge with gratitude their input and comments that helped enhance this chapter.

Team Coaching and Management

Within the training team, the training leader recognizes and appreciates each team member for their individuality and their strengths, coaching and developing skills to build the team, organized around its shared purpose. Learning about the training program starts on each person's first day and is ongoing throughout the training timeline.

- Provide a welcome to the team with clarity about the work, role, responsibilities, and how to get help.

- Plan activities where the team members get to know one another.

- See the broad team participate in reviews and decision-making about how the digital transformation training work gets carried out.

- Provide channels for peers to recognize one another.

- Manage and report about the work the team is carrying out.

- Provide timely feedback about progress or opportunities.

- Actively develop team member skills and seek to promote training staff into more senior roles.

The best digital transformation training team, regardless of size and makeup, shares values about work and quality. Each team member demonstrates a personal drive to achieve their best. They speak about their commitment to learner and business readiness and recognize their importance in achieving it. Each person has a clear role and part to play, like a musician in an orchestra with the training lead as the conductor. Outside the training team, engagement with cross-functional business leaders is essential for training leads to secure support for the training program.

Business and Digital Transformation Success

Besides learners and training team members, the training lead must attend to leaders within the digital transformation program and others across the business whose way of conducting day-to-day work will change. Do project and business leaders understand and agree with the training vision, activities, and timelines so they can provide backing? Their public recognition for early successes, their help moving work forward, and their ability to solve problems make it easier to complete training activities. These strong relationships develop when leaders *experience* how the training program, the training team's work, and the training lead will help their teams and enable transformation results *with* their partnership.

Leading with Self-Management

The ability to lead well is possible with attention to self-management and self-care in equal measure.

- Self-management "refers to the ability to manage your emotions, particularly in stressful situations, and maintain a positive outlook despite setbacks" (Landry, 2019). Maintaining a professional, solution-oriented manner in the face of extreme challenges helps a training lead shift from reaction to more constructive solution-seeking mode.

- Self-care encompasses the activities a leader regularly does for their mental, emotional, and physical health. Besides increasing resilience and helping with energy management, self-care is evident to others. It demonstrates to the team and to others "that you care to show up at your best for them, personally and professionally" (Ashley, 2024).

The next section describes best practices across these three leadership categories.

BEST PRACTICES

To help organize this information, topics are grouped by leadership category. A fourth grouping for communication covers ideas that apply across one or more of the three leadership categories.

Lead from Start to Finish

Leading the team of instructional designers and others is an ongoing responsibility that requires daily effort. From onboarding to weekly engagement throughout the project life cycle, team guidance and support make a difference. This work involves building the team while supporting each member to see all the work completed. In my experience the following tools and tactics have proved most effective in seeing a diverse group evolve into a high-performing digital transformation training team whose members enjoy working together and achieving notable results.

Onboard Team Members with Intention

First interactions always matter, and this is true when new people join the training team. Training leads can implement these activities to more rapidly establish norms and build camaraderie.

- As members join the team, gift each new team member with a structured welcome, including a plan for their first few months. Provide the following:

  » Ensure the person has a copy of their job description, including expected deliverables. Provide them with links to key information stores where project files or training templates get saved.

  » Assign new team members a project or task so they can make a meaningful contribution in the first, and no later than the second, week. This reminds each person they are on the team for a reason.

  » Equip the person with tools to support them in their tasks, including contact information for the technical help desk and even a coach, buddy, or mentor.

» Make clear attendance expectations, including a message that contractors should charge for value-added time worked, not for hours in the office or breaks.

» Set up opportunities for new team members to introduce themselves to one another, using an email, slide, portal, or other template they can populate with information about themselves, pictures from a recent vacation, a favorite quote about training, hobbies, and so on.

- Hold a training team onboarding—half or full day—if the majority of the team members onboard at the same time. Organize a collaborative onboarding process and combine it with preliminary planning about tools, technologies, and standards.

- When team members join in waves, structure the onboarding activities to see current team members support or teach those just joining.

- Talk about how everyone will work together. Are all remote? Is there a blend of in-person and remote team members? Are you all in-person with some based full-time in one place and the rest traveling in from other offices? When and how will you meet together and what is the cadence?

- Provide the team norms, values, and mission if they exist, or work together to craft and refine them.

See and Appreciate Each Training Team Member

Recognize the individual interests, training expertise, skills, technical and interpersonal strengths, and personal interests that each team member brings to their work every day.

Some Ways You Can Achieve This

- At the start of meetings, use prompts for "Who I am" icebreakers such as "My ideal dinner with friends," "A media recommendation," "A recent personal best for me is," "Would you rather be an only child or one of eight?," "My favorite vacation spot," or "The last movie I saw," to name a few.

- Explore what training team success means to each person. What's the common picture of success that emerges from the entire team?

- Take advantage of free assessments for styles, such as Myers-Briggs, Enneagram, VARK, and so on. One Myers-Briggs assessment includes relatable avatars such as "the Magician" or "the Commander" to enhance the ENFP or ENTJ labels.

The process of carrying out these activities to recognize the individuality of team members helps build mutual understanding and respect. By leveraging the different styles, traits, and strengths of each person, the team can work better together to create standard materials with consistency and a quality that reflects the talents of the whole.

Encourage and Recognize Divergent Thinking

There's a saying: "No one of us is as smart as all of us" (Blanchard, 2024). I find this to be so true, and yet it requires space and encouragement for team members to feel comfortable sharing different ways of thinking.

- In meetings, talk about how you see the team working together to share ideas and contribute to the overall team.

- Develop ground rules for working together. Include ones that require curiosity and inquiry for understanding, courage to address conflict, and encouragement to manage personal emotions constructively.

- Invite and welcome inputs to problem-solving; encourage team members to ask questions when decisions don't make sense.

- Address how concerns and conflicts will be handled respectfully. Acknowledge they will arise.

- When team members are highly introverted, be sensitive to group problem-solving activities. Instead, use surveys to capture problems and identify action steps, then review the inputs as a team and decide on the next steps.

Training leaders need their team members to feel comfortable sharing feedback and voicing unique ideas and opinions that not everyone may share.

Facilitate Team Member Recognition and Appreciation

Human needs for self-actualization and accomplishment combined with the research about expressing gratitude are helpful reminders.

- Encourage weekly recognition of team members. Some of my teams use a form to collect input weekly from all members recognizing one another. These comments were shared on each team call. All remarked upon the constructive start to the meeting.

- Recognize and appreciate team members who offer to help their colleagues.

- Offer opportunities for stretch assignments that provide growth experiences and career opportunities. More than one learning management system administrator I've worked with grew into other roles. One became an HR data analyst and another grew into a remarkable training lead and talented instructional designer.

- Have project and other key business leaders address the training team, expressing the importance of the work and the important role each team member plays in the overall team's success.

Meaningful appreciation sets a positive tone because it's motivating and empowering. This is a really helpful ingredient when the work is challenging.

Cross-Pollinate Knowledge and Skill Sharing Among Full-Time and Contract Team Members

The training team is often a mix of full-time and contract talent with a mix of instructional design skill levels. A strategy that seeks to share knowledge and develop team member skills while advancing the work is always a double win. Here are ways this can work.

- Assign each person to review one or more sets of the training strategy, tool lists, material standards, or a project asset, then "teach" it back to the rest of the team.

- Have training team members rotate responsibility for leading the weekly training team call. Rotation is useful for two reasons: Besides lightening the load for the training lead, facilitating the call means that team members can practice the skills needed to work with business and process teams to gather information and review training materials. Also, seeing one's peers model strong facilitation and presentation skills is a great way for others to learn, especially when followed by having to do it yourself.

Have Fun Together

Group lunches, mini celebrations, and happy hours are common. On one project, the team took thirty-minute game breaks to play Scattergories or Pictionary for time together. On another project, the training team members developed a running list of songs that described a moment, an experience, or a success in their work. The team enjoyed listening to the playlist during the celebration event. All of these help establish meaningful relationships among the team members, which makes the work more enjoyable.

Take Action

When team members' work is not completed on time or fails to meet standards, address it promptly. Here are some effective leadership behaviors that provide space for feedback.

- Meet regularly with each team member, even if only for fifteen minutes every week. Time is a gift, and sharing it is a leader's responsibility.

- Have direct conversations about individual performance when it's going well and not. Address any issues, even small things, immediately. Ask for others' reflections before telling them your assessment to help ease into a conversation about the work. Use questions like, "How do you think that session went?" "It seemed like this is a challenge; how do you feel?" "Would you like feedback about ____?" "What could prevent that in the future?" "What options do you see to resolve that?"

- Actively seek feedback from everyone on the team on an ongoing basis. "What can I be doing to help you or the team?" Some will be comfortable sharing constructive comments; most are not. Listen actively and ask follow-up questions. "My intention is to help complete our work. Do you feel this feedback is helpful or not?" The goal is to receive input on the team's activities for the purpose of continuous improvement. It's what you don't know, hear, or learn that will later be disruptive.

Managing the training team well is so important because the work won't get carried out in its absence. People coming together can be chaotic. It's called "storming, norming, and forming" for a reason. Facilitating the training team's work leverages management, coaching, and team-building strengths. Above all else, the training leader's job, relative to the training team, is to ensure everyone has clear direction about their role, the work, and the expectations for deliverables, as well as their quality and the timelines. With recognition of every team member as a person, how people feel about doing the work shifts. The tenor and energy within the team generate velocity to complete the work that the business and transformation need.

Build Connections as a Digital Transformation Leader

Transformation program leaders, executive sponsors, and multiple business executives are essential partners for enabling the overall training program. These stakeholders have high expectations, and the training lead needs to cultivate relationships with them by attending to the needs each stakeholder has.

Use the Stakeholder Analysis and Have Conversations

Build upon the initial stakeholder analysis to expand and engage with the circle of stakeholders you work with. Use the sample 5 Stakeholder Connection Map to identify and support the needs each leader has and keep it up to date.

On more than one project, I took advantage of on-site gatherings to approach executives, introduce myself, and ask what was on their minds about the transformation training. I've had great conversations at the table, in the buffet line, even on breaks. Besides asking any questions, it's an opportunity to provide a quick highlight relevant for them about the training work in their area. Other times, I schedule ten-minute calls every four to six weeks to have a casual check-in. My favorite way to connect with stakeholders has been the chance to volunteer together when the company offers the option. The experience of doing good provides a terrific opportunity to get to know one another. In short, find ways to connect meaningfully and foster a relationship that helps achieve training and transformation goals.

Address Stakeholder Interests

As the face of training to all stakeholder groups, the training lead must consistently communicate the digital training strategy and the tactics. The narrative and message have to address any concerns or interests specific to each business stakeholder. Every leader has a style, and the company and even functions have their own culture that must be respected. Manufacturing and sales executives are generally concerned about the time training takes employees away from their work or customer interactions. Acknowledge how these are factored into the training strategy and approach. On one project, I worked with several VPs following a transformation launch when they felt training carried out by another lead and the team was done very poorly. These executives needed to help create a *new* strategy about training success that reflected *their* perspectives and concerns. When training leads hear and respond to these needs, trust grows in the training team's ability to deliver results.

Master Leadership Communication

These communication best practices enhance all training lead interactions.

Make Verbal Connections in Conversations

Training team members and executive leaders all have perceptions and opinions that a training lead needs to know. During conversations, two-way communication occurs when there are frequent verbal bridges or connecting statements that build upon the previous thought. Without these, there's verbal sparring where each person jabs an idea or thought. Most effective training leaders acknowledge the other person's idea, demonstrate that it's heard, then *add* to it. I've had to learn this technique and am grateful for the modeling my own team members and other leaders provided. The outcome of connected conversations is stronger relationships. I have a note pasted near my computer to help me follow the prescription. Here's how to do it:

- State agreement with an aspect of, or the full, preceding statement. "I like that." "I agree." "You're right!"

- Acknowledge appreciation for the person's sharing their thinking or perspective. "Thank you for noting that." Alternatively, note the value, benefit, or helpfulness of the person's statement. "Good point." "I get what you're saying."

- *Then*, add an "And . . ." to continue with your point. "Good point. And, to add to that . . ."

- Smile genuinely.

In short, dialogue occurs when there's back-and-forth idea sharing. With trust, connecting statements evolve into "I agree with most of that" or "I disagree with that and here's why." Fleshing out differences of opinion helps everyone get things right, together.

Encourage Comments During Calls

The best ideas emerge when everyone has a say. Meetings or calls when only one or two people speak aren't necessarily as valuable as those with broad participation. You can foster this in a few ways.

- For starters, after speaking, ask an open-ended question and *then wait* for fifteen seconds for people to respond to it: "What's going through your mind?" "Is there a reaction or a concern?" "What questions do you have?" "What would you like to know more about?"

- Before a call or meeting, ask a person to bring a question with them and ask it. Often, it only takes one question for others to feel comfortable and ask their own.

- Encourage the use of chat during virtual meetings.

- Always acknowledge the value of someone's question to encourage participation. "I'm glad you asked about that." "Good question."

- If the group size allows it and it's appropriate because all know one another, ask participants by name to comment.

Answer Succinctly in Short Sentences

Answering succinctly best addresses the other person's needs. You can start by providing a yes or no response, if it applies. Add clarifying qualifiers or explanations after that. Explain your intention to answer the question succinctly and ask if there are any follow-ups. Here's an example of a succinct answer following this format: Question: "Will some people need more than twenty-four hours of training?" Answer: "Yes. A few groups of learners, based on the number of processes and activities they need to learn, will have more than twenty-four hours of training. The average across all 1,500 learners is five hours of training. Some groups of learners have a thirty-minute session. I'm glad you asked about that!" Be aware that some interpret the "Am I making sense?" query at the end of an answer as a suggestion of inferior intelligence instead of a clarity check. Instead, ask, "Did I understand your question?" or "Did I answer the question?"

Offer Assistance

Opportunities to assist others help build goodwill. Without risking the completion of your own work, a training lead can offer help across the project team. For example, training leads can help the project leaders develop a status template. They can also offer to share lists of process-based end user activities from the curriculum-planning work with the testing lead. Offering to review a communication template or review a deck is often appreciated, as are special presentations to select business teams about the digital transformation training program. While helping others is a win, training leads must also attend to their own needs.

Balance Personal Needs and Leadership

Self-care and self-awareness are practices that the training lead pursues to maintain their energy and equanimity in best handling day-to-day work situations.

Ensure a Steady Stream of Positive Leadership Messaging

Follow thought leaders on social media and sign up for leadership emails and blog posts that provide inspiration on an ongoing basis, as well as guidance and specific help to lead better through challenging times. On some really tough days, a fifteen-minute TED Talk provided the motivational insight that helped me move forward.

Be Rigorous in Managing Your Own Work

Giving continuous attention to all of the work, deliverables, priorities, and next steps involved in digital transformation training can be overwhelming. For help with this, consider the work of business and productivity strategist Mike Williams, who wrote *Doing to Done*. His ideas, practice, and easy-to-follow steps have helped me organize the many pieces of digital training leadership into achievable steps (Williams, 2022).

Seek Guidance and Help When It's Needed

You'll feel when a situation is challenging and know it exceeds your skills and ability to find a clear path through the churn. Don't go it alone. Seek out help and different perspectives from trusted advisors about how to resolve a situation. Be ever open to feedback. Remember your end goal: It's about getting things right for the learners. Seeking help may be the difference between solving the problem and seeing it fester and worsen.

Communications and caring about people, including yourself, and attending to the network of relationships form the core of effective digital transformation leadership. They matter because stronger leaders are better equipped to drive the work forward and navigate through challenging situations.

WHAT GETS IN THE WAY

All of the 90-plus "What Gets in the Way" callouts throughout *Digital Transformation Champions* represent opportunities and challenges for the training lead—and others—to resolve. However, the following two additional callouts are specific to digital training leadership on digital transformation programs. As the training lead, you'll need to be aware of these two obstacles.

Experiencing an Accountability Vacuum

There's a truism about any project, but especially digital transformations: Some people are more accountable and responsible than others. My favorite projects are those where in every meeting, someone is quick to take ownership for a follow-up, issue, or task related to their area of responsibility without being asked. This is not the norm, unfortunately. These all-too-common vacuums of accountability may reflect misunderstanding about roles or acceptable professional behavior or a business culture that tolerates poor performance.

Working Smarter: Program leaders set the tone and drive accountability across the project teams by modeling responsibility and ownership themselves. Does the program lead tell you to call or email someone else, or do they commit to getting the answer and then does so? Are roles, responsibilities, deliverables, and ways of working clear and consistently carried out by all? To request greater accountability across the workstreams, can you speak with program leaders and share your observations and examples? Always start with an assumption of good intentions and give the benefit of the doubt. Share your objective to help the project achieve its goals. "Could I get your perspective on a situation and help resolving some challenges the training team is experiencing?" Staying on top of accountability matters because there will be times when you cannot allow others to compromise the on-time completion of training deliverables. For example, subject matter inputs, security role design, role assignments to people, and training schedules are critical dependencies for training. In these situations, use status and risks, actions, issues, and decisions (RAID) to escalate and manage risks if the discussions fall short of finding an owner.

Dealing with Inconsistent Collaboration

Digital transformation training work overlaps with several other areas, including project testing, change management, communication, and other company training programs. While collaboration among these professionals is the norm, some individuals may refuse to engage meaningfully due to personal issues. In some cases, the interactions are hostile and not constructive, despite the importance of transformation training for learners and the business as a whole.

Working Smarter: Ego can get in the way of effective collaboration—just make sure it's not your own if you're the training lead. As for others, can conversation uncover concerns or the questions behind resistant or hostile behaviors? What expectations about the work and role are misunderstood? Leveraging communication and leadership skills can sometimes help secure the needed collaboration. Always act with professionalism and respect. Ask questions to better understand and connect the ideas. Reinforce the importance of working together for the business. Remember to use the word "because" to explain yourself (communication briefings, 1993a). Ask for feedback bravely and express appreciation for its being shared. Show how you have acted on it by following up with the person later. In the few instances where poor behavior persists and nothing else works, take a breath. Inhale deeply and exhale the stress, then move on and complete the work.

Final Note

Training leadership is the glue that makes everything else stick for the digital transformation training program. Leaders who are skilled, inspired, healthy, and grounded are better prepared to lead in general and especially through trying times. It boils down to strong collaboration and operating with a mindset that everyone's doing their best, all wish to succeed, and others want to step up to help realize shared goals. The next chapter covers how to help the digital transformation project team develop skills about the system and new processes to carry out their important work.

5

Equipping Project Teams with Core Knowledge

"An investment in knowledge pays the best interest."
—Benjamin Franklin

*P*roject team training is a mini project within the larger digital transformation. *Business and project decision-makers need to learn the new system and its modules and features so they can lead the transformation of end-to-end processes. This type of training typically includes system setup and configuration along with the transactional activities that are part of standard business processes. These project leaders have specific learning needs that will determine the best option for their training, usually when the transformation program starts. The training lead must help ensure a wise investment.*

BASICS

The focus of project team training is to rapidly develop technical skills and knowledge so the business leads and their teams can guide process redesign and system configuration decisions alongside the implementation partner. The training topics and information are broader and more in-depth than end users will receive, and for this reason and the fact it is needed at the start of the program, outside vendors provide the training. The starting point for project team member training is the same as the overall training approach: understand the learners and their needs, assess the training available, oversee its execution, and verify that the requirements are well met.

Project Learner Profiles

The first step is to ask who *needs* to learn the full set of system features and the business processes that the solution enables or automates. Typically, the first in line to learn is a functional workstream leader who knows the business, uses another solution, and is responsible for guiding the transformation change. For example, a senior business manager assigned to lead the transformation of a function such as quality, procurement, logistics, or customer service needs to learn how the new system functions out of the box to enable decisions about reengineering the way work gets carried out in the future. These people and others pulled from their day-to-day jobs to implement the new system and lead the transformation are typical candidates for this type of training.

Project Learner Needs

Starting with the functional scope of the overall digital transformation, identify the business areas to consider. For each type and set of learners, by function, identify *what* they need to learn. Detail the system modules, functions, data, activities, and supporting processes that are in scope for each business workstream. For example, does finance include GL, AP, fixed assets, and procurement? What about reporting? Is hands-on practice expected, or, if not, why isn't it needed? Detail what the project team learners are expected to know and do at the end of this training. Often, vendor course outlines describe a range of topics, by module, that offer a useful starting point.

Training Delivery Options Assessment

External vendors typically provide the training because the project team members get trained at the beginning of the transformation when end user training materials do not exist yet, and there are no functional trainers. Moreover, the topics in each class are more technical and cover more topics than end users will need. Common options follow.

- Often, the digital solution vendor, as part of its training portfolio, can offer an education program with consultant-level training. These in-depth trainings may span multiple courses, each taking one to five days.

- If your transformation includes very new technology and training does not yet exist, the solution system integrator may provide overviews and demonstrations.

- Other third-party vendors besides your implementation partner can be contracted to offer the training. Some of these providers are certified by the digital solution vendor to deliver training on their behalf.

The quality and experience of the vendor's training will accelerate a functional team's ability to lead the transformation in their area, so verifying the options is a best practice.

Financial Backing

Build the business case for the options and present recommendations to transformation executives to secure their support for the time and cost. Remember that in-depth technical training for the project team can cost thousands of dollars per learner. Depending upon the scope of the transformation, the size of the business teams, and the amount of training needed, the costs for project team training can be significant. Project team training is appreciated as a requirement for a more successful digital transformation.

Tracking and Reporting Needs

Monitoring the delivery and reporting on the outcomes is a necessary task for the training lead, given the expense and the importance of the training for the transformation program. Have the project team use the same feedback surveys about their vendor-led training that end users will use. Demonstrating concern about training quality and outcomes educates the workstream leads about the rigor of the overall end user training program. (See chapter 5 for more on training feedback.)

Alignment with Other Program Activities

Lastly, remember that just like end user training, core team training requires scheduling, logistics support, tracking, and reporting. Coordinate the training and ensure it aligns with the broader project timeline and activities underway to avoid conflict. Document the plan, track progress, and share feedback data. (See chapters 18 and 19 for more on tracking and reporting.)

BEST PRACTICES

Besides developing necessary knowledge and ability, well-trained project team members can leverage their business acumen and play a stronger role in guiding the best decisions about system configuration and process design to benefit the overall transformation.

Set Clear Expectations for Quality

Develop a shared vision for training quality that involves everyone, especially the training vendors. Be sure their instructors are deeply knowledgeable, skilled instructors and prepared to teach the training. Make sure those leading training can demonstrate tasks, coach others in stepping through activities, discuss the details of the business process using the system, and, finally, show others how to solve problems that arise. Does the trainer have effective visuals and provide reference materials to support the learners?

Will the learners have hands-on practice time with prepared data? Remember that the expectations for functional business trainers apply doubly to professional trainers (see chapter 17). Reinforce with vendors that the company's learners expect a quality learning experience and share the behaviors list and the post-training feedback survey you'll send to employees. Check in regularly with vendors before, during, and after each training session to reinforce agreements and expectations and to communicate delight or dismay with how the training session went.

Evaluate Day One Effectiveness

Auditing the first hour of each class provides a valuable quality check and helps provide context to the individual learner feedback that gets collected from the project team participants. If appropriate, use this opportunity with the vendor to acknowledge great training delivery. Follow up immediately to address less than acceptable training. When dealing with vendors, the recognition of excellence adds credibility when less acceptable outcomes need to be addressed. On one project with many project team training sessions, the solutions education leaders directly addressed the critical commentary because I had recognized great delivery and consistently shared learner feedback with quantitative and qualitative data.

Monitor Team Training Progress and Feedback

Update the training status, making sure to formally report on all of the core team training sessions. Report on planned and completed training. Measure overall participant ratings for the key indicators. If appropriate, share learner comments about the training. Monitor the total spend. Call out successes and add notes about any remediating actions underway. For example, if a course is low rated or canceled, is the training vendor offering a follow-on, a refund, or retraining? The training lead must reinforce the value of the overall investment and ensure that these key business learners acquire the knowledge needed to perform their roles as project team members to architect the digital transformation. Despite the planning and communication, issues will arise, and the training lead must promptly address the things that go wrong.

WHAT GETS IN THE WAY

Project team training sees issues surface that are specific to this group of learners.

Including the Wrong People in the Training

Very technical and broad process training is expensive and requires a notable time commitment from the learners, which is justified when they *need* to know the *solution*. Some stakeholders and executives accountable for the overall business function *want* to gain *awareness* of the interface and how the system works at a high level. Training participation levels and return on the investment decrease when those who do not need it are enrolled in comprehensive, expensive systems training.

Working Smarter: Typically, those assigned to the transformation program full-time are able to spend the necessary days in learning sessions because their day-to-day duties have been reassigned. Instead, for other business leaders and stakeholders who want to see the system and know how it will work, arrange demos or tailored overview sessions for their specific function. These supplementary sessions often last only a few hours and provide stakeholders with an understanding of the digital solution and how employees in their business lines will use it to carry out their jobs. Another option: Project team leads could provide these overviews after their training. Delivering an upcoming demonstration is a motivator for session participants, and they will be able to bring the transformation vision to life, which helps with overall change management.

Addressing the Absence of Developed Training

Training materials that explain process concepts, activities by role, integrations, and problem-solving take effort and time to produce. Sometimes, a course may not exist when the technology is very new. In one of my projects, I worked with a small technical consulting firm owner who offered to build the course content as a step to secure the training contract to deliver the project team training. On a different project, the project leaders and I chose to pay a vendor to develop custom content. In both instances, the custom materials never emerged because course development requires a special set of skills and significant effort over time. Today, developing custom project team training content is a DONA for me, done once—okay, I tried twice—and never again.

Working Smarter: When no course exists, work with the solution vendor or implementation partner for your project to secure "knowledge transfer" overviews. This approach carries a lower price tag because it's more free-form, demonstration-based, structured by topics, and led by participant questions and answers. Hands-on work will enhance this type of learning format.

Missing the Window of Time for Core Team Training

Project team training takes place early in the project timeline so the workstream leads have the knowledge they need to complete solution design work and prepare for testing. There is a small window of time that works, and it closes quickly.

Working Smarter: Work with the program leadership to confirm in advance when workstream leads can spend time to complete their training. Calculate the time to plan and execute the training, usually six to eight weeks or more. This includes effort to gather training requirements, review options, interview vendors, and complete the necessary legal and procurement activities. Incorporate core project team training milestones into the overall transformation project plan. Combining the two ensures everyone involved is aware of the core team training initiative: The training lead has the time and resources to develop this program, the targeted learners can plan their schedules, and project leaders prioritize project team training.

Failing to Deliver the Promised Learning Experience

While many instructors are top-notch, more than a few are not. A surprising number of professional technical "trainers" lack skills in adult learning and best training delivery. I've seen an instructor in the front of the room take a five-minute pause in projection, revisit their notes, and step through an exercise while the entire class waited. Technical consultants who try to teach without preparing and without shifting to use coaching and facilitating skills fail to see people learn, always. Even vendor instructors who know the course and materials may fail to greet learners as they enter the room, ramble and make up answers, or over-entertain instead of instructing. These potentially innocent gaffes all marginalize the training experience and prevent the learning that's needed to help the transformation project advance on time.

Working Smarter: Ask about an instructor's references when that's feasible and if there's time. Regardless—*always* audit the first hour of these training sessions. When action is warranted, take action in the moment. I did this in the example where the instructor had the class wait. I was auditing the first hour and saw that these mistakes presented problems for the session participants, who were growing more and more frustrated. I checked with the workstream lead, asked for a break, and directed the instructor to leave. I then explained my actions to the learners, letting them know I respected their time and learning experience and would secure alternate instruction— which they all appreciated. In other cases, vendor follow-ups and escalations led to credits or refunds.

On other projects, program leaders advised me to seek help when vendors failed to deliver on contracted work. Having this carte blanche made it easier for me to take action quickly to ensure quality. If you can, secure support from your in-house legal, procurement, or executive team when those options exist. These can save you significant trouble and help ensure delivery of quality project team training.

Final Note

Effective project team training makes certain that the people tasked with leading the transformation gain the knowledge about the system, options, and trade-offs to make better decisions for their business areas. This knowledge flows into and helps enhance the end user training program. Project team member training is one of many key investments that the program and business leaders make to ensure the success of a digital transformation. This and other expenses are the subject of the next chapter on the training budget.

6

Funding Support for the Digital Transformation Training Program

"Digital transformation is not just about technology—it's about people and processes. If you're not budgeting to support your people through the change, you're budgeting for failure."

—Unknown

A training budget includes the funding for the scope of the work outlined in the transformation training strategy and approach, as well as the people, tools, and services required to achieve the expected learning outcomes. In some cases, the training lead develops the budget, tracks the spend, and manages plan-to-actual reporting. In other cases, the training lead provides inputs only and someone else produces and owns the budget. In either case, the training lead must ensure the funding is adequate for both the planned and unplanned work the digital transformation training team must complete.

BASICS

The training lead may be asked to plan the workstream budget along with other leads as part of the digital transformation initiation effort. In other instances, a budget for training gets established as part of the overall business case, and the training lead may be tasked to use prescribed amounts for the work. In either case, for all months of the project time frame, a training lead should have a complete list of planned expenses by type, with estimated monthly spend.

The Right Tool or Template

Before drawing up the budget to share with others, check with the project leadership and/or the appropriate finance contact for budgeting tools and directions. A spreadsheet is the ideal tool; however, some businesses have budget software they'll want to use. You'll need to make your budget work with the business's financial language as well. Know and use the correct cost center codes to make budget roll-ups and spend tracking easier. At companies with strong cost management, monthly expenses are a budget commitment, so it's important to manage planned and actual spend month-by-month. Know all these expectations and requirements up front.

Key Items for Your Budget

Provide in your budget a line for every expense type, with expected monthly amounts, using the rules and guidance from your business finance team. A sample of common training expense types follows. Your project and company's finance policies and procedures will determine those you use.

Sample Line-Item Expenses

- *Hardware*—Capital (laptops and hardware)
- *Hotel*—Overnight travel (not conference/meeting space)
- *Labor*—Contract
- *Labor*—Full-time (add 30% for benefits, if directed to do so)
- *Meals*—Team
- *Meals*—Training events with learners

- *Rentals*—Conference/meeting space for training events, equipment, and so on
- *Services*—Editing, translation, professional voice, printing, etc.
- *Shipping*
- *Software Licenses/Fees*—Technology and tools
- *Supplies*—Noncapital technology, office tools, gift cards, flip charts, etc.
- *Training*—Core project team and training team members' development
- *Travel*—Contractors, training team members, and functional trainers
- *Others*—Items specific to your digital transformation training program
- *Contingency*—A 10% or more amount for unplanned requests and changes

Having one thorough training budget plan that's easy to update and revise from project to project is a good goal for digital transformation training leaders. You'll find that in most cases the categories of expenses won't vary much.

BEST PRACTICES

Preparing a budget is a common activity. There are some considerations that will help digital transformation training leads secure resources to deliver results.

Partner to Secure Proper Funding

The strategy sets forth the expected deliverables and work involved in your transformation training, including any additional cost-driving responsibilities such as oversight for end user role mapping, project team training, or administration of a separate training environment. The training lead needs to confirm that the training budget enables this work. In my experience, I've benefitted most when project leaders communicate the full amounts of planned funds by expense category up front and also pledge to cover the unexpected expenses that may arise during the program due to additional business requests of the training team, added business scope, or late adds for translation. Gartner-surveyed leaders who wish they had spent twice as much as they did on training so advised, "Build a case for training investment" (Phelan, 2010, p. 9). Partner with the leaders of the digital transformation about the strategy, deliverables, learner approach, materials being produced, and tools needed to complete this work. All of these factors will help determine the full budget required for your digital transformation training program.

Calculate the Instructional Designers Required

One of the most important items in the training budget is resources. Do you have the right-sized and appropriately skilled instructional design (ID) team to complete the work?

- Factor in the number of project workstreams, the processes, and the count of activities, which helps with subsequent estimates.

- Calculate estimated learning time. Use ten minutes per activity, for instance, to arrive at a total training time of, say, 100 hours of training for a specific business and process area.

- Calculate the time needed to produce materials. Use an average of forty to eighty hours of effort for an ID to produce one hour of e-learning content. For producing one hour of slide-based materials, the ID will need twelve to forty hours of effort, based on old calculations and experience. Divide these totals by multiples of forty for each ID's workweek to determine a count of IDs that aligns with the project work and timelines.

Don't forget to consider other factors that may help to determine the best estimate for overall effort and the way to meet it—for example, the type of materials being produced, the development tools, the complexity of the system and subject, the availability of knowledgeable subject matter experts, and the ID experience and knowledge of the development tools. Having *senior* IDs who are experts with digital transformation projects and multiple toolsets will enhance the overall training team and the efficient output of training material. The up-front expense of hiring a senior-level designer, whether full-time or contract, is a very worthwhile investment.

Know Training's Impact on the Bottom Line

Different companies will account for the training costs differently, depending on how the training is presented. For example, training programs that create libraries of tailored training materials that will be durable for three to five years may be treated as a *capital investment*. In this case, the business will allocate the total amount spent for digital transformation training over a period of years. On the other hand, some companies account for training-related costs as a monthly *expense*. Capitalized training programs *may* see greater comfort with a larger spend because the amounts get distributed over time. Either way, a company's finance leader makes the decision on how training expenses will be categorized. The training lead must know which method applies and whether business durability of the materials is a financial requirement, not just a development best practice.

Prepare for Unexpected Costs

To cover unexpected costs that *will* arise, ensure the training budget includes a contingency line with an amount of at least 10%. Make that percentage higher if the scope and significance of the implementation warrants it. For example, a first-time implementation will usually see ongoing changes in processes, activities, and system scope that could increase the training work and even the length of time that instructional resources are needed.

A good budget sees the training team equipped to carry out the strategy and deliver expected results. There's no time to fight for financial support for resources and tools when the focus is on completing materials, preparing functional trainers, and starting end user training.

WHAT GETS IN THE WAY

I've seen two specific complications with budgeting emerge that affect the training program and challenge training leadership.

Underfunding the Training Program

I've seen an overemphasis on price at the expense of the need and benefit of the spend. A lack of resources creates unnecessary risk. For example, on one project, I was required to make do with old training development tools and only one or two licenses—despite having a large ID team. This decision derived from a desire to save money and limited the velocity of training material production, which cost much more than the extra licenses. On another project, to save money, the program leadership asked that we hire inexperienced contractors versus senior IDs. This decision meant we needed additional time from the experienced IDs to teach the contractors how to create training materials. My time increased in overseeing their work and providing coaching and support. In a few cases, the contractors were terrific; in others, they never met the need, challenged the entire team, and produced poorer quality training materials.

Working Smarter: If, as a training lead, you own the training budget, the company has implicit trust in your ability to manage decisions about the training spend. However, when you *do not* manage the budget, add a milestone to the project plan for training funding. Regardless, use the risks, actions, issues, and decisions (RAID) log to document options and decisions, especially any that pose risk to meeting your deliverables or deadlines. Where appropriate and possible, for each deployment, work into your strategy and training approach the high-level investment cost of training as a savings for hypercare: Spend now, save later.

Not Seeing Reports of Your Training Expenses

Whether they do or do not manage the training budget, training leads must track training expenses. On one of my projects, the actual service costs didn't show as being spent in the planned month because the vendor failed to submit invoices in a timely manner. This became an issue because the unspent amounts planned for a given month did not carry over into the next period. In a use-it-or-lose-it situation, we lost the budget for that period and appeared over budget.

Working Smarter: At the outset, work with all your vendors to ensure invoices get provided monthly to meet the planned expense time frames. Make sure all invoices are copied to you. Explain your need and your expectations—you're the customer, and the vendor always wants to get paid!

Final Note

There's a finding to share from the previously noted Gartner report. Business leaders responsible for business transformation programs reported their average spend for training to be about 15%–30% of the overall implementation costs, and when programs fell short of the low end, implementations were three times more likely to run late and over budget compared with companies that spent 17% or more on training (Phelan, 2010, p.8, p.13). Budgeting, then, should be developed as a skill and talent that digital transformation training leads use to ensure the resources exist to complete the work expected of the team. Effective communication with stakeholders will help training leads obtain funds and other support and is the topic of the next chapter.

7

Stakeholder Presentations That Make an Impact

"A great presentation gives smart ideas an advantage."

—**Nancy Duarte**, Designer, Presentations Expert, and Author

igital transformation training presentations are equal parts opportunity and challenge for training leads. Every presentation—a slide-centered speaking engagement, a one-on-one call, or a meeting—is a chance to re-share the vision, communicate relevant progress, and report gaps and needs, while skillfully gathering feedback and making specific asks of colleagues and stakeholders. The need is making each one relevant so it's a step forward in building a valuable relationship. Presentation mastery is not in delivery, but in listening and dynamically adjusting to meet the needs of the audience.

BASICS

Stakeholders in the context of training presentations include any of the target audience groups throughout each phase of the digital transformation. For instance, introducing and getting input about the training approach focuses on topics about the learners, the timelines, and the expected types of materials. Speaking later to the importance of functional business trainers, the conversation addresses the needed numbers, the traits, the time they need to commit, as well as the support they need from their leaders and others to succeed. A variation of this presentation is appropriate for the functional trainer onboarding—they need to recognize who they'll teach and how, and know that a broad group of people commit to supporting them. In short, training presentations persist throughout all phases of the digital transformation, reinforcing each time how the activities that support employee learning translate to business success.

First and foremost, remember that any presentation is never about the presenter; it's always about the needs of the audience and the appropriate message for their point of view. Training leaders need to provide three types of presentations about the training in a digital transformation: the big picture, ongoing updates, and needing help.

Presenting the Digital Transformation
Training Program Activities and Timelines

Big picture training overviews occur mostly at the beginning of the transformation program when the training strategy, materials, and training tools are being decided. They explain what, how, when, and who does what to develop end user knowledge and abilities. Typically, in my experience, they are short presentations, embedded within broader program presentations. As the network of stakeholders and change champions expands, especially about six months ahead of the launch, training is a topic of great interest—because it touches so many and because it is generally understood to be critically important to the success of the launch. In particular, companies with previous failed implementations will be hyper-focused on training, at least early on. Throughout the life of the project and key stages such as the solution design, when the start of end user training approaches, and when training is finished and the go live looms, the topics of your presentations to leaders and others necessarily shift.

Highlighting What's Working

Progress overviews and ongoing updates show the digital transformation training journey and current phase. These updates signal overall status and communicate accomplishments and risks. Done well, these stakeholder presentations drive action and secure support when it's needed. The transformation leadership may provide a basic or detailed template to use for these presentations. If not, determine a framework that works to highlight key aspects of the program in a dashboard-like format that shows activities and progress with updates over time. The dashboard samples shared at the back of *Digital Transformation Champions* are meant to provide this start for you.

Communicating Issues and Asking for Help

While issues and problems are not anyone's first choice of a presentation topic, challenges do arise with every digital training program. When presenting to any of the impacted stakeholders about problems, openly address the original goal and be specific about the issue and its root causes. Then review the options and the proposed mitigation plan. Secure buy-in or get help in determining the next step. This type of presentation may be a conversation, without slides. Asking for help from stakeholders can help you obtain any needed insight and, of course, support. For example, when a vendor failed to deliver the contracted-for custom training materials, the project leads were instrumental in getting resources to use an alternate method. Always make sure to include the following elements, which are the essential components for credibly handling zigzags: Commit to the resolution, specify a time frame for doing so, and explain when updates will be proactively shared. Ongoing status report commentary is often acceptable; the lead may be asked to log a risks, actions, issues, and decisions (RAID) item and make notes until the issue is resolved.

Across these three types of presentations, some fundamentals will help.

BEST PRACTICES

A few considerations will see you make the most of any planned time you have in front of your stakeholders. These concepts can also help leverage ad hoc opportunities.

Get in the Audience's Frame of Mind

Within your allotted time, it's easy to give an update on the initiative or to know what you want to say; however, it's more important to think about what the audience wants and needs to hear. Prior to your presentation, you can ask yourself some questions culled from presentation gurus Garr Reynolds (2008) and Nancy Duarte (2008).

- Why am I being asked to speak to this audience?
- What keeps the audience up at night?
- What's the problem the audience expects me to solve?
- What does the audience expect of me?
- What do I want the audience to do?
- How does the audience define training success?
- What's the single point I want the audience to take away?

You can check your thinking by speaking with a few representative members of the audience. When your presentation is relevant to the audience, they'll listen and engage with you.

Engage with Presentations That Resonate

For the presentation to be effective and complete, you'll need to address seven areas.

1. Purpose. Be clear about the reason for the presentation or conversation. Why are you meeting at this point in time? Did others ask for the presentation? What support of stakeholders is needed for the overall training initiative at the current stage of the project?

2. Content. Visuals, handouts, decks, or other materials are often necessary components. To save time, repurpose existing content or information where you can. Sparingly create new materials. When you must, design them with reuse in mind.

3. Speaking Time. Be prepared to use just half the time planned in case those speaking before you, and any audience questions, shorten the time you have. If you are allotted fifteen minutes to speak, aim to cover all your points in about

seven minutes. Your ability to speak with brevity comes with preparation and practice, unless you're naturally very quick on your feet.

4. Preparation. The quality of your presentation depends in part on how you'll share information verbally. For every slide, note between three and five *speaking points*, and spend fewer than one to one and a half minutes covering them. Then *transition* to the next slide with words that bridge ideas from one slide to the next. For example, use a question an audience member could have, a summary statement, or some other comment, such as, "You might be wondering…" or "This is important because…"

5. Practice. Talk aloud by yourself all the points of each slide and go through the entire presentation multiple times, until the words sound and feel natural. For key presentations, have a run-through with the project leads or others to get feedback and for the practice. Time yourself.

6. Authenticity. In the context of a training presentation, authenticity means that you are sincere and open. This effect is helped when presenters use a conversational style that feels natural to the audience (Reynolds, 2023). Let emotions become part of the presentation. Express excitement when it's appropriate. When speaking to challenges, be honest and transparent about your feelings. Always recognize the team effort required for any training success and accept responsibility when it's required.

7. Audience Engagement. The best presenters maintain their audience's attention. They do this by pausing to check in every few minutes about what's top of mind and by using proven techniques.

   » Ask specific closed- or open-ended questions that get a response and generate useful information quickly. For example, a good question might be, "Did everyone receive that communication packet?" Depending on the format, to collect answers, you could use virtual or physical hands-up, thumbs-up/sideways/down. Online meetings offer polls and chat features: "We need a contact for training at your site. Could you please use the chat to share the name?"

   » State the questions your audience likely has in mind or that you've heard to shift from your topics to their thoughts. For example, "The amount of time your team will need to spend in training may be top of mind," or "Some of you have asked what topics the training course will cover and when training will start."

Over time, these techniques become second nature when you prepare for and facilitate calls. Attending to these elements helps you balance between what you need your audience to know and do and uncovering their concerns and questions.

Make Clear Asks

To draw people in, training presentations must be more than a "tell" talk through. People want to have a say and want to help. For this wisdom, I thank a program manager who taught me about making "asks" in every stakeholder presentation. What this means is you turn statements about a tell into an invitation: "We've seen this work well and want to hear your thoughts about it." A great example of when to use this technique is when you need to secure support for the *time* people spend learning new tools and processes. As an example, "Your employees will begin their training in a few months. The time is an investment in knowledge and skills development, with the payoff being transformed business operations. Can I ask your support for their having this time to learn?"

Another example is asking business executives to prepare a video message that expresses their support for the business change and their appreciation to employees for making time to learn. The video is embedded in an e-learning or a business trainer plays it at the start of a live training. Having a message like this has a positive influence on learner motivation.

In my earlier projects, I could have used asks more to publicly demonstrate the desire to collaborate. Now, when a stakeholder forum doesn't exist, I create one or seek out an opportunity to join a scheduled call so I can make asks.

Share Visuals That Tell a Story

Where there's flexibility to do so, add a visual that's relevant to the training work underway. Using a photo of an activity helps make the abstract concrete. For example, try inserting a photo of an information-gathering session or a training team working session. Later, share images of functional business trainer preparations and groups of people learning, along with notes of appreciation and highlights about progress.

Provide a Timeline Infographic

With any update, anchoring people to the work underway as part of the overall journey and timeline helps show the current stage and where training is going. Such updates provide context for accomplishments or any challenges to address. A visual with major milestones with light detail and a "We Are Here" label provides an easy way to appreciate progress and what's next.

Dig Into Concerns

It's important to be willing to pause your presentation and address any resistance that's heard. Don't just acknowledge you heard it; instead seek to understand the issue. It may be a question out of left field or a critical aside not having anything to do with the topic at hand. Take the opportunity you have on the call to follow up. Phil Grosnick, author of "Dealing with Resistance" (a chapter in *The Flawless Consulting Fieldbook and Companion*), identifies resistance as someone's indirect expression of very real concern. Being heard and understood, however, usually opens a door to working together to solve the underlying issue (Grosnick, 2001, p. 91–94). Training leads can work to overcome resistance by restating what you're hearing: "Let me see if I hear you. You've had some bad experiences with training in the past and have concerns now about hands-on practice," or "From what you're saying, it seems you may be worried that the training content won't meet the needs your business teams have." If you hear agreement, acknowledge the validity of the concern. Appreciate its being shared. Then ask, "What can I do or provide to help address these concerns?" If there is nothing shared on the call, commit to following up. Maintain an accessible list of frequently asked questions about the digital transformation training program and keep it current with concerns and topics raised on stakeholder calls.

The focus of presentations should always be creating a two-way communications forum for key leaders. Stakeholders need to be able to express uneasiness and receive information they need about end user training activities and, importantly, what they must do to support the training program. Some things typically get in the way.

WHAT GETS IN THE WAY

The misses with presentations reflect ignored opportunities and confusion that stop training team leads from connecting with stakeholders in a meaningful way.

Relying on Only One Communication Channel

Training leads who over-rely on formal presentations will limit their ability to be effective. Different communication channels serve different needs. For example, formal presentations and large-group sessions rarely work for candid or critical inputs. These are best had with one-to-one or small-group conversations.

Working Smarter: Along with formal *presentations* to groups, schedule calls or find other ways to have direct *conversations* with individual stakeholders or small groups of key people. On an ongoing basis, you can even leverage casual interactions described in chapter 4, training leadership to connect with business and other transformation program stakeholders. A direct email can work too.

Mismatching the Presentation to the Need

There are more than ten books that combine the words *PowerPoint*, *death*, and *boredom* in the title because text-only slides feel tedious to viewers. Numerous leaders, authors, and designers advocate for wordless slide designs to counter "death by PowerPoint." The gold standard is a Zen-like design aesthetic. An example is a large photo with a summary statement. I like and have used this method. With digital training, this technique can fail because the deck and slides get shared after a call, when there's no one to explain them. Getting the format right is a balance.

Working Smarter: First, understand the expectations that the business and transformation leaders have and the slide formats that they use normally and like. What's the business culture? Flex that to combine effective use of graphics and words to communicate about training. *Make sure the purpose and relevant detail of every slide are clear whether you're speaking to them or not.* When you do present, summarize the text on a screen and *never* read the text exactly as it appears on a slide. If a slide has a lot of detail, can you animate sections to help lighten the information load? Alternately, take the audience on a "tour" of the information by top-left, top-right, and so on, calling out the important highlights and noting that the slide will be shared afterward for careful review. Include a legend if it helps. Finally, never apologize for using detail. Instead, explain its purpose and value.

Preparing Poorly

Sometimes it can be a challenge to find time to prepare fully. Having the right slides doesn't matter if you haven't practiced using them. We've all seen a presenter who failed to prepare and never want to be that person.

Working Smarter: Set aside fifteen to sixty minutes to thoughtfully prepare, as the audience and the purpose of the presentation dictate. Be clear about the call's purpose, the audience's needs, and the expected outcomes. Talk through the presentation out loud multiple times. One source about tricks to ease nerves suggests physical exercise and positive self-talk (Detz, 1993). Finally, answer this: How will you know you've met your audience's needs at the end of the call?

Neglecting Perceptions or Missing Feedback

There's the saying "What we don't know *will* hurt us." In one case, after a group presentation, I followed up with a business VP about any questions I may not have fully answered during the earlier call. My request was misinterpreted as a desire to report a critical problem. This resulted in an uncomfortable call with my manager's boss and other VPs. On another project, I was surprised to hear that some business stakeholders felt that nice-looking slides in a presentation suggest decisions have been made and that input is neither needed nor desired. I began putting "construction tape" or a superimposed D R A F T overlay on some slides to reinforce the idea that things were in process and input was needed and being sought on the call.

Working Smarter: The ultimate value of working relationships is the trust that enables constructive feedback. Both sides need to feel comfortable sharing their thoughts and reactions. Remember, silence is not always agreement. When you know, as a leader, you're not getting the input you need, you must solicit it. Leadership requires the ability to take action and have the difficult conversations, expressing why they matter. Asking follow-up questions is an essential communication skill for training leads. You will need to pose questions that seek to validate your understanding and elicit any underlying anxiety or needs stakeholders may have. When you've failed to take action or taken a step you wish you hadn't, acknowledge it publicly, recognize there's a learning opportunity, and commit to doing better next time. This accountability helps establish trust and credibility.

Having a Poor Presentation Day

Sometimes, some days, despite all the preparations and even years of experience, we're just not at our best. At times, I've found myself with an unexpectedly shaky voice, which feels unnerving and undermines a usual display of comfortable confidence. We've all experienced technical issues before and during a presentation, despite setting up early. Bad days, or bad moments, do and will happen.

Working Smarter: While you can't and shouldn't necessarily prepare to fail, you can prepare yourself to respond calmly when things inevitably go awry. Pause. Recognize what's happening in the moment. Roll with technical issues; don't worry too much about them. You know your main points and can speak to them without slides. In the case of a shaky voice, usually that's caused by not breathing deeply. A few deep breaths steady me and my voice. Pause, then slow down. Lastly, don't forget to smile. I've found it helps me and every presenter carry on and do the best job in the moment.

Final Note

Every interaction a training lead has with transformation colleagues and business leaders is a chance to check in about the training vision and share relevant progress, as well as anything that's behind, while gathering feedback and making specific asks. The best presentations combine great content, effective delivery, and listening to hear needs *in the moment*. These things give your smart ideas an advantage and usually help the overall training program. The next group of chapters covers training material planning and development, a topic in which stakeholders are especially interested and involved.

8

Tools and Technologies to Power Training

"The usefulness of a thing is dependent not on what it is,
or how it can be used, but on the needs or wants of the user."
—**Mokokoma Mokhonoana,** Philosopher, Author, and Brand Strategist

Selecting the tools and establishing how the training team will use them is an early training milestone. The set of technology needs follows training delivery requirements determined from the audience analysis. These are based on the scope of what users must learn and do, the systems being taught, learning considerations, and the catalog of training material components. These must fit within the context of the overall training strategy, transformation program timeline, and budget. By analyzing options and assessing possibilities, the team can generate prototypes and document standards for quality. A systematic approach to this design activity accelerates training material development, increases work velocity, and eliminates the potential for costly mistakes and wasteful rework.

BASICS

To begin thinking about options, start by looking at the training material deliverables and the various learning tools and services that will be needed. The aim is to create a comprehensive list of *relevant*, *appropriate* components and tools so the training program meets learner and business needs in the form of effective training materials and post-training support resources.

Imagine your different learners as they will participate in the training that you and your team will provide. What will their training experience include? What materials will learners have before, during, and after their training? What resources will support them on the job? How will the training team work with subject matter experts and approvers to review and comment on training materials? The following list of options represents typical elements and some exceptional ones that may be part of the digital transformation training tools portfolio.

What's in the Training Portfolio?

This is meant to be a comprehensive list of possibilities, alphabetized within each category, to help you identify materials and tools for your training program.

Possible Types of Learning Content and Support

- Audio—music; narration using internal, professional, or AI-generated voice; single or multiple languages

- Data for training and practice sessions

- Free or for-fee existing end user training materials for the solution

- Games

- Images—stock photos, illustrations, other graphics

- Knowledge checks—those that occur during the training that are *formative* to help reinforce new ideas, and a *summative* test or other evaluation given at the end of training to verify that learners can demonstrate mastery of key concepts

- Participant guides, printed or PDF; if PDF, editable digital workbooks or read-only

- Process models—flows or process summaries

- Scenarios—day-in-the-life scenarios for training, practice, or certification

- Screenshots—labeled or not
- Simulations—providing an interactive way to step through an on-screen activity in a specific way
- Step-by-step guides—print job aids or how-to videos showing steps to complete a task
- Surveys
- Tests
- Videos
  - » Video messages from senior leaders about why the training is important
  - » Videos that provide an overview of the solution, basic navigation, and process
  - » Videos that explain key process concepts
  - » Video stories showing people in the business performing the multiple tasks carried out in the workplace as part of a process

What you and your training team select will depend on your business, learner needs, and the digital transformation.

Questions to Guide Your Toolset Selection

In addition to the previous learning components, other possible elements can emerge as the training team considers further needs.

- Accessibility and accommodation requirements some learners have—large TVs, other equipment, subtitles on videos, color and design considerations
- Content storage and management
  - » *External* for end user and learner-facing materials
  - » *Internal* for the extended training and program teams to use in creating and reviewing materials
  - » Backup copies of the materials

- Digital adoption platform for in-application performance support

- Editing

- Game platform

- Learning management system (LMS) for learner access to the assigned training, knowledge checks, completion tracking, and reporting

- Printing

- QR codes for linked references, surveys, polls, or games

- Reporting tools for end user training activities and knowledge verification

- Status tracking and reporting about training materials being produced, their review and approval, as well as end user training plans, progress, and preparations

- Storyboards for e-learning, audio segments, and overview videos

- Surveys and polls

- Testing solution providing a bank of questions and randomized answer choices for the most valid checks of knowledge

- Tracking tools for material development, functional trainer preparation, business training schedules, and communications

- Training and practice environment that mirrors a non-production instance of the solution

- Training session management, including calendar invites, for in-person sessions

- Training team communications and storage locations

- Translation

- Voice transcription

- Web storage for videos and other files

Working from a long list of possibilities, the training team can begin thinking about specific tool options and then move on to a rapid analysis before creating training material samples.

Six Steps for Rapid Analysis

At this point, there are six steps to prioritize and focus the overall tool review and analysis process. A table illustrating steps one through three identifies the needs, possible needs, and the tools that *could* be considered. Then steps four through six explain narrowing and testing the options, which the best practices detail. The goal is to test and identify the right tools for your digital transformation training program. These first three steps are illustrated in the following table and precede any sample material development.

1. Prioritize and sort the list of material and activity components into three categories: what's essential, nice to have, and not necessary. Set aside the unnecessary items.

2. For essential and nice-to-have components, document the specific need and any potential variations.

3. For each, identify any tools that are being used at the company already or that could be used to produce the component or service the need. Code the options that have cost using a variation seen with restaurant reviews: Add one "$" or up to "$$$$" or leave a blank when no additional cost applies.

Rapid Analysis

Component	Need	Options
PDF participant guides learners can interact with	No-print, digital-only training handouts with places for learners to add responses Ability to print the handout when needed	Adobe Acrobat ($) Word doc with form fields, saved as a PDF
In-application support	Easily accessed button or link to approved support materials and how-to content	Help menu link to a catalog of how-to resources in a central repository Digital adoption tool ($$$$)
Surveys	Anonymous feedback Learner-identifiable feedback Stakeholder feedback Learner tests Likert scale Open-ended text Branded look and feel Multiple choice, random	MS Forms Google Forms SurveyMonkey ($$) LMS test question feature

4. Narrow the list of options to no more than two possibilities for each item. Weight more heavily any current tools that the team members like and use. Can you eliminate tools quickly based on the cost or learning curve? Do secure-use requirements at your company mean you should avoid no-fee options[5]

5. Conduct a proof-of-concept exercise for the remaining two options. Have training team members build prototypes to test how each tool works, how much time it takes to create the sample, and how well the product meets the needs the team identifie[6]

6. To secure support from program leaders for the training program and for budgetary requests, showcase the prototypes to a group of relevant training, business, and transformation program stakeholders. When and how to do this will follow in the "Best Practices" and "What Gets in the Way" sections.

Prototyping Pays Dividends

For the training team, proof-of-concept sample creation and testing identifies any limitations a tool has or confirms its usefulness. Is the tool easy to work with and does it produce what's expected? Is there additional functionality or other helpful features? Is the tool compatible with the others being tested? How much time was required to produce the sample? Knowing the level of effort needed to create each type of material is an input to the overall material development plan the training lead or instructional design lead starts. Prototypes evolve into templates and help the instructional designers (IDs) establish standards that accelerate overall training development and help realize quality, consistently.

Project leaders and business stakeholders can buy into the digital training approach when they see examples of the materials and get asked to provide feedback early on. Their review also validates the training team's interpretation of the audience analysis and assessments about how best to meet both learner and business needs. Finally, budget support to obtain the tools the team needs to carry out the training program rarely occurs without a demonstration of value.

BEST PRACTICES

Some considerations will help the training team move forward more effectively with this phase of their work.

Use What You Have

As you review needs and options for tools, obtain the list of your company's approved and licensed software and systems. These tools are the easiest to obtain, sometimes at a lower cost or even no cost, depending on the license agreement.

Benchmark with company training colleagues to identify technologies they use, especially the more significant ones like learning management and digital adoption platform solutions. Enterprise or available licenses may exist, allowing you to use them without additional cost. Similarly, there may be available licenses for screen grab, video storage, and other tools that the training team anticipates using.

Plan for Potential Needs

Anticipate variations in needs when planning for learning content and toolsets. For example, consider whether course materials the trainer or participants use for learning could be either digital or printed. This matters if training delivery shifts from fully in-person to virtual. Reword the need: "Training course materials support both group- and self-led training" and "Participant guides can be produced and used in print or digital format." While you can flex self-paced content to group delivery by playing the course in a group setting, experience shows and colleagues confirm that converting group-based slides to *effective* self-paced training can be expensive and time-consuming when it arises as a need later on. Anticipate the need to use e-learning as a group-based tool. Better requirements help the team fully evaluate all the options.

Consider whether software you already use might have features to solve new needs. On one of my projects, to focus learners' attention, we needed to animate a graphic that listed each step in a process. We discovered that multiple free and for-purchase applications exist to produce animated GIFs. However, it was a happy surprise when we realized that PowerPoint can export animated GIF files at no additional cost—a double win because we'd already used PowerPoint to create the learner-friendly process models.

Try Tools Before Buying

Thirty-day free trials can work well, if you consolidate your testing efforts to take full advantage of the constrained time period. Either phase the start of thirty-day trials to avoid running out of time or ask the vendor for an extra fifteen to thirty days if the time is insufficient around other testing. Some vendors will extend the normal trial period; others cannot.

Check Online Reviews

When the costs and business stakes are high for learner impact, broaden the qualitative inputs about a promising option. Before choosing a tool, spend ten minutes to research online ratings and comparative reviews. For expensive tools, ask for a demo and speak with existing customers. Keep in mind that vendors seed positive comments and will make every effort to connect potential customers with their most satisfied customers. Read queries and posts in support communities. This is an accelerated activity meant to help narrow the choices, especially for the more expensive tools such as digital adoption platforms and learning management systems.

Uncover Any Pre-Existing Training Materials

Search online for preexisting content or training sessions that others offer, whether fee-based or no-cost, for learning to use the digital solution. These may be created by the vendor, a third party, or independent training firms. If those don't exist, are there others who offer training material development services for a fee? Assess the quality of any predeveloped training material, either vendor-provided materials or those purchased from a third party, and the costs. For example, generic training videos from a vendor website may or may not work for your needs. Here's the test: Will the look, feel, feature set, and story be helpful to your learners? On multiple projects, I was asked about using "free" vendor training. For both an ERP and an expense solution, after reviewing the materials, I found they included nonrelevant features or unused functionality or had a very different interface than the solution being introduced to the company. The need to provide materials that resonate with end users meant custom training content using the company's system were developed.

Most transformation programs configure a solution to meet specific business needs, tailored to the business requirements. Similarly, while training materials typically get developed from the ground up, the opportunity here is to identify existing content that can be leveraged whether it exists externally or internally. Passionate business stakeholders may appreciate the reuse of "old" system training assets or a familiar template or term. An implementation partner or the vendor may provide user-facing materials for training, with some company-specific branding.

If you use content from others, understand their licensing, copyright, ownership, and access rules. Can you download and edit these materials, or will you need to work with the vendor to make any changes? Will the links to videos and PDFs remain static? Even when a vendor oversees training and material development, assess the components against the learner needs and expectations for quality. Always clarify who does what and when and how reviews and approvals get carried out.

Adapt as Needs Evolve

As time passes, new needs may emerge or tools in your toolkit may expand their feature sets. Remain open to revisiting a decision when necessary. On one project, the approach for capturing how-to videos in the solution worked for only 85% of the planned activities. The team identified an alternate recording approach—using another tool already in the toolkit—for the other 15% with steps outside the system.

Explore Cutting-Edge Tools

Besides producing effective learning that helps prepare business employees, an ever-present goal is to be efficient, be smart, maximize impact, and even delight the learners. The technology landscape and training development tools continue to evolve, along with learner expectations. A new tool or new feature in an existing tool may solve a problem or satisfy a new learner preference. For example, thanks to the popularity of podcasts, audio is frequently cited as a "would like to have" request. Generative artificial intelligence is a major factor in learning tool advances. Amazon's Polly software converts a script to audio, and Synthesia uses artificial intelligence to generate a lifelike speaking avatar for video and audio embedded within training. These technologies are being embedded in training software tools. As you assess your needs, also look at the newer features to assess what makes sense given the cost, time, and requirement constraints of your digital training program.

Seek Efficiencies

Digital adoption tools embedded within major solutions or hosted ones such as WalkMe and Whatfix, or even chatbots, provide learners with support within the system interface. This assistance takes the form of a help menu or widget whose content is produced using a custom tool. When first launched, these typically expensive tools were less versatile and did just one or two things. Now they generate multiple forms of helpful output and even training content such as job aids and videos. In some cases a screen cast video can be repurposed for simulations or tests. Other digital adoption tools produce content into multiple languages. Explore AI features embedded in training tools and how they might accelerate your training material development. A low-cost option is to consider ChatGPT for creating custom music clips and images and accelerating training material development in myriad ways. All of these solutions warrant investigation and testing to determine their value for your business learners. Those tools with large annual fees may require analysis for return on investment and actual cost savings in creating and maintaining training materials.

Plan for Sustainability

As you evaluate different tools, factor in post-launch considerations for upkeep and costs. Who will update the materials? What's the trigger for knowing updates are needed? Some cloud-based solutions see ongoing monthly or quarterly application updates that could require changes to the training materials. Will the tools you selected make this work easier? Harder? Is a practice environment needed after launch? Will simulations be preferred? These business decisions and requirements get addressed during the review of options if not already answered in the training strategy or as a lesson learned from an earlier implementation as part of the training closeout process, discussed later in chapter 20.

Hold Show-and-Tell Demos to Build Buy-In

Present the prototypes broadly and repeatedly to select project and business leaders for their review and feedback, and even approval. This should be a formal step in the tools selection process. When leaders and budget owners can see what's being produced and hear about the trade-offs and alternates that were considered and why the tool is recommended, they are more likely to provide purchase support. For instance, being able to speak to the time it takes to use a tool and whether that's more or less than an alternate option helps justify the recommendation and garners support for its purchase, especially if there's a cost difference.

Log Decisions

As decisions get made or revised, the training lead and those conducting the analysis must remember to document their notes, findings, and callouts for reference later *when* questions arise. Note the options, test steps, considerations, and approvals about the tools and platforms in the forum that's best for your project. This could be a risks, actions, issues, and decisions log, a status document, a strategy update, overviews on a page, or a combination of these tools. A lead ID makes updates to the material development standards and templates. The LMS administrator documents steps to use in working with that system.

Use Tool Selection to Foster Team Collaboration

Engage the training team in brainstorming components and considerations. Note that a group discussion about these lists, needs, and options is especially effective when the training team includes a blend of full-time, contractor, and offshore team members. Once the list is prioritized and scaled down, divide the testing and proto-typing among the IDs to leverage the team's thinking and gather diverse input.

Here's an example: On one of my projects, a major vendor awarded our team a best practice recognition for use of prototyping a portal for the digital adoption support information. Three team members took two weeks to coordinate a usability-based survey that asked business learners about their expectations for the look, feel, access, and naming for the knowledge platform. A raffle of several large-screen digital TVs to everyone giving feedback incentivized high response rates to a thirty-minute survey. The final portal design was very different from what several IDs had initially considered and resonated well with the learners. Taking time to gather user input usually helps realize a better solution.

Be aware of some watch items as you carry out these activities.

WHAT GETS IN THE WAY

Reviewing needs and options for training material development requires effective scoping and focus, always tied back to the audience, curriculum, and training strategy.

Overlooking the Core Training Requirements

An incomplete list of components or needs will require new analysis and testing of options later, when training development may be well underway. Not putting in time before building training materials means you risk reworking them later. For example, a late requirement for audio voice-overs on screencast videos may not be possible or not easily supported if the initial tool selection didn't consider the needs for audio.

Working Smarter: Set aside time to compile the components and needs, capturing all the suggestions, comments, and feedback from training team members and other project and business stakeholders, factoring in the learner considerations and current training models in use. Then, and this is the key, anticipate shifts in needs. Revisit the lists periodically throughout and after the initial launch and identify opportunities to better support learners, especially if yours is a multiyear transformation program and the learner feedback warrants doing so. Even smaller efforts warrant a scaled-down version of their exercise.

Failing to Manage Time and Effort

Sometimes, brainstorming and multistep analyses can generate excessive work that balloons beyond a reasonable time frame or return on the effort. You want to avoid overcomplicating the analysis.

Working Smarter: Limit the proof-of-concept period to a few weeks and not more than a month. Narrow the brainstorm list quickly, but keep refining it based on tool complexity, costs, effort for training, time reviewers would spend, effort to keep content current, and, always, value and impact for learners. This helps ensure a right-sized effort and set of tools aligned with the expectations to see business users learn new business processes and a new solution, appropriate for the degree of digital change. Doing so also demonstrates the training team's ability to deliver materials and manage its uses.

Ignoring Security Policies

Internal security requirements may change your approach for accessing and using a product. Some businesses require an IT administrator to install every application and update. Some freely available tools and sites may be blocked by a company's IT security team. Some businesses restrict service providers from certain international geographies.

Working Smarter: Start with the company-approved list of tools as a best practice. Then involve IT in the review of the prioritized list of needs and options, *before you test*.

Overlooking the Fine Print

Hidden surprises may cause fees, format incompatibilities, or extra work later. For example, cloud material development for e-learning, some video, and other tools involves annual fees and proprietary file formats that lock you into ongoing fees and may limit your ability to export the materials for use elsewhere.

Working Smarter: Be aware. Anticipate the need to change vendors in the future. Know whether you can export content or whether you'll need to rebuild. Identify the options for conversion or export and document any ongoing license costs with the budget owners. For large-fee tools, can you cancel the contract if business needs change? What's the termination period, and are there any fees?

Delaying Documentation of Findings and Results

Assessing possibilities involves experimentation, by design. The tool selection exercise involves hypothesizing, then asking and answering questions by working with a tool's features and by building prototypes. An ad hoc approach to capturing notes and documenting the finds will delay the team's ability to produce standards and templates, covered in the next section. For instance, the optimal window size for video recording has to be determined, then consistently used across the team of IDs. Testing reveals the ideal standard setting for producing learner content. Not all teams document their findings and decisions.

Working Smarter: As part of the proof-of-concept planning phase, decide on and communicate how the team will capture notes about settings, options, and observations and where these will be stored. Planned well, these notes are the start for development standards and speed template creation.

Penny-Pinching, Pain-Gaining

Digital transformation projects typically involve very high monthly spend rates that make the cost of training tools seem relatively inexpensive. Even so, in some cases there's an odd push by business budget owners and others to limit the spend on training tools or extra licenses. On one project I led, a key business team lost trust in our training team because we were authorized to use only an older version of a tool to produce a key type of training that was misaligned with the business leaders' expectations for highest-quality, enhanced output. These leaders brought in their own ID, who used the latest toolset to generate training on our behalf. It would have been less costly in terms of time and dollars if we'd just gotten the software licenses.

Working Smarter: Coach project and business stakeholders to consider the cost of better tools versus the time and costs to produce materials with older tools. Reviews of proposed tools and sample training materials with key stakeholders help align expectations about the output, quality, and need. While challenging, if business leader decisions do limit the set of tools for training, identify specialist team members who can become experts and cross-train a backup. Never skimp on having a learning management system for assigning, tracking, and reporting on training completion. My first large-scale digital implementation saw end user training tracking handled with an Excel spreadsheet that took multiple people more than a day every week to track learning for about 1,500 learners with only a 70% confidence rate in the accuracy of the data. That was a definite DONA: did it once, never again. An LMS is a success factor for digital transformation training, and I now highlight it in every digital transformation training strategy as a requirement.

Accepting Legacy Tools Without Evaluation

Digital transformation project and training teams may inherit a set of tools, or a solution vendor may bring their own set. The training lead must assess the inherited or assigned tools to ensure they meet the needs for the current digital transformation training team, the broad group of stakeholders, and the learners. Assuming these will work—failing to review and test what's available against your list of assets and needs—is a mistake.

On one of my projects, the leaders required the training team to track and report material development using the same system used for system configuration and testing defects. This tool required an administrator to set it up and required an additional log-in step for each user. The IDs felt the effort required to communicate their progress was excessive. The process really broke down when business leaders providing approval needed to log in and provide their sign-off. Fewer than 20% of approvers actually did that. The remaining 80% generated their approvals via email, IM, or a phone call, requiring someone else on the training team to manually advance the development stage in the system, wasting time. These issues unfortunately confused the actual progress and challenged my ability to report accurately about the status of training material development.

Working Smarter: When handed a set of tools or templates, review them and assess their value. Ask, "What can be better?" and "Will this work for our needs?" as well as "What are the simpler alternatives?" Look at learner and business feedback and leading practice knowledge for ideas to enhance what exists. Review the list of existing tools and materials—inspect what you expect. Test to see what works or could be more efficient and effective.

Here's an example: On another project, I inherited a model where the functional trainers needed two documents to teach. They had to use a text-heavy instructor guide with manually inserted slide images and also hold the participant guide. It took a lot of time and effort for the training team to produce and maintain these two assets. The details were helpful to the functional trainers, yet having two documents was a challenge to teach with. At that company, to help the functional trainers teach better and to reduce development effort for the training team, an ID redesigned the PowerPoint slide deck to be a multipurpose document with simplified instructor guide details in the PowerPoint notes page. Because the materials were in one document, it worked better for all and could be more easily maintained.

If training is outsourced, carefully review the vendor's list of training components and tools to understand their approach to training, learning, and measurement, and how complete it is or is not.

Final Note

In my experience, going through this process is essential because it's an up-front investment with multiple benefits. It forces a holistic consideration of what the training team will produce and ensures broad alignment across key groups of training stakeholders, both of which are necessary for digital transformation training success. It's not uncommon for business leaders and project colleagues to have experiences with marginal digital training as their norm. By showcasing the training components and tools within a framework of business and learner needs, the training team helps its program and business

---

stakeholders appreciate the *whole* of a quality digital transformation training effort. In particular, prototypes shared during stakeholder show-and-tell sessions generate helpful, necessary feedback. Samples of the training materials also help bring the training vision to life and garner support for the team's work to see all learners prepared and confident to use new systems and carry out work in new ways. Effective training content design and consistently crafted materials are the topic of the next chapter.

9

Frameworks for Quality Content and Fast-Track Development

"Consistency is what transforms average into excellence."
—Unknown

his chapter explains the foundations of digital training material design and tools that aid its development. Specific considerations and organized steps see best informed decisions about the form and structure of your training materials. The team creates and uses prototypes to test the design and get feedback from others, then sees them evolve into material templates. The training team members must define specifications, establish rules about how to use the tools and what quality means, then document these. Together, these elements see quality training materials produced consistently and as efficiently as possible so people can use them to learn the new system and processes to carry out their work and as reference after training.

BASICS

Training material tools that embed guidelines and guardrails allow the team of instructional designers (IDs) to advance with relative independence. These reference materials explain the team's decisions about how to produce materials and use the tools. The place to begin is with the terminology, grammar, and visual guidelines, or *style*, which underlies all the training team's materials.

Style Rules for Communication

Step one when creating materials is to create a style guideline document. A style guideline summarizes decisions about grammar, word usage, and branding. For example, school students get introduced to style as a way to cite references in papers, using either Associated Press (AP) or *The Chicago Manual of Style*. Similarly, E.B. White and William Strunk Jr.'s *The Elements of Style* advocates a timeless approach to clear writing. Corporations often develop their own brand book combining visual and communication directions for employees.

Your digital training style guide builds upon existing models and then includes notes and specifics relevant to the digital transformation. Typical components for a training style guide include these elements:

- Cross-reference to the company guideline or another style guideline
- Specific decisions with examples for punctuation, capitalization, numbers, and spelling
- Branding (color, font, logos, etc.) and how it relates to company and program standards
- Specific information about text hierarchy font, size, and color (headings, sub-headings, text, etc.)
- Image usage and whether to use clip art, vector graphics, and/or lifestyle photographic images, along with preferred sources the IDs should use, a company library or an online catalog such as Getty, and the proper attribution for images accessed by online search results or from a fee-based service
- Acronyms that apply to your digital transformation and how to use them—first time spelled out with acronym in parentheses, for example
- Word list and where the master glossary is maintained and how it should be linked to the training materials—seek to minimize updates to materials with links to a master glossary

Some of these choices and decisions about structure and branding get embedded into *templates*.

Content-Boosting Templates

Templates encode as many of the style decisions as possible and also incorporate standards for using a training development tool. As you build out drafts for each type of training material, explore how it can be templatized to help reinforce the style standards for every training material object. For example, the following can all be templatized:

- *Slides, documents, job aids, videos, process, and explainer graphics.* Update the structure of titles, subheadings, fonts, color palette, margins, page numbering, and spacing so that an ID can use the standard layout settings without having to worry about looking up the correct setting and manually adding the format every time.

- *E-learning components.* This includes slides, blocks, graphics, engagements, and so on.

- *Storyboards.* Besides formatting, embed standard language and even instructions to help IDs build the material, with ease and accuracy.

During the planning stage, the team works with prototypes of each training material type. This work is an up-front investment where each example can evolve into a template. Using templates sees IDs more consistently create training materials. Along with templates, training team *standards* ensure that materials share a common look and feel and that they function the same across all transformation business process areas.

Specification Standards

Standards include recipes and technical specifications as well as content placeholders for building training materials and using the development tools. These rules may or may not be embedded in a template, so it's important to document them as well. They may be incorporated into the training style guide or stored separately in a technical standards document. Having specifications collected and maintained in a central place makes it easy for IDs to access and reference them.

These elements of training documentation can evolve with each phase of the training program. They result in a more uniform use of training development tools necessary for producing a body of quality digital transformation training materials. Quality materials are more helpful to learners and have durability well beyond a single go live. Document items such as the following:

- Branding color RGB and hex codes
- Screen resolution for ID computers to use when capturing screen prints and video recording
- Video recording window size and rendered size
- Export settings: SCORM, PDF, GIF, and so on
- Settings about standard graphics and video recording
- Development standards for every tool used to create the materials, including how-to notes or links to online resources
- File and folder locations and rules for storage, including where IDs can find the training resources and where to place their own materials
- Learning management system (LMS) usage, steps, and reports
- Structure and the process of the training material
- Training environment details and data setup steps
- Template catalog: describing the item, its purpose, and link to the master file or template for each document, with links to samples

Together, all of these details help instructional designers, the LMS administrator, and others produce training materials. Consistency makes the materials easier to understand, and therefore benefits the end users and business teams who rely upon them.

BEST PRACTICES

When creating style, templates, and standards for your digital transformation training program, build upon what exists, then use and create what best supports the expectations for your training program. Validate the prototypes, then develop and maintain your documentation with rigor.

Build from the Company's Style Guides

Knowing the business foundation will help you create tools the end users will easily understand. Typically marketing or another department produces a communication standards document that details the company's brand, look, feel, and text guidelines. Look in the company's style manual for instructions about use of color, font, imagery, voice, punctuation, and tone for the company's brand. Reviewing these guidelines is the starting point for the design of all transformation training materials.

Reference Free Technical Writing Standards

Digital transformation training teams can benefit by referencing an existing guide. Both Google (2024) and Microsoft (2023) have effective models to refer to as a start. These guides illustrate the basics of technical writing that should be considered as part of your training material development approach. Digital transformation standardization requires the use of the same words for the system elements. Interface and action terms are especially important because standardizing how IDs will reference the on-screen objects and give instructions for their use provides early seeding of the language about new ways of working. Doing this with the project teams encourages adoption of the new language well ahead of end user training and helps support the business change with clarity in messaging.

Brand Beyond the Transformation

The style guide you use will document decisions about graphics appropriate to the digital training initiative *and* to the company as a whole. In some cases, the transformation program may have its own branded look, feel, and logo. In other situations, the company brand applies. Either way, the training materials should be usable beyond a single transformation go live date and their longevity must be a strong consideration for training material design. Company logos, unlike transformation logos, usually live well into the future. Consider company branding with the system colors to define the training look and feel. For one program I worked on, we chose a generic black/white/gray scheme to enhance the relevance of training materials among uniquely branded subsidiaries who would be learning a new tool and processes.

Consult Design Talent

Enlist the assistance of graphic design colleagues or a service or even AI to help create a company-resonant look and feel. Senior IDs often produce very visually effective materials, and it's true that there is often no budget for graphics support. In my experience, when a design professional assists with training material design, the overall quality and outcomes are always superior. Design guidance for visuals, color selections, and page layout gets converted into templates so the team can produce higher-quality materials, easily and with consistency, again and again.

Hold Reviews and Get Approvals

Project team colleagues and key business stakeholders must review and be asked to provide feedback about the material structure and design—ideally before more than 5% of the training material gets created. Their input improves and enhances the assets. After that point, changes and rework are time-consuming and often error-prone, even eroding progress in the overall material development work. An incentive for this review is that early samples of training materials show business and project stakeholders what the learners' experience will be, gaining support for the training approach and the team's work.

Track the Progress

Plan a milestone to receive approval for the design of training materials. Track and document the reviews and sign-offs key stakeholders provide for the learner-facing training materials, including prototypes and templates. I have needed formal sign-off for the method to track training material completion, the subject of chapter 12, "Quality Assurance Through Material Reviews and Approvals."

Keep Design Documents Updated

As new learnings emerge about what works or doesn't, have the training team update the style guide, standards documents, and templates. For instance, let's say that despite testing and a developed standard, there's learner feedback about the way a course played in the LMS. Their input necessitates two updates. The first is to adjust course settings in the LMS. The second is to note in the technical standards document the settings and explain the change. Track changes to standards and add dates and initials so the team has an ongoing record and can trace the enhancements.

These best practices will help the training team develop a useful set of instructions that will help accelerate the creation of training materials. There are also common challenges that might emerge in the work.

WHAT GETS IN THE WAY

Omissions and lack of attention to the details will weaken the guidelines and guardrails that course developers rely upon for training material creation.

Having No Style, Standards, or Templates

On some training projects, often those where training is last minute, there is no time or effort put into predevelopment planning. The outcome is an unfortunate mishmash of training material types. The inconsistency of materials can make it difficult for learners to use them. Though it's tempting to save time, it's usually a mistake to skip this step of documenting style and standards and building a template for every tool. You'll pay for it later when people struggle to learn new systems and processes.

Working Smarter: A consistent look and feel across your training materials helps to build confidence in the quality of the training content among learners and also project and business stakeholders. Given the impact, ensure the training team has time to produce templates, ideally before the initial launch. Make sure to build in time to use lessons learned and feedback from others.

Taking a "Ta-Da" Approach to Training Material Design

You're not looking to do a surprise reveal of your training materials, but rather to create something that reflects the needs learners have and the feedback stakeholders offer. Failing to get feedback from program team colleagues and a broad group of business representatives creates a behind-the-curtain perception of the training team's work, which erodes credibility and can create a vacuum of critical support.

Working Smarter: Build consensus as you work and continue to share details about the plans for training materials. Use stakeholder presentations to explore resistance and collect feedback. I recall an executive at one company who walked around with a binder of models and diagrams. Throughout his day, in hallways, in the kitchen, in every meeting, he made an effort to talk about the work underway to collect questions and feedback from a variety of people in different functions and roles, to great effect.

Thinking Everyone Understands Iterative Design

Individuals vary in their backgrounds and ability to see a model and recognize it as a prototype. Not everyone can view a rough draft and see the diamond for the rough edges. This fact explains why one input on the Stakeholder Connection Map (sample 5) is tolerance for rough drafts versus final-only materials.

Working Smarter: Modify your process by getting to know your stakeholders. Collect ongoing input about their expectations and sense of progress. Assess their preference for giving feedback about design. As time with them allows, explain the early material design and development process. Are they a reviewer or approver? What training materials have they liked? Send periodic updates or set up times to check in with them, hear needs or questions, share where you are, and communicate any needs for their support. When you share draft materials, explain that you seek and need their feedback at the early stages to improve the final training product.

Lacking Candid Feedback

Feedback is more than a proverbial gift; it's a necessity. Without it, your efforts as a training lead may fall short or fail. The key is to figure out how to work together to get it right for every learner.

Working Smarter: Chapter 4, "Training Leadership for Lasting Impact," includes a section about training engagement with the business and project team leaders. The importance of building strong relationships among these key groups is that it develops the partnership and fosters trust that sees these stakeholders willing to provide candid, timely feedback that benefits the training program. Likewise, the IDs must seek ongoing feedback from their subject matter experts (SMEs) and business process teams.

Using Varying Terms Among the Different Teams

Even with a style guide, templates, and a job aid of terms, I've seen SMEs and others who helped refine the labels for on-screen objects and ways to instruct people ignore their previous work or use cute terms like *hamburger* or *spaceship* to describe objects on the screen during important demonstrations to stakeholder groups. Remember, the digital transformation introduces a new language for new ways of working. When people use multiple terms for the same thing, the understandable result is confusion.

Working Smarter: Ask program, workstream, change, and communications leads to model the use of correct terminology. Ask IDs to assist their SMEs in learning the terms and ways to describe interaction with the on-screen elements. For example, to illustrate the need for common terms about the new system interface, show a visual of the system interface. A commonly used screen for that business team will work well. Label the key objects with letters and ask your transformation program colleagues what each is called. The variation is always a shock. Have a gift card or "bragging rights" as the prize for most right answers. The range of inputs usually leads the team to an awareness of the need to know and use correct terms. The exercise also provides an opportunity to reinforce the agreed-upon terms, which leads to better internal and business-facing communication.

Assuming All Designers Use the Templates, Standards, and Style

Whether the team is a mix of senior, junior, or newly trained IDs, it's a fallacy to assume that just because the resources exist, they'll get used. Validate use, understanding, and application among the team.

Working Smarter: IDs can showcase their progress with demos to their training peers on group calls. Their doing so helps illustrate different ways of solving the same instructional challenges and also ensures consistency in the use of the tools. To further drive compliance with standards and use of templates, a checklist-based peer review at an early 25%–50% completion stage of materials is a best practice. Later, 75% material completion stage reviews and show-and-tells verify completion progress, quality, and consistency, pre-training. This later review stage is way too late to check for the first time whether templates and standards are being used correctly.

Final Note

Together, the style guide, templates, and standards about the use of development tools allow the training team to produce strong materials that see people learn new process steps and how to use the tools to carry out their jobs in new ways. The work crafting these documents begins during testing of the products as part of the team's initial planning work. As the list of all the expected training components and decisions made about the development tools and templates for creating each, the overall training material development plan gets created. Managing material creation is the topic of the next chapter.

10

Blueprint for Developing Training Materials

"A goal without a plan is just a wish."
—Antoine de Saint-Exupéry, Author and Aviator

*T*he development plan—the listing and details about all the training materials being created—is a very visible training deliverable with multiple uses. The development blueprint gets used to plan, manage, track, and report on the training team's timeline and progress creating the entire set of materials. It can serve as the basis for the number of instructional design resources the team needs to produce the planned training content. The plan is also a tool for identifying risks and gets used to escalate requests for assistance to program and business leaders. The plan helps leads track achievements or challenges in reaching major completion milestones, and these can signal the health of the overall digital transformation project. The best plan enables consistent, accurate reporting.

BASICS

A development plan is a file, often a spreadsheet, list, or database. The training lead drafts a high-level list using the business case and the transformation business lines, along with the processes and activities noted in the curriculum plan. The instructional designers (IDs) add in the details based on the training material components needed to support training for the breadth of learners and locations for each functional area and audience type. A basic training material development plan details the size and count of all the training items being produced. It must be filterable and should accommodate changes and various calculations. My perspective is that a spreadsheet provides training leaders with the best option. I've also seen SharePoint lists work well, although this can require extra steps to export and massage the data, which new tools help automate.

Structure and Purpose of the Plan

Determine the layout of your training material development plan with some basic considerations.

- *Structure.* Organize the details based on the digital transformation by business processes and activities.

- *Components.* List the training materials needed as appropriate for each: video, e-learning module, slide deck, job aid, practice activity, etc.

- *Use.* Determine who will use the tracker. Who can add content items? Who can update percentage completions?

- *Traceability.* Confirm that progress reported to business leaders can be tied back to data in the plan and that changes to listed items are recorded. Adding a tab to contain lists of the deleted items and notes about additions is helpful when questions arise.

- *Timelines.* Detail the estimated and need-by completion dates for the materials.

- *Assignment.* Establish who has responsibility for managing the work of updates to the plan.

- *Ownership.* Ownership. Finally, for all the objects being produced as part of your digital transformation training program, assign who is developing each. In one case, the team added a column for identifying the internal peer reviewer for slide decks and participant guides; there was a "-" or "NA" for a video or job aid that didn't require it.

- *Special Requirements.* Lastly, include any project-specific details you need to track. For example, on one project of mine, the program leaders expected the training team to report progress on a weekly basis. The development plan included columns for estimated completion rates and dates.

This level of detail about the creation of training materials provides counts and details about the ongoing progress for completion, review, and approval against the overall program timeline.

Key Elements to Include

For each process or business area, list the full set of materials that the training team will produce. The opportunity lies in avoiding complexity and finding the simplest way to plan, track, and report progress. I recommend doing so using the following steps:

1. Start with a list of all the *process areas*, because they tie to the transformation scope and team structure. Moreover, for these areas, you'll have accountable and responsible leaders who are on the project and within the business, and who can help drive progress when it's needed. Add "Training" and "Program" as additional process areas for overviews and navigational content that apply across all workstream areas.

2. For each process, list the *subprocesses*: For example, in finance, you might have AP, AR, and GL.

3. What are the *security roles* or *jobs* involved in carrying out activities related to each subprocess? Within AP, there is perhaps a manager, a supervisor, and a processor, and the activities each role performs would involve different work activities. This step may need to come later for your digital transformation if it's a first launch.

4. List all the *training material components* the team will produce. Revisit the final list of materials the team identified in its earlier planning work. For instance, are you producing training slides and participant guides, or an e-learning module? What about post-training knowledge assessment tests for certain groups of learners?

5. Determine the *criteria for percentage completion reporting* for every training material component in your plan, whether a module, lesson, or bank of test questions. Completion percentages should indicate a pre-agreed-upon set of progress metrics to simplify tracking. For instance, 10% could mean the material is drafted and 70%, 75%, or 80% could mean the final draft is out for final subject matter expert (SME) review. The use of 100% should mean printed or published and ready for end user training. See "Best Practices" and "What Gets in the Way" sections for ideas about completions.

6. List the *final courses* that will be created from the modular content.

The modules, lessons, job aids, and learning components will be consolidated into role- or job-based sets, depending on the grouping of tasks that people carry out in their daily jobs. A good development plan helps track the overall body of work so the materials are ready for each learner group's start of end user training.

Fitting the Pieces Together

Effective digital transformation training materials include the same components regardless of the instructional designer. Your development plan may include the following details or consolidations based on completion and percentage details:

- Objectives for a training that teaches a set of process-related activities
- Model of the process
- Overviews about the process to provide context about how to correctly complete key tasks in and out of the system
- Listing of the steps or activities that make up the process
- Task-based, how-to job aids or videos
- Practice lessons and activities
- Glossary of key terms, data types, and system or process concepts
- Questions that test for comprehension of key concepts, tied back to objectives
- Any review games

No one plan design will fit every digital training need. The Training Material Development Tracker, sample 8, is a starting point you can use in building your own.

The most useful development plan is neither too detailed nor too high level and works for the IDs to plan and track their work. A well-managed document ensures data accuracy, and the training lead can use it for consistent, reliable reporting about training material development progress.

BEST PRACTICES

A few activities will help craft a useful training development plan.

Define Your Completion Percentages

Clarify the meaning of percentage progress for each component listed in the plan, for example, storyboard, slide deck, knowledge check, and job aid, that the team determined it will produce. What does 10% mean in terms of drafting, content build-out, and progress? If the training or a workstream lead sees a learner guide listed as 50% complete, what would that reflect in specific terms for content, formatting, reviews, and readiness for training? How do peer reviews, SME reviews, updates, and approvals factor into the progress definitions? Where can these definitions be found? Discuss these with the entire training team so everyone has a common grounding for these important training material development milestones. Document them in the training standards guide and refer to them frequently during team meetings.

Report Progress Each Week

Tracking and reporting weekly about material progress allows everyone on the training team and on the project to see advancement and respond to shortfalls as they emerge. Provide early and ongoing updates about overall completion by each process or department, against and relative to expected milestones aligned with the program timeline. For instance, training material completion always accelerates during testing as the system and final processes become real. To meet the overall timelines or changes in development scope, the training lead may need to request support to complete development in specific areas. Ongoing, consistent reporting about progress establishes credibility that proves valuable when support is needed for transformation leaders.

Track and Report Count Changes

Rigorously track changes, both adds and deletions, to counts of the learning objects in the plan. Digital transformation process redesigns often see late decisions and changes about who does what. This necessarily impacts the training content because it's tied to the activities that people carry out in their work. These changes can drive consolidations or splits of modules and lessons so they remain relevant from a learning perspective. Corresponding counts of training materials being developed get reported as deltas in the weekly project status and as part of the training plan on a page. See sample 6 and sample 8 for examples. IDs are the first to recognize changes and will communicate these important updates in the development plan.

Plan for Modular Development

Often, common, shared content can be repurposed across multiple trainings for different learner audiences. Besides functional overviews and a common how-to-navigate course, other material may be relevant for users in different functions as part of an end-to-end process training. For instance, accounts payable details about when the customer gets billed relative to shipping may be helpful for the sales, customer service, and fulfillment teams to know, too. For content used in multiple courses, determine how to account for it once, without double- or triple-counting its development. At the same time, factor into tracking and calculations any additional rework that may be needed.

Manage Tracker Access

If the tracker is an Excel file, restrict or limit the number of people who can edit the official tracker and/or restrict edits to specific areas to ensure accuracy. On smaller projects, as training lead, I've made all the updates in the tracker based on one-to-one check-ins with the training team members. On one large program, a lead was hired to coordinate all of the work carried out by the IDs. In most cases, using Excel and SharePoint lists, experienced IDs make updates themselves.

Boost Efficiency

One CIO I worked with extolled the importance of reserving the right to work smarter. A good place to start is checking in with the instructional design team. Avoid burdensome, duplicate progress tracking and reporting efforts that take away from their time developing training materials. Ask the project and workstream leads for ongoing feedback about the value of your reports about training material development. I've been delighted when others share ideas and we've implemented suggested changes. In short, continue or enhance what works; rework or eliminate what doesn't.

Identify Business Risks

The development plan can show progress relatively between the different business teams. Helping clear the roadblocks in developing materials is most often a transformation business leader's responsibility. Some leaders easily grasp the importance of every additional percentage point and the collaboration required to achieve it. In other cases, leaders may ignore the looming chasm. Until the team achieves 35% completion of materials, the 50% milestone is unattainable. The development plan can be used to model the risk to meeting milestones by projecting the current progress trends over time, as a discussion or graph. I've used both to get leader help in closing progress gaps.

Flag Resource Gaps

The development tracker can be used to calculate an estimated time and cost to produce the body of training materials, based on earlier prototyping or industry estimates. For example, do you have enough IDs, or are there too many for the planned content? I've used the development plan to successfully secure additional IDs, explained in chapter 6 about budgeting. The tracker is also a useful tool for reallocating work among under-utilized IDs.

Address Root Cause for Any Stalled Content

At some point in the program timeline—typically, as the start of training approaches—unfinished system configurations or process decisions mean incomplete training content. A course has to be finished, approved, and possibly translated for training to start, even when certain information is unavailable. For instance, on one project, with the workstream lead's agreement, the ID left a placeholder slide with a graphic and a callout that more detail would be provided. The ID will know this well in advance and can call out the delay when certain percentages do not advance.

Consider Other Factors to Bypass Problems

Every business and transformation has its unique needs. Two of these are universal and deserve your attention.

1. *Version control and recoverability*—Are duplicates of an ID's work maintained in multiple places, automatically? How will materials get backed up, how can earlier versions be recovered, and has the team tested this for each type and storage location?

2. *Training material maintenance*—How will responsibility for ongoing updates to the materials be handled after they get approved and used in training? Will a business team or a training department take ownership? Based on the answer, it may make sense to engage that team in the planning of what's being produced and how, or add a milestone for the handoff in the broader plan to track the exchange.

Despite all of the planning, care, and ongoing attention, there are challenges with managing, tracking, and reporting about digital transformation training material development.

WHAT GETS IN THE WAY

Four issues with training material creation tracking and reporting reinforce the importance of a controlled development plan.

Misunderstanding Progress Reporting

Progress for training material advancement gets reported as an overall percentage, with breakouts by each business or process area. Changes in transformation business scope or other details that add items to the list affect the count of training objects. This in turn will drive *decreases* in reported progress percentages. Examples include the following:

- Additional functionality in the system, additional subprocess areas, or added security roles will increase the count of training material objects being developed. This will therefore *decrease overall progress* when the change is first reported.

- Early plans for processes and activity counts may reflect inefficiencies in the current state. The redesigned process may eliminate content and decrease the overall count of learning objects. However, *when those objects were further along than others*, the change will *decrease the overall training completion percentage* when the change gets reported.

Working Smarter: Maintain a log of changes to the training development plan and document all updates that affect completion percentages in status. "Backward reporting" when progress seems to be going in the wrong direction—for example, when last period the team reported 45% and the next period there's a 40% completion—requires both a status footnote and verbal explanation. Similarly, it's also problematic if one week sees an unusual bump up in completion. "Why not every week?" leaders will wonder (and some will even ask). Finally, know that when the change in object count is more than or equal to 10%, conversations about resources will be held, either to review excess capacity or because the team needs support. Chapter 18, "Progress Updates That Keep Leadership Informed," continues this topic.

Delaying Build or Decision-Making

Digital transformation is a significant undertaking. Business teams determine how work gets carried out in new ways using enabling technology, often with changes in jobs and functional responsibilities. Sometimes, these hard decisions do not get made until very close to training, during training, or later. Without a finished system or detailed process, the training team can't produce materials to help people learn the new work steps. These delays or gaps show up on a tracker as behind-target training material completion rates, relative to other areas. They also show up as missed milestones.

Working Smarter: Listen for these situations in weekly calls with your IDs. In the best-case scenario, the program leaders will appreciate the issues that underly the delays in completing training materials and will work behind the scenes to help see decisions made. In the worst case, the business team is not publicizing the issues behind the delays and may claim the ID is not accessing available materials and information. Managing these situations is part of stakeholder engagement and resistance management. Talk with program and workstream leaders at the start of the training program about how to handle any delays in material development that reflect pending process or system decisions (see chapter 4, "Training Leadership for Lasting Impact"). One option if completing 100% is required: Move the items that can't be finished into a separate bucket of post-training, hands-on practice session topics for the process team to lead when the business decisions or system configurations are ready—sometimes weeks after the launch.

Varying and Inconsistent Completion Reporting by IDs

A team of IDs I managed on one program had varying skill and experience levels, came from different cultures, and reported their work progress differently—*despite common, agreed-upon criteria and a structured team member onboarding program.* As a result, a key business team disagreed with overly optimistic completion rates over a period of weeks. This doubt created a public credibility gap for training that ultimately drove additional daily administrative tracking and weekly reporting cycles for the IDs and the training lead. These issues came down to my not spending enough time reviewing the IDs' early work, another DONA.

Working Smarter: Avoid surprises by spending time weekly with each ID and looking at the materials being created. On team calls, have each ID give show-and-tell demos of their materials to validate reported progress and share great work. Look out two months at a time and track velocity for each ID and the team; do this by calculating a baseline where X hours worked generates a Y percentage increase in completion. Do note that this velocity calculation varies depending on the experience of the ID, the project type, training material development scope, as well as the stage of the project. Also see chapter 11, "Information Gathering with Subject Matter Experts," and chapter 4, "Training Leadership for Lasting Impact."

Overcomplicating the Development Plan

Early in my training lead work, my training material development plans were too detailed and took too much time to manage for me and the IDs. On a later transformation, a tailored SharePoint site met the development, tracking, and reporting requirements; better yet, the ID team liked it, especially the auto-generated updates feature for shared content. Unfortunately, program leaders required the team to use the same tracking and reporting tool the program's system developers were using. Updating two tools added administrative effort, took more time for the IDs, and failed when approvers would not log in to the program's system.

Working Smarter: The best approach is to draft a model, then have the more senior IDs "kick the tires" and help refine it. Right-size the development plan up front, by reviewing the tool and its use with the IDs who will provide updates and use data to guide their work. Ask the project leaders who count on the progress data for feedback. Discuss with the training team and others any anticipated changes in the count of objects and how these changes will be communicated in status and training reporting. Reserve the right to adjust the structure within a month of using it. Note lessons learned along the way in the training standards documentation or risks, actions, issues, and decisions (RAID) log to reference for the next deployment.

Final Note

Beyond describing all the content items the training team will produce and the work involved in creating the digital transformation learning materials, a good training development plan serves other uses as well. Besides progress tracking, the best development plan helps IDs work together with their business transformation team, the topic of the next chapter.

11

Information Gathering with Subject Matter Experts

"By asking targeted questions and the right questions from
the right sources, training and development professionals can
make information relevant and meaningful for our learners.
This translates to on-the-job performance."
—**Michele Medved,** Technology Instructional Designer and Author

Often, while decisions are being made about the training materials to produce and
the tools the team will use, instructional designers (IDs) and subject matter experts
(SMEs) also begin working together to review the solution and how work will get
carried out. These interactions begin ideally when the solution is being reviewed with
business teams. Sometimes, the conversations begin later, during project team testing.
These sessions rapidly evolve into ongoing working reviews over months, during one
or more weekly calls. There is a formula to this relationship: Many processes and steps
mean more system activities and screens to learn. The different learner audiences and
security roles determine the needed training materials and, ultimately, the time they'll
spend working together. SMEs importantly help the IDs clarify and describe who does

what within the organization and in the system and also understand when, how, and why. The ID and SME partnership is central to the learners' ability to succeed.

BASICS

Material development for a digital transformation training program begins with the curricula. Initially, the scope of processes, subprocesses, and the technical solution determine the tasks people will learn to do their jobs. Once this framework is established, the training team IDs will get assigned to develop materials for one or more process areas. The digital transformation program includes business process teams or workstreams, each with one or more designated SMEs who help the IDs produce the training materials. The role of the SMEs is to answer the IDs' questions about new processes. SMEs also show the IDs how the new system gets used to complete key activities the various user roles will perform. The strength of the partnership between IDs and SMEs shows in the progress of training material development and its overall quality. Gaps in this important relationship can result in rework and remediations that add time and cost—and risk—to end user learning.

In my experience, a planful, structured approach to the ID/SME working relationship helps the information-gathering process achieve its outcomes. There are the six steps I recommend and that my training colleagues confirm.

1. A Smart Start with Preparation

The ID pre-reviews documentation and resources. To understand the new ways of working, system activities, handoffs, and which security roles perform which tasks, the assigned ID begins by reviewing existing documentation including functional and technical design specifications, process flows, requirements, and use cases. Attending solution confirmation workshops and demos or watching the recordings of them is often helpful background to begin organizing the content for training materials.

2. Introductory Overview Session

The assigned training team member schedules and holds a kickoff or initial meeting with one or more SMEs designated for that process area. The training lead may join the meeting to answer strategy questions. Topics of this call include a subset of the training strategy and an overview about working together.

- The types of materials that will be created
- The learner audiences and the topics of the materials—the high-level curriculum plan with the included processes and activities
- Roles and responsibilities of the SME and the ID, as well as the functional business trainers, in reviewing content
- The review and approval process
- Training team requests and SME inputs about working well together
- The training material development milestones relative to end user training

A strong kickoff sets the stage for a great working relationship.

3. Calender Invites

The ID schedules the information-gathering and information-review sessions as agreed to in the kickoff.

4. Pre-Call Agenda and Questions

Two days before the first session, the ID sends an email with the agenda and expresses appreciation for the SME's time. The agenda should include specific topics or questions, if possible. These sessions focus on a process and system area, emerging from the ID's study of the process diagram and the technical, functional, or other documentation. IDs stepping through the activities in the system are especially valuable preparatory steps ahead of the working sessions.

5. Post-Call Follow-Ups and Thanks

After the session, the ID sends a summary with decisions, actions, and next steps—again, while appreciating the SME's help with the work and time. The follow-ups and any actions must be clearly stated. For example, *Jaime provides answers to Suresh by X date*. Typically, SMEs and IDs both get post-call "homework." IDs will schedule the next calls, incorporate inputs, and so on. This actioning helps maximize the value of limited meeting time, which is best used for discussions or questions and answers about information not available elsewhere. I often see training and process team leads copied on this communication to keep everyone informed.

6. Consistency Strengthens the Relationship

Steps three to five repeat over months. Eventually they conclude when final reviews and approval of the digital transformation training materials are complete and ready for the start of end user training.

The ID and SME demonstrate mutual respect and show ongoing appreciation for each other in the best cases. Ultimately, the actual progress of material development against the training development plans and major milestones reflect the effectiveness of their work and the strength of the partnership. For greatest success, consider some best practices.

BEST PRACTICES

Hold a Great Kickoff

Develop a set of slides or a micro-learning that all IDs can use to explain to SMEs the purpose of information gathering, the timelines, the materials, the progress percentages, and the roles and responsibilities in the digital transformation training initiative. This information comes from the strategy or approach. The purpose of the kickoff is to explore expectations about training and create a common understanding about the work being completed. Ask questions to help ensure a two-way conversation.

- Highlight key aspects of the training strategy relevant to the information-gathering activities you'll be participating in with the SMEs. Ask, "Does this feel right?"

- Recap the approach to developing role- and process-based training materials to most helpfully support the various learner types in the process area. Ask, "What is missing here?" "What else should we consider?"

- Review the audience plan on a page and focus on the relevant processes, locations, groups of learners, and preliminary training timelines and how these align with project milestones such as test cycles and the launch date. Ask, "What else is there to know about these groups of learners?"

- Review the curricula and training materials being produced for the workstream. Explain the standards for materials and how they help the learners. Ask, "Do you have any training materials that are used today?"

- Explain the material development cycle and why the reviews and sign-offs are essential milestones. Ask, "What questions do you have about reviews and sign-offs?"

- Review roles and responsibilities and any time estimates required of the SMEs, and how that will change over time. Ask, "Is this what you were expecting?" or "Do you anticipate any challenges with the timelines?"

- Note whether the SMEs will be asked to undertake a single review, or if both a preliminary and a final review are planned. Ask, "Who else must review materials or provide input as consulted parties?" Sometimes other reviewers include the functional trainers and various business leaders, even project leads.

- Explain what reported completion percentages mean, when to expect them, and who else has or will review the materials.

- Agree to "Ways of Working" (the final and perhaps most important step).

  » Set expectations that the ID needs to create training material drafts.

  » Confirm that the SME answers questions, demos system use, and reviews the materials.

» Clarify the SME's preferences for working together: X hours or minutes per week and which day(s).

» Set the expectation that a meeting can get moved if needed—and that the teams will avoid canceling a meeting altogether—to remain on track and not fall behind.

» Agree on the storage location where meeting notes and files will be kept and have the ID provide a link.

» Reinforce that the ID will always come to a working session prepared.

» Explain that the ID commits to communicating before and after the call to help move the work along.

» Agree upon the first working session call date and time and the topics.

This initial call will carry forward the strong start to a great working relationship between SMEs and IDs that the kickoff creates.

Prepare and Accelerate

Preparation before every call ensures best use of SME time and ID effort. IDs must ask for, read, and digest background materials so SMEs don't need to explain information available elsewhere. Documenting questions and sharing them in advance helps SMEs get ready for the call so material development advances. Moreover, when IDs prepare, it helps foster a great working relationship built upon respect and collaboration. The working relationship can be so strong that the ID is treated as an extended member of the business process workstream. One ID was mentored by the functional VP and was eventually offered a role on the business team as an SME.

Communicate and Follow Through

Accountability develops credibility and trust on all sides, a foundation of the best partnerships. Being accountable in this context means IDs must be responsible for their work and follow through on commitments to SMEs. Specifically, they do the following:

- Send or post the agenda and questions in advance.

- Follow up by email with actions and the next meeting time after the call.

- Communicate proactively: When necessary, ask for help or renegotiate timelines before a timeline passes.

- Secure support (again, proactively) to meet development progress targets for the training materials.

- Ensure agreement on status reporting about the progress of workstream training material development.

Ensure IDs Take Charge and Manage Their Work

The best IDs plan their work and manage it like a project using the training development plan as their start. They set out to achieve milestones based on their scope and business area, the materials being developed, and the individuals they work with. With planned activities by timeline, they can quickly flag potential risks and escalate issues so that they get resolved in a matter of a few days, not weeks. These highly effective IDs finish great work on time, even early, and can step in to help colleagues.

Discuss What Great Work with SMEs Looks Like

Does everyone on the training team know what great looks like? Discuss concrete examples. The best IDs learn from their SMEs. They gain deep knowledge about the business, the transformation, and the new system. This understanding evolves from asking questions and follow-up queries after hands-on work in the system. When IDs do their homework and prepare, they are appreciated more as partners by SMEs. One ID on her project arrived at the first working session with an outline for a course she created by repurposing the process and system documentation, all of which awed her SMEs. Always thinking about learners ensures IDs bring a useful perspective that can help the business team identify missing steps in a process. The SMEs and business team value and respect these notable contributions that an ID makes. Share this vision of partnership with the IDs during their team onboarding.

Encourage IDs to Show Gratitude

Gratitude is important and appropriate. SMEs have a full set of responsibilities, if not a regular full-time job. They may not have knowingly signed on to help develop training materials. Accordingly, the IDs must acknowledge and value the time SMEs spend helping to answer training questions and review materials.

Be flexible. Recognize that SMEs wear many hats and get pulled in many directions. Find ways to work together that support information gathering. One ID felt enormous frustration with SMEs arriving late to her meetings. She talked to me about escalation and punishment. With coaching, she found a way to refocus on a mutual respect for one another's time. She sought an alternative meeting schedule and she and her SMEs developed friendships outside the program. In addition to direct appreciation during meetings and in follow-up emails, IDs and the training lead can use status notes and group calls as places to acknowledge the notable help SMEs provide that advances training material work.

As in all working relationships, the most effective see a shared goal, clear understanding about roles and responsibilities, mutual respect, and great communication. Just as the strength of the partnership results in better-quality training materials completed on time, the converse of challenged relationships is also true.

WHAT GETS IN THE WAY

When timelines are very tight, transformation SMEs may be pulled and lack time to work with training. If gaps exist between an SME and ID, agreed-upon ways of working falter and training material development falls behind or the quality suffers. Here are some watch areas.

Conflicting Priorities and Lingering Delays

An SME's other work can take priority ahead of the training team's needs for their time and support. The lack of SME inputs about how things work or timely reviews of material drafts means that the training content may be incomplete or inaccurate, or not ready before the planned start of end user training.

Working Smarter: Project leaders can help balance priorities across the digital transformation. When training content creation remains among the top four priorities along with system build and testing, the workstream leaders can rearrange work assignments so SMEs can complete tasks for training material creation. With a little effort during crunch times, even fifteen minutes twice a week helps an ID advance training material progress. IDs and training leads must watch for these conflicts before they become irreversible. This is covered in chapter 18, "Progress Updates That Keep Leadership Informed."

Underperforming SMEs Stalling Progress

This situation is similar and yet distinct from the previous example where SMEs have conflicting priorities. Some SMEs may be overwhelmed or overworked, and unable to provide time or the help an ID needs. Instead of finding an alternate SME to support the training material development, they do nothing, and the training status changes from yellow to red. When an SME's unavailability extends beyond two weeks, this delay usually creates unacceptable risk. A colleague reports that on one project, SME delays were so challenging that multiple IDs quit in frustration.

Working Smarter: In my experience, in the worst cases, SMEs who consistently failed to follow through on training work, despite project leadership support, were disengaged from the transformation and the delays for training were symptoms of other issues. After two weeks, I will work with both the ID and the business transformation process leader to address the issue and secure an alternate SME. Business process team leaders can often identify a replacement SME or, in the interim, they themselves may step in and answer questions. Sometimes, technical team members can fill gaps in SME availability to help with using the system. The point is to not let the situation linger and to quickly engage others in finding a knowledgeable backup.

Navigating Difficult SME Relationships

SMEs are human—they represent the range of workplace colleagues we've all encountered. On occasion, some may continually miss or be late for sessions, or accept interruptions during them. They may never complete agreed-upon tasks. They may be distracted, or communicate poorly, or not at all. These situations require a different approach than the one you would use for the unavailable SME.

Working Smarter: Remember, for every challenging behavior, there's a human explanation. Your initial meeting secured agreement for how you'd work together. Since people are usually more alike than they are different, finding common ground that honors the challenging behavior constructively is the key to moving forward. Here are some examples of ways you can respond to some common problems with SMEs:

- *They're late to meetings.* "I notice you're often late to this call, and I wonder if it would be more helpful to you if we could find a different time to meet?"

- *They're not completing reviews of training materials.* "Would it help to delegate your course material reviews to someone else right now so we can continue to advance our work together?"

- *They accept constant interruptions.* "I see how much others besides me rely on you and your time. Would it be more helpful for you if we met in a conference room away from your office? Meet at a different time, earlier or later in the day? Shorten the call time and meet twice a week instead of once, when you have blocks of time to dedicate to the training discussion?"

- *They're uncooperative or resistant.* "Your knowledge, expertise, and help are so important. We won't have training for the end users without your input. What can I do to make this process easier for you around your other work commitments?"

- *They want to write the training materials.* "I love your passion for helping create effective learning materials—it's mine too! I count on your help reviewing the materials I'm creating using the standard templates we reviewed at our kickoff. I could really use your help creating practice scenarios and test questions."

See Salvatore (2015) and Medved (2022) for additional tactics. The goal between the ID and SME is always professional collaboration, respecting the designated roles and responsibilities each has.

Bridging Knowledge Gaps Hindering Progress

The SME assigned to help the ID should be one of the people most knowledgeable about the new technology and reengineered processes. While it's very rare, on several transformations I've seen the ID be the only one who can piece the specifications together and work in the system performing the activities. The issue becomes apparent and highly problematic when no one from the business can answer questions about how the transformed business process will work, who will carry out which activities, how the system fields get used, or the correct data elements to use. This gap in knowledge and the vacuum of detailed information signals problems for the digital transformation, especially when it's a core business process. For training, it means the materials may remain incomplete or lack key information.

Working Smarter: Chapter 5, "Equipping Project Teams with Core Knowledge," explains how business SMEs gain the expected knowledge to guide the transformation. When gaps in ability exist among the business process teams, the training lead needs to escalate them to transformation leadership carefully and with sensitivity. Training material completion may be placed on hold. As a tactic in this situation, hands-on practice can be enhanced with more detail about process-specific how-tos that are not in the training materials. It's not ideal, especially for the learner. Project leaders may choose to provide on-site hypercare support provided by technical resources in these rare cases.

Straying from the Proven Approach

In the training material development partnership, an ID may also fall short. Some IDs shift their methods when they shouldn't. This affects the timeliness, the quality of the training materials, and, sometimes, the learner experience. Unfortunately, no single type of ID falls into this group of underperformers. I've seen senior, junior, onshore, offshore, and employee IDs, as well as direct and third-party contract professionals, deviate from the agreed-upon standards for ways of working with SMEs to gather information and produce training materials. In one case, the workstream team overran a junior ID and dictated their preferred approach for bullet- and text-heavy slides, even though the template design and development standards emphasized a better approach. Sometimes, IDs allow the process team members and SMEs to draft the materials rather than doing the work themselves. Unfortunately, it only takes one misguided ID to negatively impact the entire team because work that strays from the plan results in marginal training material that will make it hard for the functional business trainers to use. This difficulty will also challenge end user learning.

Working Smarter: Have each ID show their work to the broad team on group calls within the first four to six weeks. As training lead, review the work as a quality check: Have IDs open their files during one-to-one check-ins with you. Monitor completion status. Watch for slower progress completing materials, relative to the other IDs, as a signal of a potentially underperforming ID. If an ID offers ongoing excuses or explains delays as awaiting handoffs from the process team for a second week in a row, follow up. Work with the ID to understand the issues. Does it make sense to join the next call the ID has with the SME? Provide the ID with support to resolve problems and always hold team members accountable for their deliverables. Lean in to what may be difficult, recurring conversations. In the worst case, I've had to ask other IDs to step in and help complete the materials.

Final Note

It takes time to translate process and system information into training materials that people can use to learn how to do their jobs. SMEs help IDs clarify and describe who does what within the organization, as well as when, why, and how to carry out key tasks using the system. Their relationship can be developed and nurtured to ensure the SMEs and IDs have joint ownership of content they're both proud to share with learners and business leaders. The materials that the SMEs and IDs produce must be reviewed and approved at multiple points, the topic of the next chapter.

12

Quality Assurance Through
Material Reviews and Approvals

"Inspect what you expect."
—**Paul J. Meyer,** Founder of the Personal Development Industry

Q*uality training materials require two things: the working partnership between the instructional designer (ID) and subject matter expert (SME) and, just as important, internal and external benchmarking. These reviews, feedback checks, and validation at different stages of material design and production mark important progress milestones. The culmination is the business sign-off for course readiness to use in training. Without these review steps, risks mount. Training content may be incorrect or not accepted, or could ultimately fail in helping people learn new ways of carrying out their daily work. Reviews and formal sign-off—early and ongoing—help garner support and fans for the training effort and the business's digital transformation.*

BASICS

Earlier chapters describe the importance of partnering broadly to make certain the overall training program succeeds. The training strategy sets forth a means to identify the learners and describes the way people will learn to do their jobs differently and the tools and materials that they will have. Ongoing reviews of these training material drafts ensure that the content is accurate, is complete, and meets agreed-upon standards. A final business owner approval validates their readiness for use in training. The various stages of material review and approval follow.

Standards and Specifications

After rounds of presentations with project and business stakeholders, most often the digital transformation program manager and the business sponsor approve the training strategy and material development plan. The items they review and approve include the following:

- The audience analysis, with details about the groups of learners, by business and location

- The process-based courses and topics that the groups of people will need to learn to do their jobs, along with any distinct needs they have for training delivery, language, and accommodation

- The types of training materials being created and all the tools used to create, provide, and track end user training

- The approach for who reviews and approves the training materials, and where decision-making authority lies

Digital transformation leader approval is important because the scope of the work they agree upon determines training resources, budget, and the timeline. Chapters 1, 2, 3, and 6 include notes about these because up-front alignment helps avoid chaos later.

Quality Checks Against the Guides

The training team is responsible for ensuring the materials that the team members produce conform to the established instructional and design standards. Each training team must determine how best to accomplish this among its IDs. The following describe typical examples of these activities.

- IDs may conduct peer reviews of one another's materials at a specified stage, using a checklist previously created from the standards document, explained in chapter 9, "Frameworks for Quality Content and Fast-Track Development."

- The training lead may conduct quality reviews of the training materials as an accountability check ahead of a major SME review milestone.

- Depending on the volume of training materials being produced and whether the timelines are compressed, the training lead may bring in a proofreader to review the materials for grammatical and formatting errors and adherence to standards.

- Others in the business or from the transformation program's change or communications teams may assist with reviews using a checklist of what to confirm.

However they're carried out, the goal of these internal reviews is to quality check the materials across all the business processes and workstream functions.

Nailing Accuracy in Process Steps

While consistency and standard checks are the responsibility of the training team, assessing content *accuracy* falls to the business. The process leaders on the transformation program and their functional SMEs have this important responsibility. Their regular review sees the materials developed with ongoing checks about how well the information reflects the way the system works and how job tasks will get carried out. Once all the materials are prepared and ready for a set of learners as a course, approval for readiness to use in training rests with one person—typically a single business workstream executive leader. This person normally has the responsibility to sign off on the training materials, verifying that they correctly incorporate process and system instructions, that they provide necessary opportunities for practice, and that the tests of knowledge are appropriate. The training strategy documents who has final approval responsibility. This topic is also described in chapter 3, "Responsibility and Decision-Making Clarity Drive Success."

Some considerations will help realize best outcomes across all these quality checks.

BEST PRACTICES

The activities that result in effective reviews underscore clarity about responsibility and the importance of efficiency.

Keep Reviewers Informed at Every Stage

Business and project teams benefit from explicit detail about all the steps involved in producing training materials and what each person is being asked to do. I recommend you do this by diagramming the process for training material creation, reviews, percentage stages, and approval sign-offs. In your diagram, note who is responsible at each stage and the expected turnaround time. Show the progress percentage at each stage as well. I've produced this visual in different formats— as a table, an infographic-style process map, and a Visio process flow with swim lanes. While business culture and project documentation standards may dictate one model over another, in my experience, a tabular format seems to work best across all audiences. When done well, the exercise of sharing the model and collecting feedback about the activities and stages helps educate everyone about the stages, steps, and who is responsible for what.

Align Training with Business Learning Standards

Outside of the digital transformation training team, the company's learning function will be most informed about training best practices, how people learn, tools, templates, and approaches that work well. The experience and knowledge these teams have make their feedback especially valuable for the digital transformation training program, *even where the types of training are different*. For instance, those involved in leadership or sales training at the company have much to share that could benefit a digital transformation training program. Make connections and have conversations to seek input, use the feedback, and build upon existing business training norms. This approach ensures the materials and the digital transformation training program leverage what's known about best supporting the company's learners.

Automate Feedback Collection

Gathering necessary feedback from SMEs about materials can be done easily and be efficient for material development. This model sees the ID share a link to a draft of course materials with comments in context, and the ID can review and incorporate suggestions. This functionality is listed as a consideration in chapter 8, "Tools and Technologies to Power Training." Saving time with effective collaboration benefits everyone.

Track and Document Approvals

The formality and structure of sign-off approvals depend on the type of digital transformation, the business culture, the business stakeholders, and the audiences impacted by the change. I've used verbal and email approvals, signed documents, and digital sign-offs. Factor in the time that approvers will need and ensure that whichever method you use does not in itself introduce any risk for delay.

There are some watch areas for quality assurance activities.

WHAT GETS IN THE WAY

As I reflect on my own experiences, poor communication and lack of accountability pose the greatest challenges for training material reviews and approvals.

Missing the Right Stakeholders in Prototype Reviews

Even when stakeholders are not formal reviewers or approvers, they may need to be consulted or informed on material development at stages along the way. These reviews help business leaders recognize the training approach, the components, and how the materials will be used to teach their teams new ways of working in the digital transformation.

Working Smarter: Conduct broad reviews with the business stakeholders you identified alongside the learner audience analysis (see chapter 2, "Learning Topics and Audience Insights for a Strong Foundation"). Do this when the components, tools, and technologies and training material design are being determined and feedback can more easily be incorporated. To gather feedback, conversations are ideal. Surveys can work, too, when you need to collect more individual inputs than limited time and large group presentations allow.

Sharing Responsibility for Final Approvals

Final course approval is a big responsibility. As such, some people would prefer to share the accountability. However, this means waiting on two people to work approvals into their schedules instead of one. Having more than one responsible approver risks timely completion of course materials and preparation for the start of training.

Working Smarter: Identify the single, designated approver who must provide the sign-off. In some cases, this business executive is closely involved and has been an SME as the course and its components were completed. In other cases, the designated approver is a senior executive whose direct report has been the process workstream leader or a key SME. In those cases, the executive relies upon the delegate who has already reviewed all the materials and verifies to the leader that their approval can be granted. Having a single accountable business leader is a best practice, not just for material sign-off. Digital transformations identify single business owners and drive greater accountability for processes and key performance measures part of the overall change.

Overstepping SMEs and Others Acting as IDs

Business SMEs are responsible for describing to the training team members how the new processes work and how the system and data enable it. Sometimes, for example, these key business resources may try to replace the approved training material design and instructionally sound template with painfully long paragraphs of bulleted text *because they prefer it*. This type of unauthorized "improvement" can happen despite evidence that text-heavy "wall of words" slides decrease learning effectiveness (Clark, 2010). On another project, managers not involved with the details of the new process design and the system pulled out hours of approved content because they felt their team didn't need to know it, creating serious delays in adoption after the launch. When needed content gets removed or the materials are ineffective, people cannot learn what they need to do their jobs.

Working Smarter: The training lead may need to step in and help the ID explore underlying concerns that prompt people to make changes to the approved templates or content. In one case, the business team wanted both their functional trainers and the learners to have detailed notes. A compromise was reached that produced longer-than-average practice guides while the training materials matched the approved standards. In the other instance where key content got removed, the risk was communicated in advance to transformation and workstream leaders who nevertheless and, unfortunately, could not sway the local business team before the go live.

Being in the Dark

Silence is not agreement. Never assume (note the warning: ass-u-me) that when you hear no feedback, everything's fine. Rather, there's likely something to know. In one instance, business leaders did not understand the purpose of a sales training layout mock-up and assumed it was a final design. Feeling that their needs were not being met, executives hired their own training coordinator and ID to create materials. The business ID and I had to support and work with these new people, in addition to handling all the other planned work.

Working Smarter: In all training presentations, reinforce the importance of feedback—especially constructive feedback. Have pre-presentation conversations with key stakeholders to collect input early on. When you hear concern, don't defend; lean in and ask questions to understand. Listen to hear the need behind the words. Ask transformation leaders to validate what you and the IDs are hearing. Getting things right by working together helps the overall program succeed.

Rushing Through Reviews

When things get rushed or pushed to the end, there may not be time to complete internal quality check reviews before materials need to be approved and produced for the start of training.

Working Smarter: Plan material production and set milestones that incorporate time for the training team and SME reviews, as well as the final approval stages, as detailed in chapter 10, "Blueprint for Developing Training Materials." Monitor the progress of training material completion to ensure the planned time remains available to complete training material reviews. Use early "show and tell" checks among the training teams on weekly calls to provide any course correction that's needed.

Final Note

Business thought leader Ken Blanchard is credited with calling feedback the Breakfast of Champions to describe the importance of broadening perspective about how our performance conforms to expectations, or not. Applied to digital training material creation, reviews, quality checks, feedback, and final approval ensure that the materials will meet or exceed the expectations for upskilling the company's talent and that they are ready for final production steps, the topic of the next chapter.

13

Final Material Production with Editing, Translation, and Printing

"Expect the best, plan for the worst,
and prepare to be surprised."

—**Denis Waitley,** Motivational Speaker, Writer, and Consultant

There are final steps before the training products are 100% complete. Editing, translation, and printing, one or all three, are typical final treatments for training materials. These may be required because of learner needs or business specifications. In many cases, a single service provider may be the best option, and some may even offer multiservice discounts. Key considerations are volume of materials and how tight the timelines are. Whether internal or through a vendor, recognize the value of conducting tests to validate your selected approach and confirm the turnaround times, quality, and costs.

BASICS

As part of training material development, additional editorial, translation, and printing steps may be needed to reach 100% completion for some of the components.

Each service is addressed separately in this chapter, beginning with editing. Consider the need, identify the options, and assess the trade-offs of working with an outside vendor or handling the work in-house. Depending on the volume and timelines, a strong vendor partnership may be your best choice. In other cases, internal resources may work better and be more cost-effective. The major risks are timing and capacity to complete a large volume of work in a usually compressed time frame.

Polishing for Quality and Clarity

An editorial review is not the same as a subject matter expert (SME) review. SME reviews of materials ensure the *accuracy* of the training content. For example, are the process and series of steps in the system described correctly? Editing ensures the *quality* of the materials—whether they use language accurately and appropriately and in line with style guidelines. The quality assurance process for training materials has different types of editorial reviews.

- *Peer review* comes first. It's a quality check for alignment with the business's style and training development standards. For example, are the templates being used correctly for the different types of materials? Are core concepts of the style being applied such as capitalization, punctuation, and formatting? Are reported progress measures in line with the agreed-upon measures? This review typically occurs in earlier stages of training material development, and the training team members are best suited to carry out this benchmarking review. This was covered in chapter 12 about material reviews and approvals.

- *Proofreading* happens just before materials get produced. It involves a final review of the training materials for obvious errors in grammar, style, or formatting and for conformity to standards. The training lead may carry this out or it may get outsourced to an external editor.

Translating for Global Reach

Translation is the process of converting reviewed, edited, and approved materials written in one language into another so all learners may comprehend the content without language barriers or cultural bias. When translation is legally required, the training budget and strategy must include it. The high costs and additional time required for translation and subsequent reformatting of materials mean that this aspect of the training program has to be carefully planned and well-managed. The following factors impact the cost and quality of a translation.

- Length and format of the original materials because pricing is typically handled by word or page count.

- Translator qualifications, certifications, and experience level, which can affect both speed and quality.

- The availability of a company glossary of already translated terms and phrases, or a tool that the editorial team creates so that over time the amount of actual translation decreases, along with the cost.

- Automation, which some translation services use to decrease costs while maintaining quality. Alternately, common tools like Google Translate provide internal options, although the work then requires review and proofreading to validate the accuracy of the translation.

- Complexity—when the materials being translated include screen objects and technical terms, decide if these need to be translated or not. Translating on-screen labels and field names adds significantly to time and cost.

Inputs from the business teams and even HR about requirements will inform these decision points to guide quote requests from editorial services.

Choosing Between Digital and Physical Materials

Although digital tools allow the creation of portable document format (PDF) files, my own experience and input from colleagues confirms that paper handouts continue to be largely preferred for in-hand reference and for practice exercise instructions. The purpose of the handout and its benefit to the learner determine the content and also the format. For example, if the job aids and step-by-step instructions are easily accessible within the application, a printed version would be less useful. Alternately, when the learner guide will be a post-training desk resource, either an editable PDF or a printed version may make sense. If you print materials, these are some things to think about.

Print Format Options and Pricing

The likely number of materials is the first thing to consider. Then, the length, format, function, and cost considerations will help the training lead determine the binding, layout, and final output of printed training materials. Consider the learner and the materials. It's not helpful to have forty single-page handouts and a booklet. The participant guide should be all-inclusive of information, reference, and practice content. Some different output options include the following:

- Double-sided printing with a corner staple is the lowest-cost option, yet it may feel unimpressive, like something anyone can make at home.

- Coil and other specialty bindings cost more. We can all agree that they look great. However, booklets generated this way are the most expensive. When it's time, they are hard to recycle and for virtual sessions will need to be printed and shipped out.

- A lower-cost option to coil binding is saddle stitching. This format sees 8.5-by-11-inch pages organized into a booklet created from an 11-by-17 tabloid sheet with two staples on the inside. This format has page limits, and you'll want to make sure the staples hold when the pages are turned and folded back to avoid the materials falling apart.

- For other binding options, work with your printer. They're the experts.

- All-color printing is most expensive, yet it may be worthwhile, given the impact of the business initiative and the company culture. Some printer technologies allow for color on specific pages like the title page and some on the inside, which provides polish at a lower cost than all-color.

- Heavier weight paper can be as impactful as color, and, while it costs more than typical paper stock, it may be a worthwhile investment for your training materials. Based on type and length, a document printed on heavier paper with grayscale can be as effective as and less costly than all-color on a lighter weight paper.

- When you get quotes and samples from your printer, keep in mind that translated documents can be 10%–25% longer than English for Spanish, French, German, and Arabic (Transperfect, 2013).

Confirm both business leader and learner expectations for material output, then look at samples and determine an estimated per book cost, including materials, to use for the training budget. Having both cost and estimates for the time to format, print, ship, and receive the materials—whether produced internally or externally—allows for smart planning so that materials are in hand for the start of each training session.

Digital Documents

Often because of company culture, environmental concerns, and cost or time considerations, a PDF version of the handout may be requested instead of a paper printout. These are now easy to generate from all applications. If learners need to interact with the digital PDF to type answers and other information directly into it, the document can be converted into a form-like, editable PDF. You'll need a specialized tool and additional time to build these. To find efficiencies, test the options during your prototyping phase. For example, Word form fields are easier to convert into editable areas. Finally, a PDF can be made more book-like with flip-book creator tools, if that page-turning effect matters for the learner audiences and business leader expectations. I've seen sales team learners prefer an extra wow factor.

As you think about how your learners will interact with the training materials, some considerations will help this work go well.

BEST PRACTICES

Planning and preparedness are important activities to realize the final outcomes for training materials that you and others expect.

Start Smart by Weighing Quality, Speed, and Cost

When looking to produce materials, start with the tools, vendors, and contacts your company's communication or marketing department already has in place. Could the vendor your HR, communications, or sales department use help produce training materials? Is there special pricing in place already? Supplier setup and legal arrangements are easier when you can use previously approved vendors and services. Negotiated pricing discounts and better service-level agreements may be available as well. Even when you establish your own vendor relationships, negotiate volume pricing and turnaround times. Set clear expectations for quality.

Prepare Thoroughly by Testing Everything

Make no assumptions about editors, translators, vendors, formats, handoffs, or timelines. Validate everything early on by using the tools, people, or services several times, before the crunch of end user training material production. Questions to ask team members and vendors include the following:

- Does the *peer review* include a complete checklist, tied to standards, that people can use to easily document adherence or deviation from the expected norms?

- Does a *sample translation* resonate with the intended audience in regard to terms, language, and communication effectiveness?

- Is the *print or PDF quality* acceptable to business leaders and representative learners? Get explicit feedback.

- Do the *editable PDFs* meet expectations, and will they actually get used? If learners are going to print off their own copies instead of using them digitally, based on observed preferences and behaviors with other learning programs, revisit printing.

- Are the *turnaround times* and *costs* for each type of output in line with the estimates? These are necessary data points for budget management and having the materials on hand for end user training.

- Verify the internal *quality check stages each vendor uses*. How does the vendor address errors? Does work fall within the service levels? Who helps when there are issues—do you have the mobile phone numbers for your primary vendor contacts?

These are questions to ask and types of experiences to learn from early on, well ahead of go time. I worked with a vendor to overcome initial print and translation issues and forged a multiyear partnership that became a success factor for our transformation training program by working through these things.

Protect Materials with Security and Copyright Standards

Your materials are proprietary and should be treated securely and copyright protected. This is intellectual property owned by the company. Details to keep in mind include the following:

- *Copyright.* When you distribute materials to outside vendors for printing and translation, the work agreement typically includes a nondisclosure agreement (NDA) that assures confidentiality. In addition to having an NDA in place, copyright the pages of all materials and work with your legal team for an appropriate proprietary and confidentiality footer.

- *Secure Transmission.* When sending files, ideally you have a secure site to use to upload materials to your vendor, rather than emailing them. If you email, use your email system's option to encrypt or password protect the email. A secure upload site is the typical, easiest approach for sharing documents for printing and translation and may be a deciding factor for selecting one vendor over another.

Companies as a norm wish to protect their business information. Training materials that describe tailored business processes and how to use configured systems are confidential intellectual property and need special protection.

Set Development Standards with Translation in Mind

When your audience analysis suggests the need to translate, your style guide must reflect this decision. Using active voice and easy-to-read, shorter sentences makes for easier translation (and generally for better writing overall). The consistent use of style guides is also critical. A few other considerations apply to make the text more translatable and comprehensible.

- *Avoid jargon, idioms, cultural references, and any slang.* For example, references to "the bottom line" or popular movies or characters may not be understood broadly.

- *Data and information changes.* Will all dates and phone numbers need to be translated to reflect other countries' formats?

- *Instructions for system screen elements.* In rare cases, there is a need to translate on-screen objects, labels, and data. If not, specify that screen elements remain untranslated, a decision that saves much time and cost. If people will work with an English version of an application, translating the on-screen elements can be confusing for a learner.

Keeping learner needs front of mind and testing translation, output, and editing options are best practices that will see quality training materials produced for all learner audiences and ready on time for their training.

Some watch areas deserve consideration.

WHAT GETS IN THE WAY

Experience has been the best teacher about the most common issues that arise with training final quality and production steps.

Assuming In-House Is Always Best

Just because the office has a multifunction printer or a printing services group does not mean they offer the lowest-cost option for producing materials or that they may be able to support your volume or timelines. At one company, the in-house print team prioritized by requestor; this meant that a sales or CEO request would always get prioritized over any digital transformation training jobs in the queue. We almost missed getting the materials in time for a training in one case. Another time, despite commitments that the volume and due dates could be supported, the staff expressed frustration with the amount of work and the tight timelines.

Working Smarter: If your company has an in-house printing team, get quotes early on and run tests to evaluate quality and turnaround. A single multifunction printer is actually the most expensive option for generating booklets, once you factor in time, labor, and materials. I ran an experiment producing color, saddle-stitch training materials and documented that the cost per booklet printed in-house was more than double what a printing service would charge. In-house options are probably best for backup—not if, but *when* you need it.

Overlooking Capacity Needs

Getting all the training materials completed usually involves a wave of work at the end, very close to the start of training. Individuals and small firms will be challenged in managing the rush of translation and printing work that arises at this time as part of a typical digital transformation training program supporting 1,000–5,000+ learners and all their course materials.

Working Smarter: In my experience, multiservice companies have the resources ready to handle the work volume and tight timelines with better consistency and accuracy because of rigorous quality controls. This is true for both translation and printing. Even so, it's best to overcommunicate about the volume and details about the work that's coming, its progress, and any delays. I start this communication during initial calls, based on early audience analysis numbers and the known program timelines. Besides volume, revisit and reinforce expectations about the agreed-upon turnaround timelines in the contract. Pace the work out by submitting what you can for reviews, edits, translation, and printing when it's ready; avoid holding everything with the thought that you'll send it all together.

Ignoring Vendor Insights

When you have a strong vendor partnership, leverage their expertise. In one case, I received internal business direction to have materials printed near the work locations, nationally and internationally, which was the initial approach and agreement with the printer. My printer chose instead to print and ship from a single plant. My program leadership challenged me to change the printer's practice because it appeared counter to the agreed-upon approach and seemed more expensive. In this case, the printer's decision benefitted my needs better.

Working Smarter: Provide business leadership with the data behind the approach. Working with a single plant to print all the materials ensured the highest-quality output. The single plant and its staff understood the material, final format, timelines, and, most importantly, quality specifications. As a result, they were best equipped to *consistently* produce materials that met expectations and were on time. Keeping the work at one location also allowed a strong partnership with the vendor, who went above and beyond to resolve the few issues that did arise. With discounted shipping rates, this approach provided the lowest cost as well, which program leaders also appreciated.

Failing to Validate Translation Quality and Resonance

On the surface, translation seems as straightforward as converting one currency into another. However, language dialects, structure, style, and vernacular mean that you must confirm that the translation style works for the learner audience. I've seen both experienced independent and multinational firms whose translators misused words and phrases. In one case, a Spanish translation was accurate, but incorrect for business use. In another case, the translation tone and word choice were formal when the original was not.

Working Smarter: Early on, after a translation is complete, coordinate a review with a representative from the learner audience. Have one or two people who represent the learners or their management team compare both language versions to assess accuracy, consistency, and quality. Repeat this later. I also recommend having a representative of the business review the change communications that precede training as well as the vendor's glossary of terms. Translation requires learning, which is why the glossary of translated words and phrases is so important when using a service.

Assuming Translation Equals Communication

Translation isn't always the end point. Sometimes, additional steps are needed to effectively communicate training concepts. I've seen lower-than-average read rates for translated communication and training materials when clearly the business expects the opposite. In other cases, low literacy rates among some learners mean that the written word in any language is less effective than hearing and doing.

Working Smarter: Refocus on the need. How will learners whose first language is not English best learn and use the new system and understand processes? Will the translated materials be helpful? When the literacy rates may be low and the application interface elements remain in English, consider alternatives to translation. Might having a trainer and coach fluent in the first language better meet the needs of the audience? This is a necessary question to ask and answer in partnership with transformation, business, and HR leaders.

Final Note

All the time and effort spent planning, designing, and working with others to create training materials is not the end. Final production is like the sprint at the end of a race to reach the finish line and requires maintaining best form once the training materials have their final review and are approved for use in training. The next chapter addresses the topic of games, a final consideration for training delivery.

14

Games to Engage Learners

"Learning happens faster with play."

—**Colin Snow,** Thai Chi Master and Instructor

Meetings and trainings often incorporate game-based activities because they add excitement with fun, friendly competition. Games vary in cost and the effort needed to design and play them. A business may use a gamified experience to introduce the case and communicate a vision for the digital transformation change to all employees. During digital transformation training, games can be effective tools to help people practice their recall of new information and also demonstrate their understanding of key concepts, both necessary steps for learning. Best of all, games can make training enjoyable, and it's my observation that better learning occurs when people feel good.

BASICS

We know learning requires repetitive practice to see new information become knowledge that people can ably apply on the job. Systems training involves many new terms, a new digital interface, many screen elements, and new types of data. Mastering new processes involves recognizing the sequence of activities, who does what, when, and where to find information about how to perform a task correctly. The practice of recall, application, and use of all this new material involves a variety of activities, discussions, and hands-on practice. Games provide a fun way to let learners make sense of and organize these new concepts for their own use (Stolovitch & Keeps, 2002). Friendly competition—structured, scored, and time-based activity—injects a sense of delight and joy into the practice of working with new information.

Exploring Options for Learning Games

The right games can help workplace learners with the following elements of building knowledge.

- *Recall*—The ability to retrieve recently learned information such as terms and key screen elements. A "trivia" challenge sees either groups of learners work together or individuals compete to correctly answer questions.

- *Skill Development and Reinforcement*—The opportunity to practice using the new system, see the effect of choices and decisions, and get feedback. A scavenger hunt game carried out in teams of two ensures a driver and navigator partner together in working through screens and "collecting" items on the list.

- *Demonstration*—The chance to show ability to use the new information correctly in context or to complete a task. An example of this involves timed problem-solving with a "case study" completed as either a group or individual activity.

Traditionally, school homework, projects, quizzes, and tests provide similar opportunities to "practice" accessing and using new information. Games have become common at school for the same reasons they are liked in the workplace—they're effective and fun. While some games played in school settings are also workplace-appropriate, the game, its instructions, and rules about how players complete activities must be relevant for the business audience and learning purpose. This balance requires consideration of the audience and their needs along with the game and its purpose and effectiveness for the task. Moreover, the time needed to develop a game and the costs to do so are additional considerations for the overall training material development effort.

Selecting the Right Game for Your Needs

Game formats include a range of options. They can use technology; be board-based, paper-based, or voice-only; involve body motion; and even rely on a system demonstration. Whatever the format, the game is a contest with instructions and rules where individuals or teams compete against one another for bragging rights or a prize. To be effective as a teaching tool, a game must help achieve the expected learning outcomes and resonate with the audience and work for the person facilitating the game. I consider game formats in three categories: *simple, midrange,* and *complex.*

Simple Games: These types of games use flash cards, quizzes, and matching activities that take a short amount of time to play and create. Simple games are best for recall and concept reinforcement. They can be free or low-cost to produce and require less than a few hours for instructional designers (IDs) or functional trainers to plan and create. There is often no cost to play. Brainstorming low- or no-cost game options and choosing the best for the situation is a productive collaboration activity for functional trainers and IDs as part of the later stages of material development.

Midrange Games: There is a continuum between simple and complex game types with varying costs and time needed to develop and play. I've worked with IDs who use e-learning development tools to create interactive games that people complete on their own as part of their self-study experience. The development tool is already on hand—the cost is the time to create the game. Online game platforms enable engagement from a phone or laptop with a preset list of questions, scoring answers by speed and accuracy with a leaderboard of results. These systems may have license fees for the number of both game developers and players. Again, if it best supports the learning experience, it can be a worthwhile investment.

Complex Games: Complex games are experiential for the learner and are time-consuming to develop and play, so they usually have a large price tag. These types of learning games support the process of teaching and learning through the game play itself. Discovery learning activities or learning through action can involve meaningful, context-rich visuals, as well as motivating experiences that engage decision-making to build knowledge about and motivation for changes (Paradigm Learning, 2023). One example is a day-in-the-life business simulation game where a team of business leaders use a sample instance of an enterprise resource planning solution to carry out the cycle of business processes from planning, ordering, receiving, producing, selling, invoicing, and closing the books (Baton Simulations, 2011).

Discovery games are another high-end group gaming experience. These are large-scale games that involve technology, print materials, or a combination. At one company, a large-sized visual illustrated elements of the business transformation, and this was the backdrop for group-based play with card prompts and tablet inputs for scoring. This sophisticated game experience was facilitated by business leaders and representatives from the company that helped develop it. Employees across all functions and roles played together at every location in groups and developed a common understanding of the business change through discussion, questioning, and the gaming experience. These complex types of games require many months to a year to design and create. They carry a sizable price tag that reflects the effort involved. However, this type of game is a foundational change management tactic for some digital transformations with large-scale changes that involve all business lines and employees. When employees play discovery games, they develop a better understanding about the drivers of the business change, the functions affected, why change is necessary, and the business gains that will be realized in achieving the transformation. This information helps employees appreciate their role in the change. These complex games are typically outside the scope of digital transformation training, although the training strategy and messaging can repurpose some of the game content.

But how does the best game for what you're trying to achieve get selected or created?

Choosing the Right Game Format

Consider the combination of factors that influence the optimal game for each situation in the learner's digital transformation training journey.

- *The time frame available for a game.* Are there ten, fifteen, or thirty minutes available for a game in the training schedule and agenda?

- *When the game will be played.* The end of a topic or the end of a morning or afternoon of training creates natural opportunities to review a set of information and topics covered earlier.

- *The number of learners.* How many people will play determines how to structure the competition. For smaller groups, learners compete against one another. Pair-based teams work with six to twelve participants. Competition among teams of three or more works when there are nine or more learners in the session. The average class size gets identified during the audience analysis and early training planning. Ideally, the game instructions can be flexible based on the number of learners in a session, although counts of people matter for some games.

- *Who creates the game.* Training team IDs have the time, skill, and tools to develop more sophisticated games. Functional trainers may also create games that facilitate review and readiness among those they teach as a way to deepen their own learning. Manage the decisions about the type of digital transformation training games as part of the overall training strategy and material development plan. Ensure business and project leaders endorse this approach and support any budget needs and best practices.

BEST PRACTICES

When designing and developing the right game, take the following into account.

Focus on the Audience

Games are like other training materials—they help distinct groups of learners organize new information and demonstrate understanding of concepts. As a result, they have to be audience-relevant.

- Some groups of learners prefer activity.

- Labels, clues, and instructional language must also be audience-appropriate in game materials.

- If the learners' jobs involve moving all day, a game with physical activity may resonate more than games that involve only sitting.

- When a game is designed for speakers of multiple languages, ensure active voice and simple instructions.

Ensure the learner needs remain top of mind during game design because games help validate that one or more learning objectives have been achieved.

Adapt Classic Games into Activities

Many popular games can be modified and used to enhance digital transformation learning. For example, trivia and even a simplified *Jeopardy!* game using a PowerPoint or Google slideshow will see teams of learners work together to review terms and concepts, and to organize information. Activities like these engage learners and help create a more effective virtual or in-person training environment. In another example, an ID on my team created a modified Game of Life for onboarding new training developers. It introduced the training development life cycle with all the challenges and major milestones. It was a midrange game, taking about a week for her to create and just over an hour to play in person. The participants found it humorous, educational, and a great team-building exercise.

Use the Wealth of Online Resources

A multitude of cost-free or low-cost game ideas and development tools exist online. Popular game platforms like Quizlet, Gimkit, Edpuzzle, Kahoot!, and others offer free or inexpensive opportunities to enhance learning. Functional business trainers I've worked with found free online tools and created crossword puzzles and word searches they used as review games with candy prizes. Their learners noted these games positively in post-training feedback.

Whatever the type, the best games provide review and practice opportunities tied to specific training objectives that help people by providing an appropriate and relevant learning experience. When learners have the skill to "play" and "win" at a game, they demonstrate their ability and show that the game is successful.

WHAT GETS IN THE WAY

Selecting a game seems fun and easy, but missteps are possible. Here are a few.

Skipping Game Testing

Nothing is worse than a game that falls flat because some of the components are missing or because people don't understand what to do. Testing a game reveals these deficits and helps prevent unpleasant surprises.

Working Smarter: Even when timelines are tight, pulling together a sample group to test your game is a step that can't be skipped. Make sure the necessary pieces are in hand and the instructions are clear. Confirm that facilitators can introduce the purpose and instructions and that learners can successfully complete the game so that it accomplishes its purpose. Ideally, functional business trainers, your early learners, test each game and instructions, providing feedback about what works and doesn't. Improve or remove the game from the training, as necessary.

Choosing an Overly Complex Game Platform

Bandwidth and internet connectivity are not always guaranteed. For this reason, I've seen well-tested games fail just when they're most needed. The more graphics a game uses, the more bandwidth it requires. Choosing a technically complex game may tax your system and carry unnecessary risk.

Working Smarter: Avoid cloud solutions that are challenging to set up, are hard to use, or don't integrate well with your training presentation. Always keep a local copy of your files. If your game is web-based or digital, always have a nontechnical backup prepared. For example, if you're using a cloud-based game platform, have the questions prepared and shift to a group-based trivia game format in the event of technical issues.

Overloading with Games

Games become lame when they're overused. For instance, signaling the end of a section with the same review game quickly feels repetitive and even tedious. Instead of exciting learners, it will prove demotivating (Brandon, 2023). There is no one game that meets every learning need, and including games just to say you have them will backfire.

Working Smarter: Games are learning tools. Combine a variety of activities for a terrific training experience. Remember that a conversational activity with another learner where each person shares two to three things learned, one to two things to know more about, and one question is also an effective review of the material and concepts, without the competitive aspect of a game.

Playing Games Incorrectly

During one game session, I didn't have much time, so I opted to skip a step in the game instructions—I did not ask teams of learners to choose a name for their teams before starting the game. Though I can't be sure of the reason, I did notice that the participants showed low effort and lacked enthusiasm. The game, that day, was not a win. However, I witnessed a different group, with the same audience type, playing the same game after receiving the instruction to choose team names (a few-minutes exercise). In the second situation, the participants enjoyed the competition and enthusiastically played to accomplish their goal. Investing that extra time seemed like it made a difference in creating team cohesion and rapport.

Working Smarter: Instructions matter. After all, the game designer created them, and tested them, with effective team play in mind. For the best chance of success, stick with the planned introduction, instruction, and rules that others have validated. Ensure the functional business trainers do this as well.

Assuming Games Need a Big Budget

Don't let a lack of budget be a reason to opt out of having any games. Many effective learning games are cost-free.

Working Smarter: Remember, learning games don't have to be hard or complicated. A game is effective when learners can shift their thinking and processing as part of the training program. Think of games as a type of review activity or friendly quiz, components of education. A game adds competition that can bring energy and excitement to the review.

Final Note

While games are not a requirement for digital transformation training, learners generally welcome them, and they are easy to create and implement. Best of all, when functional trainers create them, with or without ID assistance, they reinforce key concepts and deepen their own learning. In all cases the success of a game as a training tool relies on the functional or other trainer who facilitates the learning, the topic of chapter 17. The next chapter looks at the very important topics of measuring training effectiveness and learner readiness.

15

Metrics for Learner
Knowledge and Confidence

"There exists a common and costly myth that if there are ten to fifteen people in a room with an 'instructor' at the front using a whiteboard or projector, something productive called 'training' is going on."

—Ruth Colvin Clark, Digital Learning Researcher, Author, and Practitioner

An effective digital transformation training program will prepare learners to work in new ways, see them ready and reasonably confident for the change, and equip them with reference materials to guide them on the job. Their learning is the goal, so an equally essential training program deliverable is measurement. Learners' ability, knowledge, and preparatory experiences involve multiple checks, confirmations, and demonstrations. These occur both during and after training. Along the way, the results communicate progress and drive action to close any gaps, while also highlighting successes to celebrate.

BASICS

This chapter is a bit different from the other chapters and is also the longest. Rather than providing brief overviews and checklists, it goes deeper, introducing tenets from change, adult learning, and learning assessment fields. The purpose is to provide a holistic framework with which to ensure your learners are ready, prepared, and then able to successfully work in new ways. If your background sees you knowledgeable in these topics, skip ahead to "Best Practices" and "What Gets in the Way."

Learning Assessment as a Transformation Imperative

One of the leading practitioners of learning evaluation is James Kirkpatrick, who explained the importance of learning measurement. Assessing learning throughout a person's training and skill development journey is how the training program demonstrates business value (Kirkpatrick & Kirkpatrick, 2006). The starting point is an understanding of what is meant by learning, since that's what's being measured.

Learning in a Digital Transformation

Ruth Clark consolidates the *what* of learning as the effort required to "transform information from instructors, workbooks, or computer screens into new knowledge and skills in long-term memory" (Clark, 2010). She identifies four key human processes involved in seeing information become working knowledge.

- Focused attention
- Engagement that promotes processing
- Management of the mental cognitive load
- Ensuring learning of new information can be used and the needed details retrieved on the job

The design of the training materials addresses some of these elements. Additional considerations for assessing the learning that occurs while people participate in training activities are covered in this chapter because *how* adults learn is only half of the equation for designing and delivering effective digital transformation training programs.

Malcolm Knowles is another notable adult learning author and one of the first I came across. He shared principles that describe *why* adults learn (Knowles, 1996). He identified six factors necessary for adults to acquire and use new knowledge, listed below as they apply to the variety of digital business transformations.

1. *Adults have a need that motivates them to learn.* The fact the business is transforming and jobs are changing provides compelling reasons to learn a new system and new ways of working.

2. *Adults approach training with a task-oriented and problem-solving mindset.* The focus of training must support day-to-day work tasks they perform on the job, both "happy path" and problem scenarios.

3. *Adults bring life experiences to the training experience.* Prior learning experiences, good or bad, along with work and life situations affect people's ability to learn new ways of working, and these must be considered and attended to during digital transformation training.

4. *Adults are motivated to learn by both internal and external factors.* Personal motivation to learn new things and the desire to be successful in the workplace positively influence learning.

5. *Adults need to see themselves as self-directed learners.* The ability to guide their own learning shows up in the questions people ask or requests for more practice, for example.

6. *Adults need to know why they are being asked or required to learn something.* The "so what" of a topic helps learners attend to the information, especially when it's a key task they perform. "Today it's done one way; tomorrow you will need to do it this way" is an important component of digital transformation training.

In short, all business training programs address the elements of both lists. The *Digital Transformation Champions* strategy, audience analysis, curricula, materials, functional trainer approach, and training delivery components combine all these important considerations. How and when to incorporate measurements about whether learner needs are being met and the extent that expected learning is happening or not occur in multiple ways throughout an end user's training journey, sometimes repeatedly.

The Right Timing Matters

Learning is an iterative process that requires time, repetition, and practice for recall and reinforcement of new skills. Therefore, evaluating end users as they carry out their digital transformation training is also an ongoing activity with three key types of evaluations.

- *Learning checks.* Learning checks ascertain how attentive learners are *during training*, as well as their ability to recall just presented information. Later, the learning check activities provide learners with the opportunity to retrieve facts from long-term memory or look up the information and apply it during training.

- *Knowledge assessments.* In contrast to learning checks, a knowledge assessment is often a one-time test where the learner demonstrates their ability to apply key concepts based on the learning objectives. This gets delivered to end users *after completion of their training*. It's the equivalent of a final exam.

- *Feedback surveys.* These repeated check-ins with learners identify what their experience has been, how they feel, and how well their needs as adult learners are being met, *each time* they have a structured training session.

There are different ways to design and conduct each assessment type.

Learning Checks During Training

Checks for learning can be questions, activities, or games. They are valuable because people have to make sense of what they hear or read about new processes and features of a new tool. These activities see learners talk about the new information and determine what it means for their day-to-day work, or apply the information to scenarios. Some common options for learning checks include the following:

- *Queries, prompts, and nonsystem activities.* These types of learning tests are called formative evaluations because they occur during training and test *developing knowledge.* These particular checks help learners to focus and explore their understanding. Whatever format you choose, the learning checks should provide opportunities to make mistakes and reflect on their own work situations. Wrong answers, clarifications, and the chance to question the new concepts all help learners reinforce the desired outcome. See *Telling Ain't Training* (Stolovitch & Keeps, 2002) and *The Ten-Minute Trainer* (Bowman, 2011) for learning check ideas.

- *Hands-on training in a practice system or with a simulation.* No one learned to walk without falling down, and no one gains mastery using a new system without hours of practice. Adults must step through lifelike tasks in a test system, *even when the interface is simple and straightforward.* Watching a video or reading a job aid is informational, though, and does not provide the necessary engagement that results in learning. A simulation may suffice. Hands-on practice is necessary. This learner check gets interspersed with self-paced e-learning or during facilitated training sessions—avoid lumping hands-on practice into one session.

Post-Training Assessments

Carried out after the end of the structured training and the conclusion of multiple hands-on practice opportunities, a final knowledge assessment helps learners and the digital transformation stakeholders feel confident about learner readiness for the go live. Will Thalheimer famously simplified learning as a formula during a talk about our brain's difficulty in staying focused to learn and recall new information: Learning = Remembering - Forgetting (Thalheimer, 1996). He was instrumental in my adopting the use of a final exam because it helps learner motivation during their training knowing there's a test of the new knowledge.

The after-training test is a set of structured questions that sees learners recall information and demonstrate their knowledge in an "open-book" format using available resources. The subject of these tests includes process steps, system tasks, data, and details about performing the job. The business selects the minimum passing score for all end users. Most transformation programs require a passing score of 80%. These are so important to the business that, sometimes, a successful test result is the requirement for learners to be granted access to the production system. These summative assessments measure knowledge retention for a set of expected learning objectives once training is completed. In some cases, when the work is critical, select groups of learners will be tested twice or more.

Feedback from Learners About Their Experience

At the conclusion of each training interaction, a survey allows learners to give input about their learning process. Surveys measure quantitatively and qualitatively how learners are feeling. The questions may be numeric or text-based. For example, the set of questions based originally on an ASTD Job Aid "Taking the Pulse Survey: Change Readiness" (n.d.) that I've evolved over the years is shared as sample 9, Learner Insights Survey. I always include a place for learners to communicate any needs or requests they have for assistance.

These measurements help the training and transformation leaders assess how well learners are prepared for the go live date and beyond.

Industry Models for Measuring Learning and Readiness

Within the fields of change and human performance, different approaches exist that are relevant for thinking about digital transformation learning measurement at a very high level.

Change

Woven into my own training leadership practice is the ProSci change methodology and the powerful notion that organizations don't change; people do. The ADKAR model of awareness, desire, knowledge, ability, and reinforcement offers a straightforward way to think about successfully helping people navigate their own change journey. Training supports the knowledge and ability aspects of the change journey. Gaining competence in new ways of working enhances desire.

Kirkpatrick–Katzell Model

The renamed Kirkpatrick–Katzell Model (Thalheimer, 2022; Kirkpatrick & Kirkpatrick, 2006) identifies four "levels" for learning measurement that culminate in observable business impact, the purpose of the digital transformation training program.

Level I—Reaction. Do learners feel that their training experience was valuable and relevant to their work? Did they feel actively engaged? Did the expected activities take place? Learning checks and feedback surveys are two tools for measuring reactions. Additionally, manager conversations and functional trainer observations are other data points about learner reactions.

Level II—Learning. Based on the objectives and outcomes of the training program, how confident do learners feel? Can they demonstrate understanding of the ideas and apply the concepts to scenarios? How did the training develop the expected skills and abilities? Multiple-choice tests can be used to evaluate this level of learning, per Kirkpatrick. In digital transformation training, the learning checks during training and the knowledge assessment after training both measure learning.

Level III—Behavior. Can the learners apply their knowledge to simulated situations? Can learners explain their new knowledge or demonstrate their skills? Post-training observations, interviews, or additional certification exercises can effectively show a learner's ability to apply new skills to work-like situations. In digital transformations, functional business trainers provide a demonstration of their ability to explain concepts and show how to use the system and the training materials to lead training with their peers. Business leaders may dictate that select learners in key roles have a "day in the life" certification exercise added to their training journey to further test their ability.

Level IV—Results. Does the business realize the intended outcomes? Keep in mind, there's normally a dip in productivity after a launch. A key measurement is how long it takes learners to capably carry out their jobs using new tools and new processes. Charles Fred terms this the "cycle time to proficiency" (Fred, 2001). While the length of hypercare, the transformation-supported stabilization period just after the go live, is one indicator of user proficiency, the better measures are better business KPIs and service-level agreements.

In one ERP deployment for which I was training lead, after two weeks, the company experienced its second-highest shipping volume of all time. In another ERP deployment I heard about, hypercare lasted more than a year for many reasons, including a training program that failed to achieve the intended learning outcomes. Moreover, the program leaders did not appreciate the need to factor into the go live decision the end users' lack of readiness. On a project I led—one of my favorites—after three days, it was clear the users were fluent with new tools and processes without issues, so the hypercare period concluded rapidly. The close of hypercare signals the end of the program and starts the clock on seeing a return on the business investment in the digital transformation.

Performance-Focused Outcomes

Since the 1960s when the Kirkpatrick–Katzell Model was introduced, most have embraced the four-level structure, including the American Training and Development organization. An alternate model focused on performance has emerged with strong proponents (Thalheimer, 2022; Shank, 2021). This model advocates for a different approach to gathering feedback, illustrated as Option B on the second page of sample 9, Learner Insights Survey. I attempted the use of performance-focused questions and found that the cautionary notes applied: It takes more time to develop, more time for learners to complete, and more time to evaluate the results. Consequently, I've returned to the more standard approach illustrated in the first page of the sample.

To summarize, these three aspects for assessing learning are included in this section as fundamentals for measuring digital transformation training. Learning checks, knowledge assessments, and feedback surveys provide necessary insight about the learner audiences at multiple points. Snapshots about these metrics are an important update for program and business leaders.

BEST PRACTICES

This section groups the ideas about leading practices by assessment type and timing.

Plan Learning Questions to Reinforce New Ideas

Testing learners during the training occurs with planned, simple questioning and structured activities. For best results, functional business trainers need to be trained to utilize the following techniques:

- *Repetition.* Very few of us grasp new concepts after a single broadcast of a key point. Make sure the key ideas are checked multiple times and in different ways.

- *Skilled use of questioning.* Questions can help learners focus and also process new ideas. During training, prepared questions and group discussions help learners recall and reinforce new concepts. *Closed questions* have a yes/no or right/wrong answer: "What is the button I should select on this screen?" or "What's the next step?" These keep the learner focused. *Open-ended* questions invite thinking: "How is this similar to what you do today? How is it different?" Reflection and discussion among learners allow them to connect new processes and activities to knowledge they already have.

- *Recollection of information.* Recall sees learners retrieve from notes or memory new information. This is another necessary aspect of adult learning. Games are especially engaging ways to work together to practice recall, the focus of chapter 14.

- *Application of concepts.* Show a screenshot or a short video. Ask questions about the situation: "What can you say about the equipment order, based on the information on the screen?" or "Can the transaction be submitted as is?" or "Will the billing go through as expected?"

- *Reference and use of key resources during training.* Encourage "cheating" to look up information because finding answers is a best-practice on-the-job activity. Knowing there's a place to easily look up the *correct* answer helps the learning process by decreasing stress and supporting the learner's moment of need (Gottfredson & Mosher, 2012).

- *Help and encouragement.* A key benefit of person-led training is the human coaching element. Answering questions, correcting wrong answers, and confirming key points of understanding all help the learning process. Invite and appreciate *all* learner questions: "Great question; glad you asked!" Be comfortable when you don't know the answer: "We'll have to learn about that together. I don't have an answer, so let's add that to the parking lot. I commit to getting you the answer." Then follow up to find the information and share it with others. This approach reinforces the fact that new users will have support as they come up to speed and that we learn together.

All of these learning check activities can be incorporated into the training materials. Additionally, learning checks are at the core of the facilitation, presentation, and demonstration skills that functional trainer preparation seeks to develop, covered in chapter 17.

Provide Hands-On Experience in the System

Digital transformation involves new technology, and learners have to practice using these tools to be able to carry out work using the new system, features, and data.

Effective Practice

Hands-on practice requires a lifelike system. The data elements should be realistic. There should be planned practice scenarios with hands-on exercises. The point is for people to feel comfortable making mistakes while they learn to use the system to carry out the tasks of their jobs. Usually, there is a *training environment* that is a copy of the testing environment. Other times, learners carry out practice using the *testing environment*.

Simulations That Can Be Flexible

When a training instance of the solution is unavailable upon demand, an interactive recording can be developed so a learner can step through a model of the activity. This option is ideal when the workforce is unable to gather for training. For example, Gulfstream used tablets and simulations for their on-the-ground crew who could not physically gather in training rooms to learn new procedures and system tasks. They won an SAP education best practice award for their approach (SAP, 2011). Medical device training experts advocate for the use of simulations to maximize the learning experience for medical practitioners whose available time for training is very limited (Haugen & Woodside, 2010). Be sure to develop simulations that appear realistic and function like the actual application in terms of letter case, selection areas, and navigation. I have seen learners very frustrated by inflexible simulations that required a click in a specific area, not the full button, or that required text input with exact capitalization. The learners failed in attempting to complete the task more than they succeeded because of a poor simulation.

Design Effective Post-Training Assessments

After-training tests measure what learners know and can do after their training and practice. The goal is to determine whether they learned what they need. Can they demonstrate this understanding? For multiple-choice questions and other format options, there are important considerations. Following are some guidelines.

Carefully Craft Questions Tied to Learning Objectives

Create multiple questions for each task- and outcome-based learning objective. A well-written stem question should make clear what knowledge is being tested. It should feel relevant and be answerable, with thought. Answers should include effective distractors. Poorly written questions confuse and frustrate learners instead of reinforcing confidence with a demonstration of knowledge and recall. Patti Shank's book *Write Better Multiple-Choice Questions to Assess Learning* is a terrific resource.

Standardize Objective and Test Question Quality

Ensure the instructional designers (IDs) on the team are well-versed in writing objective- or criterion-based questions. Consider a training team workshop about doing this. Update the standards and templates to incorporate the key ideas. On one project, an ID prepared and presented a short course about writing criterion-based test questions for his peers that required they practice writing both learning objectives and knowledge assessment questions for their assigned digital transformation training content. It was effective and very productive.

Include Media

In addition to word-based questions, media can be used effectively to assess learners' knowledge about the system or procedural learning. Use system screenshots, short videos, and situational questions like "What is the next step to take based on the screen and data entered?" or "What action will clear the alert that's visible on the screen?"

Opt for Open-Book Tests

Learners should be able to complete their tests using support materials. Doing so mirrors how they'll work on the job, where making use of job aids, training materials, and other support resources is encouraged to accurately carry out tasks and work, as designed in the reengineered processes.

Develop Post-Training Questions During, Not After, Material Development

Have the IDs write practice activities and test questions as they build out materials. It's much easier for IDs to create learning check and knowledge assessment questions during material development because the objectives and content remain top of mind. It also works well to ask functional business trainers to come up with relevant hands-on practice scenarios and to provide supporting practice data instead of tasking them with creating test questions, an ID responsibility.

Secure Business Decisions About Expectations

For a first launch especially, to ensure appropriate planning and resourcing, program leaders must communicate their expectations for pass rates and post-training assessments so they get communicated as part of the strategy. Is the required pass rate 70%, 80%, or 100%? How many times can a test be re-taken—three or five times? What happens if someone cannot pass the test? Must training and the test be completed before access to the system gets granted? Some businesses require training and a passing test result for access to use the system. Others do not. Find out executive expectations so you can plan accordingly for budgeting and reporting purposes.

Use Technology to Provide Valid Tests

A test that presents a varying set of questions whose order of answer options get randomized enhances the overall validity of the assessment. When the correct answers get continually re-sequenced, the test is stronger and answers cannot be shared. Ideally, your learning management system (LMS) has features for building questions and generating a random test from a bank of questions. Alternately, e-learning tools can be used to create a bank of questions as a SCORM object. This is a consideration in the learning tools selection process, addressed in chapter 8.

Certify Critical Learners After Training

In addition to a post-training knowledge test, many businesses have seen superior people readiness with additional observation- or group-based certification tests. These are often called "day in the life" activities. In my own experience, I've seen these focused on high-stake tasks, jobs, or business areas. They are always specific to the work that a select group of people do. The certifications include straightforward scenarios as well as problem-solving. Day in the life is meant to mimic real-life work and involves a combination of discussion and in-the-system demonstrations of ability. Best practices for this follow.

Identify the Preferred Day-in-the-Life Certification Test(s)

Business leaders will decide if and how to certify their teams and which format they prefer. Day-in-the-life certifications come in a variety of options and can be very different across the business functions. Here are the most common formats:

- *Daily work.* Select sample scenarios for key tasks related to a specific job or role. Use system activities and an explanation of the process to verify learning. The certification validates a learner's knowledge and ability to apply it correctly in day-to-day work.

- *End-to-end walk-throughs.* Have various learners get together and talk through all the process steps and demonstrate use of the system for various activities to validate readiness at a site or within a business team.

- *Practice labs.* Provide a physical space set up like the work environment where learners come and practice before or after work or during breaks. Logistics warehouses may find this approach especially helpful when the lab is situated near the lunchroom and there's someone present to facilitate the practice. For example, imagine a mock setup of shelving representing storage locations. Learners can use scanners or the system to practice receiving and checking out inventory using new handheld equipment. I've seen business teams require every learner to participate in multiple sessions in a post-training practice lab. A mock setting is especially useful if some learners complete training more than two weeks before the go live, or if the go live date gets pushed out.

- *Manager conversations and demos with team members during meetings.* Any supervisor can request a team member to "show me" or "tell me." Ask, "How do you enter an order in the new system?" or "What would you do in the system if _____ occurs?" or "What report tells you _____?" or "What materials will help you look up _____?" or "Where do you go when you need help with _____?"

- *Business-driven exercises.* Groups of business team members step through the full end-to-end processes with people demonstrating and completing key tasks. For example, on one of my deployments, finance coordinated a mock close with representatives from all the teams. It was so effective as a preparatory and validation activity that the business teams repeated it a second time. The hypercare period for the finance function was a nonevent with 100% end user adoption.

These post-training certification activities, whatever form they take, notably benefit the business. Accordingly, document any potential final certification activity as part of the audience analysis, even if it's a potential and not yet confirmed. The placeholder signals that business leaders and their teams can consider whether it's beneficial to certify select groups of learners, and how to carry that out.

Have the Business Take Ownership of Group-Based Certification Activities

Business-driven certifications versus those led by change, communications, testing, or training achieve better outcomes. Ultimately, business ownership for people readiness is a bridge to the adoption of new ways of working that sees the expected business results and ROI because the business leaders have steered their teams through the transformation.

Include Typical Problem Scenarios

Whatever the format, include common scenarios that come up in the course of work, including problems and exceptions. These "problem path" examples truly validate learning when users demonstrate how to address the issues that will arise on the job. These should have been taught in the training and also reinforced during hands-on practice.

Use Certification to Identify Needs for Launch Support

All certification activities, but especially the group-based ones, flag system issues ahead of the launch. There may be individuals or groups of learners who need help with specific tasks. Functional trainers or the transformation team can assist with technical or data questions. They can also provide coaching and close the gaps ahead of the launch. If this is not possible, place knowledgeable project team members on the ground for the first few days of the launch. Everyone wants to succeed.

The earliest certifications should be of functional trainer readiness to work with end users.

Functional Trainer Assessments

Your functional business trainers are the early learners, so their readiness must be evaluated using a different set of performance outcomes and expectations. While both end users and functional trainers learn the processes and the system tasks, functional trainers require an additional set of skills: the ability to demonstrate use of the system, then present the content to their peers and facilitate group sessions *that result in effective learning outcomes*. Their timeline is different as well. Functional trainers must be fully prepared five to six weeks before end user training starts. Their knowledge and abilities are best certified with a thirty- or forty-five-minute mock training of what they will do with learners, including a system demonstration and exercise facilitation. An added benefit of these early training demos is that they can generate excitement within the business for the program and for the start of end user training. See chapter 17 for more information about functional trainer preparation and assessment.

In every training session and with each group of learners, it's important to ask how they are doing.

Use the Insights from Feedback and Test Results

People in training sessions may look confident or appear to be struggling. In both cases there's value in asking people about their learning and how they feel. Measuring learners' experience and sharing the results provides an important snapshot for the entire digital transformation program.

Sequence Feedback Surveys Before Knowledge Assessments

Collect feedback before the final knowledge assessment test. Doing so avoids biased data related to feelings about taking the test, rather than the experience of learning.

Ask the Same Questions Repeatedly

Competence and confidence grow over time. Feedback a learner provides after the first training session *should* be different from what's reported after the final training or hands-on practice session.

Take Action When It's Indicated

The feedback may suggest that some learners need help. In my experience, exception data pointed accurately to legitimate gaps that had to be addressed. For example, learners indicated ongoing confusion and a need for more practice because they had not worked hands-on in the system, despite expectations that they would. In a few cases, the questions were misread and mismarked. People said, "Oh, I misunderstood the question. I thought one meant I agreed, instead of disagreed." In other cases, language and literacy possibly challenged a person's ability to complete the survey, which is a flag for their overall learning. Identify before training starts who will follow up directly with the learners. It's usually the local training coordinator who developed the training schedule for the business function, and almost never the training lead.

There is much to know and apply in measuring the learning for a digital transformation. Be aware of a few watch items that compromise insights about readiness and learner needs.

WHAT GETS IN THE WAY

Sometimes, learning checks and feedback don't happen or don't get done properly. Here are some of the reasons why and some ways to safeguard against that.

Failing to Check for Learning During Training and Practice

Functional business trainers have the important responsibility of carrying out the ongoing learning checks during training. Simply talking at learners without allowing them time to react, reflect, or synthesize what they're doing shortchanges their mental processing. At worst, a lack of engagement prevents learning.

Working Smarter: Training material templates can include "Learning Check" sections as a design norm to signal it's time to recap, review, and confirm understanding. "Train the trainer" programs for functional business trainers teach and practice facilitation skills that engage participation, question asking, and discussion about what's changing. Through their own learning and practice, the functional trainers experience the value of learning checks. They get to practice asking, answering, and responding to questions, and playing games to see how they promote learning. The key is having learning checks modeled and *experiencing* the value themselves to then turn around and use the tools with the end users they're teaching. Audits of the first few sessions also help ensure that the training incorporates questions that aid learning and hands-on practice.

Lacking Structured Practice Activities

Learners need to reinforce their learning with organized, logically sequenced activities. These should have a purpose, clear steps, and expected outcomes. I've seen situations when the functional trainers "wing it" while introducing a concept, which adds confusion and unnecessary stress. In contrast, when the activity scenario is clearly introduced and supporting data exist in the system, learning occurs and confidence grows. For instance, an example of a hospital billing scenario would involve made-up patient data, actual medical services, and sample costs. The functional trainer would guide learners through the training exercise as planned. These scenarios and supporting data should exist in advance of training. It can be hard, if not impossible, to wait until the day before a scheduled session to compile a set of activity scenarios and data for hands-on exercises. The review activity won't be done well, and the lack of preparation negatively affects the learners' experience.

Working Smarter: Your training material development plan should consider how to develop practice scenarios and supporting data. Think about ways to capture practice scenarios and be flexible about who creates them. Does it work to incorporate scenario planning into the subject matter expert (SME) information-gathering sessions? Is it better incorporated into the functional trainer onboarding or their development process? Can the transformation process teams help? Are there other project assets that could be used, such as test script scenarios, use cases, or today-to-morrow changes from change impacts? The best options vary depending on things like the process teams, the length of time functional trainers have to prepare, and the amount of material the ID needs to create. Collecting these examples and ensuring the data exist is a collective effort that pays off for the learners and is measurable in their feedback and their knowledge assessment results.

Having Weak After-Training Tests

Learners dislike questions that are too simple. Conversely, they will feel stressed by those that are too challenging. Tests will put learners off when drag-and-drop or other engagement quiz features are overused. Likewise, an overreliance on text-only, true-false, or multiple-choice questions feels tiresome and provides limited insights into learners' comprehension and ability. On one transformation, the tests that the business and workstream teams validated were deemed by learners as "too difficult." On my first program as a training lead, end users were completing some of the post-training assessments *before* training because they were so easy. To be truly effective, tests must be valid and passable by most learners once they finish their training.

Working Smarter: Plan early and think about learner knowledge tests during the tools and technologies review. Consider how best to test the types of learner tasks or the learning outcome in a way that works for the learners and appropriately tests their knowledge. For example, if the assessment is problem-solving in a particular case, use a scenario or a screenshot. Based on key business metrics, which user tasks and activities are impactful? What questions or examples provide insight into learners' ability to correctly carry out the steps? The more meaningful for business work the questions are, the better they confirm knowledge.

Posting Tests That Don't Work

Questions can fail to function as expected. Usually, this occurs when the test question gets built in either the LMS or another tool. Correct answers get marked as incorrect or incorrect answers as correct. A learner choosing what they know is the right or wrong answer receives an alert that their selection is wrong. This frustrates learners and creates a negative feeling about their learning experience.

Working Smarter: Ensure tests get validated in the LMS or other platform *before* they're assigned to end users. Ask three to five people who know the correct process and system to complete the test and confirm the question and answers are correct or that the simulation performs as expected. Tell them to try to "break" the test—by changing answers, going back, clicking here and there, and so on. Testing the test makes it an effective user assessment. No one wants users to remember how frustrated they felt because the test didn't work.

Designing Tests That Miss the Mark

Avoid having too few or too many questions. Tests are not one-size-fits-all. Requiring every knowledge assessment to have twenty questions will be a challenge for short courses because there may be only three key learning objectives. Having a standard seven questions for a final knowledge assessment for hours of training will omit important learning topics.

Working Smarter: Establish a standard and use the learning objectives to develop knowledge assessment questions. First, as part of training standards, determine the number of final test questions based on one or a combination of the following: the length of training time, the number of key activities the role performs, and the criticality of the role. For example, for every hour of instruction, plan to draft one to two possible questions and have the knowledge assessment use one. Tie every question to an essential learning objective. Track the creation of these questions in the training development plan.

Testing Before Getting Experience Feedback

On one deployment, learner feedback about their training experience and the materials was collected *after* the knowledge test. Instead of training reactions, the data revealed how learners felt about taking a test, which very few people like doing. It was nearly impossible to separate feedback about the training from the testing experience. That was a DONA.

Working Smarter: Capture feedback about the course or training *before the knowledge assessment*. Post-class feedback from learners helps validate that training met their expectations—for them, it's a no-stress survey, meaning it may yield helpful data about their training experience. The knowledge assessment has a passing score requirement that the business sets, usually with a limited number of retake attempts. You can see why people may feel frazzled and focused on that experience if asked afterward.

Adding Assessment Requirements Late in the Project

The need to avoid repeats of past disasters may motivate some business leaders to demand high scores for testing, additional practice, and even post-training certifications with separate reports about training activities. If these additional requirements get communicated late, there can be challenges in meeting the need. Certifications may require additional training team effort, more time to coordinate test reviews and approvals, and extra LMS administration. This all comes at a time that conflicts with other planned work for end user training.

Working Smarter: The business expectations and requirements for all learning assessments should be part of the training strategy or approach, the topic of chapter 1. At this early stage, the effort and resources to support the work can be factored into the overall resource plan and training budget. When late requests get made, explore the concerns and issues behind the asks. Perhaps having the business coordinate a certification activity directly would be the best course. If the task falls to training, communicate any potential risks to other end user training activities.

On one project, a "day in the life" certification exercise for all learners got introduced shortly before end user training began. The certification activity was a do-this and tell-me-about checklist of tasks for people in specific job roles, built out and scored in the LMS. While very effective as a final documentation for learner preparation, these checklists added time for question development, LMS administration, SME review, and final approvals. Translation requirements were another consideration. Additionally, there was coordination needed to identify who would spend time with the learners to review the items and score them, then train these individuals in how to use the checklist. The reporting effort to summarize results was another added activity. The training team was already very stressed to complete planned training materials, knowledge assessments, and other training preparations. The certification work required extra hours in the evenings and on weekends. On another project, a key business leader requested a different view of learner activity that added several hours of time every other day for additional reporting. In both these cases, training team member attrition resulted because unfortunately additional resources were not forthcoming to help with the extra work.

Practicing in the Live Production Environments

To learn a new technology, a person has to be able to make mistakes, without fear of breaking anything. Digital business systems integrate with sales, production, financials, and reporting metrics in real time. As a result, inputs and mistakes made in the production environment by new users who are learning the system introduce errors that require cleanup work. For this reason, training and assessments should *never* take place in a production system for users learning to carry out transactional work. This may be a change for some functional teams where on-the-job training in the production instance has been the norm.

Working Smarter: Hands-on practice needs to occur in a non-production environment. Normally this is a specific training environment or the testing environment. In other cases, it's a simulation built to mimic the way the activity works in the production environment. All these options for practice see learners comfortably build their confidence and have the ability to pass their post-training test. Normally business leaders will allow only skilled and tested users in the production system for data and transaction quality.

Final Note

Assessing learning involves multiple checks, confirmations, and demonstrations, both during and after training. The training strategy should describe the selected or recommended learner assessments. It must also explain how tests and certifications will measurably demonstrate learners' ability relative to both the business goals of the digital transformation and the specific learning objectives, by job role.

Because learning gets measured, it can be reported. Along the way, sharing results about end user learning communicates readiness and spotlights any issues. The ultimate test of the effectiveness of the learning is how well people can do their jobs and demonstrate proficiency. Before that, however, the goal is to measure *predictably* how learners will perform at launch. It matters: When learners report the training feels relevant for their jobs, that they worked hands-on in the system, and that they feel confident to do their jobs, you'll more likely see rapid, successful adoption of new ways of working in the business functions. "The staff look like they've been using the system for two months," one transformation leader reported, walking the floor on the first day of a go live. This very positive outcome of training is dependent on some key activities and deliverables that others are responsible for, the topic of the next chapter.

16

Training Dependencies as Boosters, Not Barriers

"It does not do to leave a live dragon out of
your calculations, if you live near one."

—J.R.R. Tolkien, Author

Work that others perform directly affects training in a digital transformation. Training is highly dependent on how the transformation program operates— and particularly how its leaders manage technical and process scope, priorities, risks, actions, issues, and decisions. Moreover, deliverables produced by people outside the training team affect the completion of training work and preparation of learners. This chapter describes seven dependencies the transformation training lead must oversee to achieve the results expected of the training program.

BASICS

This chapter introduces dependencies for training and learner success in a digital transformation training program and how to talk about them in training overviews, then rigorously track them throughout the project phases. Samples 1, 2, and 6 illustrate how to report about these dependencies.

Seven Critical Dependencies to Manage

From my own experiences and inputs from training colleagues, these are the critical dependencies that the training lead and the entire training team need to call out and monitor. The list is organized by importance. Your own list may be shorter or longer.

1. Functional Trainers—the Critical Dependency

Simply put, the critical dependency for launch success is the group of people who are culled from their business teams to teach and prepare their peers. These individuals may be called *lead users*, *super users*, or *functional trainers*. Functional trainers are the ambassadors to the business, and the success of learning depends on their ability to use the training materials to teach people new processes and how to work in the system for carrying out daily tasks. Moreover, they translate current business steps into new process activities.

A great solution that is well-tested and documented, with high-quality training, can be negated by an ineffective functional trainer. Learners will not succeed if the person tasked with teaching or supporting them cannot accurately talk about how to complete an activity, confidently use the system, or effectively lead people through hands-on practice. Functional trainers get identified well before end user training begins and are early learners of the system and processes. Their work and responsibility are much greater with an instructor-led training approach, lighter when there's a combination of e-learning and follow-on practice sessions. In both models, functional trainers first develop their own knowledge and ability so they can then help their colleagues learn and practice new ways of working. Chapter 17 addresses functional trainer best practices and what gets in the way of preparing this key group of business transformation change leaders. I include it here as a dependency for training because the business identifies and makes these people available. Moreover, the transformation workstream team members teach functional trainers how to work in the new system to carry out redesigned business processes, another dependency. Having strong functional business trainers sees businesses realize lasting transformation.

2. Completion of Process Design and System Build

Training material completion is dependent on having a configured and fully tested system that functions as expected to enable the workflow of new processes. These steps include clarity about screen design, data, and who performs which tasks across the process activities. This seems obvious: When processes are undefined or the system is incomplete, the training team cannot finish creating training materials, nor can functional trainers learn new ways of working. Often, these issues emerge first as process-specific delays in progressing training materials. As delays continue, training materials remain partially complete. In the best-case scenario, placeholders flag pending decisions in a way that indicates they'll be communicated during training or at a later time. In other cases, business approvers will not sign off on materials because there are gaps about who will carry out the work or the system configuration remains undecided. In these situations, business leaders may have to delay the launch date.

3. End User Security Roles Design and Mapping Them to People

A security role defines the process-based activities a person can perform in the system, as well as the screens, fields, and data that are available based on the work they do in their job. The timeline and designated owners for role design and coordination of security role assignments is another important dependency for training. Training materials explain how work gets done and by whom. The ideal digital transformation training strategy holds that people learn those aspects of the process and the specific tasks they need to know to do *their jobs*, based on the security roles assigned to them. Lists of each role and the activities enabled, along with counts of people assigned to each role determine the logistics of end user training. The time frames, size of classes, number of sessions needed, and weeks required to complete training and practice are based on the number of activities people need to learn, based on their security role assignments. Some people have multiple roles assigned to them. Transformation programs that align cross-functional work to role-based thinking for solution design, configuration, and testing help minimize pre- and post-launch issues. On one transformation, after the go live, there were 1,500 role changes because the importance of security design and user assignments was misunderstood. Worst of all, some people did not receive the training they needed, and others were confused to be placed into classes they didn't need. Security role design and careful user management matter for individuals, business operations, and training.

4. On-the-Ground Business Contacts for Training Execution

The best outcomes for learners, functional trainers, and overall readiness occur when the business identifies training coordinators for its functions and sites. Someone at a geographic site or on a functional team is best suited to coordinate the training and practice schedules by working with local managers around business priorities. These contacts are the local people who "care" about transformation training for their business teams. During training, they help the business trainers and ensure logistics are in place, resolve any day-of training matters that arise, and follow up on missing or incomplete training. They are also the ones who take action when learner feedback requires it, and handle other training-related needs for their business team. The digital transformation training lead cannot effectively carry out this role, even in a backup capacity. It's like asking the digital transformation program lead to teach a course—that's not what they're prepared or supposed to do.

5. A Training and Practice Environment

A robust, functioning copy of the digital solution with the in-place configuration, security roles, and data must be available for learners to use for hands-on practice. On some projects, training receives a standalone environment. It is not as up to date as the TEST environment and requires separate administration, especially when users are provisioned by name instead of using generic training accounts. On other projects, training shares the TEST environment with named accounts and security role assignments. This works best in my experience because the system remains up to date with patches and, most importantly, functional trainers can more easily carry out testing and prepare for training in a single environment. It also can help verify user setup is accurate. In other cases, high-fidelity simulations may be a better hands-on practice option when there are a few key activities that users need to learn. In an earlier example, Gulfstream developed simulations and used iPads for their staff in an award-winning training program (SAP, 2011). The key to overseeing this dependency is working with program leaders and the system implementation partner to identify options and select the best environment or platform so learners can practice using the system. Based on that decision, others follow: who and how it will be kept up to date with ongoing and final system changes, user setups, and support during training sessions get made and the resources provided.

6. Change Communications

Before they attend training, learners and their managers need to receive clear and comprehensive messages about today-tomorrow differences in their business processes. These messages should introduce the new system and identify manual tasks that are being automated, as well as any changes in who does the work. The wins of the changes get highlighted, and any interim processes get noted. The overarching purpose of these communications is to prepare people by introducing what is changing and why. This information establishes a clear need and motivation to learn new ways of working, important for a person to have before their training session.

When training materials are "durable" and used for three years, the messaging about what is new and different must get conveyed with pre-training communications. I've led deployments where training was asked to embed change communications into the training materials themselves. In these cases, training was stale after the launch. Think about new hires and people changing jobs without any context about old processes or the legacy system. Their learning effort is more complicated as a result of having to learn with materials that focus on old ways of work. Therefore, highlights about change delivered weeks before training starts are a change management and communications deliverable that sees learners and their managers aware of why training matters. Well-prepared functional trainers do a brilliant job bridging today-tomorrow concepts during the training sessions.

7. Business Requirements for Training

The business stakeholders must decide early on about requirements for training. For example, for which security or job roles is training required? What is the passing rate for a post-training test—70%, 80%, 90%, or 100%? Will materials need to be translated? Who is responsible for approving training materials for each process or business area? Will post-training certification be required for some or all roles, and if so, who will develop it and conduct the sessions? Will there be additional day-in-the-life testing before the go live to verify readiness of people in critical business roles or end-to-end processes? How many functional trainers will there be and when will they join the program? All of these decisions determine how the training team completes its work—and in the case of certification, they may increase the number of materials the team needs to create and the efforts for which the functional trainers may be responsible. These decisions are needed when the training strategy gets refined and training material development gets planned.

While these dependencies are known and can be tracked as cross-functional milestones and monitored by project managers, best practices will help the training lead and instructional designers (IDs) receive the information, decisions, handoffs, and resources needed to realize the training program outcomes.

BEST PRACTICES

The following items address communication and work across the transformation business teams and with those responsible for the dependencies.

Build the Case with Emotional Connections

Illustrate the point about why a dependency matters with compelling backup. Tell stories with consequence and impact when introducing the interdependencies and how each makes a difference for the learners, the business, and the digital transformation program. Here are a few examples:

- Misses with role-mapping assignments raise specific questions from learners during their training: "Why am I in this class? This isn't my job." Worse, they won't have the correct system or the knowledge they need to carry out their jobs, and hypercare issues will arise quickly .

- There's a story about one deployment and two plants with vastly different training coordinators that illustrates the importance of this role for a business team or site. At the site with a dedicated and committed training contact who actively supported the functional trainers and the learners, training took place as planned, with little variation. Learner feedback was very strong. In the other case, the expected training did not occur, and the resulting lack of knowledge created unacceptable outcomes for the people and the business. The differences between the two coordinators showed up early with training schedule creation delays and class rescheduling. Functional trainers reported issues, which low-rated learner assessments confirmed. Then during hypercare, metrics about business operations at each plant showed that the one exceeded expectations and the other fell far short, not surprisingly.

Poignant stories help convey why project and business leaders need to appreciate the importance of training dependencies.

Enhance Visibility by Adding the Dependencies to the Project Plan

Give visibility to the interdependencies by naming them as "Training Receives" tasks or milestones. Tasks can have 1%–100% progress; milestones on a plan are either 0% or 100%. Some program leaders and project managers will recognize the importance of tracking the list of dependencies. Others may reluctantly agree to discuss them and will benefit from stories about why they matter. Either way, adding your dependencies in the overall project plan as tracked items will help ensure that the training team receives the necessary deliverables. Consider making these dependencies entrance criteria for the start of training or go/no-go decision criteria for the business teams. I also suggest including dependencies in business readiness dashboards, as well as your RACI if you have one.

Document and Report Risks

Despite escalation and discussion, there are many times decisions fall outside a training lead's circle of control or even influence. Acknowledge the decision, assess the risk, and take appropriate action. Log a risk or decision in the risks, actions, issues, and decisions (RAID) log with the implications from a training perspective. Include any steps that would mitigate the risks. For example, not having a learning management system creates a large margin of error in training completion reporting and requires excessive effort to manage enrollments and training tracking. Likewise, if business leaders choose to delay the onboarding of functional business trainers or decide they must both teach and carry out testing, there may not be time to fully prepare to perform all of the tasks the transformation leaders expect. Functional trainers will feel very challenged. Sometimes, with additional data, decisions do get revisited. Other times, the teams work together to make the best of the situation.

While there is usually no direct responsibility for the seven dependencies, the training lead can influence their delivery with overcommunication. Sample 6, Digital Transformation Training Status at a Glance, shows how to report about these items and communicate progress or signal issues to a broad audience. Update the dashboard quarterly, monthly, or weekly, as needed.

WHAT GETS IN THE WAY

Unfortunately, many things can prevent the training team from receiving these handoffs in a timely manner. A few items deserve attention for their negative impact on the digital transformation.

Mismanaging System Role Design and Assignments

Two types of projects may see notable challenges with security role design and assignment of roles to business end users. Initial digital transformations where the processes and system are new are one example. Understaffed projects are another. A lot can go wrong if security role design, maintenance, and user assignment are not well-managed.

Working Smarter: Request that transformation program leaders take action to benefit the business process, training, testing, change, and communications teams. Explain that having someone on the transformation team doing these things can help the business see a more successful launch.

- Provide a centrally managed list of end user security roles, described in a way that makes it clear to the multiple transformation teams what people will and won't be able to do.

- Include the details about what each security role enables in terms of activities, screens, fields, data, and any reports.

- Document the process, timeline, and "owner" for the design of each role, and also who is responsible for carrying out the matching of people to the security roles.

- Provide a documented process for requesting access to systems and the information needed to "provision" people to a system environment. In best-managed transformations, there is a structured form provided.

- Maintain a central list of the learners assigned to one or more roles and describe the process and communication about changes in roles and assignment.

- Report about ongoing changes to the security roles and the counts of people mapped to each to help coordinate training logistics.

- Keep security roles an early focus of the entire program because they enable new ways of working and determine the training and communication that people need.

Lacking Support for Coordinators

If the person identified to carry out key tasks to bring the transformation training initiative to the business team gets behind or cannot carry out the necessary work—like building schedules for training and practice—everything will fall behind. Even worse is a schedule that business leaders do not see or validate so it gets changed after training starts. In one instance, a key local training contact was assigned temporarily to cover a demanding operational role, leaving no time to support the site and employees with their transformation training. There were significant issues with the training. Because people were unprepared, it was challenging after going live as a result, and adoption was delayed.

Working Smarter: Ask business leaders to designate the right people with time to carry out training coordination tasks. Hold a short kickoff call with this group of people to welcome them and emphasize the business importance of the work they'll undertake. As with the other milestones in this chapter, add these to the project plan: training coordinators identified and onboarded, training schedules created, training completed, and so on. Communicate via status when gaps emerge and request support. Sample 10, Training Preparation and Learner Readiness Dashboard, shows progress by learner audience for the training activities that others carry out.

Failing to Send Learners Communications About Process Changes Before Training Starts

Business teams need awareness about how work that gets done "today" will change "tomorrow" for specific tasks and job roles. The negative consequences are far-reaching if communications are not prepared or they're sent to the wrong people because role-mapping assignments are incorrect. Inaccurate change communications mean that managers cannot provide an accurate overview to their teams about transformation changes. Moreover, those who attend training may be confused and unclear about why they are in a specific class.

Working Smarter: Experienced change management teams normally document, track, and coordinate communication about business changes the digital transformation will introduce by business, process, and job/security roles. This level of detail enables targeted communications about the new ways of working in a transformed business model. The training lead and IDs must understand the change impact tracker structure and its links to security roles—the training materials should reflect these decisions. Also, IDs need to see the drafts of these documents and know when change communications will get sent. Ideally, the timing is two to four weeks before training starts. In the strongest transformation programs, the change, communications, testing, training, and workstream teams collaborate to share resources that help each team accomplish its goals.

Final Note

Fundamentally, managing these dependencies well is a function of training leadership. Poor or ineffective leadership only exacerbates the consequences of not having key dependencies in place. Chapter 4, "Training Leadership for Lasting Impact," reviews the basics, best practices, and how to manage more effectively through the most common leadership challenges. Because it is the number-one training dependency and the key factor for learner success in a digital transformation, the next chapter is about selecting, developing, and supporting functional business trainers.

17

Business Trainers as the Essential Factor for Transformation Success

"You're asking people to give up pieces of who they are in order to grow into what you hope they can become."

—**Kerry Bunker,** Executive Leadership Coach, Author, and Speaker

Human endeavor and commitment are inspiring, and for digital transformation, it's the secret sauce for success. I've seen hundreds of people step up as functional business trainers. In this important role, they are early learners developed to lead their colleagues through training and hands-on practice, ultimately realizing the promise of digital transformation. Having functional trainers helps drive adoption by seeding knowledgeable resources among business teams to help the business achieve the expected outcomes. How to identify, develop, coach, and support digital transformation functional trainers so they can excel in their critical role is the focus of this chapter.

BASICS

Business leaders make the decision about having businesspeople deliver training as an input to the digital transformation training strategy. Instructional designers (IDs) typically do not deliver the training because they know the *new* state of working, not the *current* system and process steps or the day-to-day specifics of the job. When learning something new, it helps to have someone answer questions about how it varies from the process and way things work today. For this reason and others, having trainers from the business functions is the best model for digital transformation training programs. Functional trainers deeply understand their business area. They learn the new processes and system and how to teach their peers using the training materials and tools. Executive support for the functional trainer model helps ensure the right people get selected, have adequate time to develop their skills and build knowledge, and receive recognition for their notable contributions. How to select the right people, develop and support them in carrying out their work as business trainers is well-understood starts with their work.

Core Responsibilities of Functional Business Trainers

Business and program leaders make decisions about what the business trainer role entails. All functional trainers learn new processes and new technology. Their other tasks may include all or some of the following:

- Reviewing draft training materials to ensure the content is relevant for their business areas

- Preparing practice scenarios, reviews, questions, and, if needed, data for training and practice sessions specific to the work people perform in their business areas

- Attending "train the trainer" preparation and committing to deliver a sample course session to be "certified" to teach others

- Leading training sessions, demonstrating how to use the system, coaching learners, and facilitating hands-on practice sessions—in person or virtual

- Conducting testing—observing or carrying out user acceptance testing (UAT)

- Providing overview demonstrations to business stakeholders

- Engaging actively in *all* functional trainer group sessions

- Providing ongoing feedback about *their own* preparation, learning, and readiness to teach others

Not everyone is well-suited to take on the responsibilities of the functional trainer role.

Employees with the Right Stuff for Training

In addition to possessing a deep understanding of the business, functional trainers should possess the traits and strengths that will help them carry out their work in this stretch assignment role. These characteristics are detailed in the upcoming "Best Practices" section. Functional trainers become important champions of the change as they learn the new system and reengineered ways of work. To succeed, besides having capabilities, they need time to learn and practice and perform their functional trainer tasks without regular duties getting in the way.

Key Questions for the Business Trainer Program

Digital transformation initiatives that reassign people from their normal day-to-day work for a period of time to join the project team. Invoke decisions about how functional trainers will engage with the program, how their skills will be developed, and the start and duration of their time commitment.

- *Assignment effort.* Are functional trainers fully or partially dedicated to the project? Those assigned as functional trainers on a part-time basis need the greatest attention and the longest runway of time to become prepared because their day-to-day work priorities compete with transformation support work.

- *Timing for onboarding.* When will functional trainers be released from their day-to-day work to support the project?

- *Skill development.* Who will take the time to teach the functional trainers about the system, data, and process? How will their knowledge and progress be formally assessed and reported?

- *Train the trainer.* What is the structured approach to ensure functional trainers can effectively lead training among their peers? Will they be certified as ready to teach?

Remember that functional trainers—arguably the most critical factor for end user training and business adoption—must be carefully selected, onboarded, trained, and well-supported to carry out the activities they get tasked with. It takes the right people as functional trainers and a network of people to help them.

Trainer Preparation and Support by Leaders

Functional trainers receive important support from a broad network of project and business leaders.

- *Business Executives.* Selection of functional trainers and decisions about the time frames get made at the highest levels to help ensure the overall digital transformation program succeeds and business operations meet or exceed KPIs.

- *Workstream Leads and Subject Matter Experts (SMEs).* These are the primary points of contact for functional trainers, typically teaching how to use the new system and answering questions about how work will get carried out tomorrow.

- *Business Leaders.* They speak to the program's importance and recognize the role the functional trainers have in supporting the launch.

- *Transformation Program Leaders.* They ensure functional trainers are fully engaged with their digital transformation program business teams to build knowledge and carry out their other responsibilities.

- *Transformation Training Team.* IDs will share training materials and may incorporate business trainer feedback. The training team members coordinate the functional trainer development program, including train the trainer, their certification assessment, and often facilitate community calls with the broad group of trainers to see them prepared before training starts and supported during training.

- *Managers/Supervisors.* A functional trainer's manager supports the person in their project role by reassigning work to others so they can participate and engage as early as they need to. Managers can also prioritize digital transformation work if conflicts arise when the person has both day-to-day work and functional trainer responsibilities.

- *Others.* Testing, communications, and other transformation program teams will engage with functional trainers based on the tasks the business trainers are asked to carry out.

Criteria for Training Delivery Abilities

The training team must prepare and share standards for training delivery during the onboarding that functional business trainers receive. These standards get use as certification criteria for their being able to teach their peers. Ensure the functional business trainer is prepared and able to do the following:

- Demonstrate knowledge of the processes and system they support

- Demonstrate knowledge of the course(s), training materials, and all resources

- Create an effective training environment and facilitate learning—make sure they have:

  » Communicated expectations, objectives, and goals

  » Managed time and the classroom

  » Demonstrated preparation to work with learners

  » Encouraged participation and discussion about new information

  » Used appropriate question and discussion techniques and managed a parking lot

  » Demonstrated professionalism and respect for every learner

» Demonstrated in-the-moment flexibility and effective problem-solving

» Led effective hands-on, in-the-system practice

These delivery behaviors become the basis for your train the trainer program objectives, content, and activities.

Identify When a Business Trainer Isn't Needed

Not all transformation learning gets supported by trainers from the business. Functional business trainers support multiple learners rather than just a few. For example, when only a *few* people perform unique or highly technical tasks, knowledge transfer sessions rather than end user training make greater sense. These workshops get conducted by the solution vendor or the project team. Participating in testing provides the expected hands-on practice. Other end users with one task to carry out—for example, business leaders who need to approve requisitions and invoices—can learn from a communication or short self-paced instructional video rather than having a functional trainer assigned to them.

Titling Your Functional Business Trainers

Like a person's name or the name of a transformation program, the label used for business trainers matters in most instances. Functional trainers may be called *lead users*, *super users*, *facilitators*, *functional trainers*, *change agents*, *ambassadors*, or another term. Have business representatives choose the term that will resonate the most with functional teams and the business trainers themselves.

Create an overview of the functional trainer program. See sample 11, Business Trainer Overview at a Glance, for one way to convey the purpose, major milestone activities, responsibilities, and counts of learners and functional trainers. While the approach to using internal talent as trainers is common, unfortunately not all functional trainers succeed in their work. The following best practices identify what is known to help them succeed.

BEST PRACTICES

Best practices for a functional trainer program that achieves its objectives start with clarity about what they will be asked to do, selecting the right individuals, and then carefully attending to their development and their performance.

Select the Best Trainers

A functional trainer has a visible role and a sometimes daunting set of responsibilities. To set them up for success, select them based on their strengths and proven ability. The best functional trainers are avid learners who value and enjoy helping others. Other abilities and traits are necessary as well, in my experience. Here are some examples of what I've seen to work best and what to avoid.

Traits to Select For

For your best chance of success, look for people who have the following traits:

- Personable and respected by their peers
- Technically proficient and knowledgeable about the business
- Positive in their outlook, with a can-do attitude
- Comfortable with ambiguity, change, and continuous improvement
- Professional in their demeanor
- Natural problem-solvers who seek solutions
- Able to say, "I don't know"
- Comfortable speaking with confidence in group settings

Watch Characteristics

For the best chance of success, do not choose individuals with the following:

- Lacking the desirable traits previously listed, even though they *have time* to be assigned to the digital transformation (Phelan, 2012b)

- Uncomfortable with unknowns and ambiguity

- Uncurious and complacent—they identify problems and expect others to solve them

- Overconfident or arrogant—they lack humility

- Too senior to be effective as peer instructors to others; executives or senior managers do better as workstream leads or sponsors rather than functional trainers

These lists are a starting point. Do the functional trainers in your transformation program need to speak another language? Do they need experience working with learners who require accommodation? Expand and refine these starter lists with input from your company's HR team, executive business sponsor, and workstream leads to agree on which traits of business trainers that will best support the digital transformation.

Confirm the Needed Number of Trainers

Once the list of possible functional trainers is culled, determine the number you need to onboard. Gartner provides a rough formula of one business trainer for twenty-five to thirty learners (Phelan, 2012b). My own and others' experiences qualify this recommendation based on the learners and the content being taught. Review the following topics and adjust the teacher-to-student ratio as appropriate.

- *Amount of New Knowledge.* Consider the degree of change and the number of processes, tools, systems, and activities people must learn. This complexity determines the needed counts of functional trainers. For example:

  » On one project, a group of learners in planning had the greatest number of system tasks and business process steps to learn. They required more individual attention, and the ratio was one functional trainer to five learners.

  » Conversely, some tasks are simpler to teach to larger groups. Reading labels with a scanner involves just a few steps and a few activities.

Those performing these tasks often work in large teams across multiple shifts. A single functional trainer per shift can effectively help twenty-five or more people, before launch and as an on-the-job support coach after.

- *Learner Needs.* Specific needs that learners have can alter the ratio. For example, the audience analysis calls out languages and accommodations, which should be considered as a factor in determining the number of needed functional trainers for one area. Particular needs may increase the number of functional trainers required for a site or group of learners. For instance, a customer service training saw an additional functional trainer added and dedicated to a few learners to fully support their unique needs.

- *Locations That Functional Trainers Can Support.* Counts of the functional trainers should factor in physical locations. For example, there may be forty learners in total spread across five sites more than four hours apart. If the goal is for functional trainers to be local contacts for end users, then in this type of situation, the count of needed trainers could increase to one for each site.

- *Backups.* Having a few more functional trainers at the start is a recommendation since there is often attrition.

The next step, after determining the count and selecting the final pool of functional trainers, is to communicate and onboard them to the program and begin the process of developing their skills.

Communicate Monthly Time Commitments

For each assigned responsibility, identify the expected time functional trainers will spend working on the related tasks and when. Make sure that all the functional trainers understand their expected time commitments, by month and phase of the digital transformation program. Be transparent about what's known and what might change.

Build Trainer Confidence with Strong Preparation

The functional trainers need to learn a great deal on a tight timeline. There are essentials to share with them at their onboarding about how they will be supported in carrying out the responsibilities they're assigned.

- *Basics.* For each assigned responsibility in the functional business trainer program, identify the elements and criteria for success. For instance, when training sessions are being led, what's the rubric for expected observable behaviors and skills that promote learning? Specifically, map out how they will develop and demonstrate these abilities.

- *Train the Trainer Program.* This is the training that sees functional trainers learn to teach their colleagues. They experience what their colleagues will learn from them later. For train the trainer to be effective for *digital* training, the transformation training templates and tools, including the learning management system, must be used to teach functional trainers about training delivery. Resources and courses exist online for teaching train the trainer skills (ATD, 2024), and many books exist about the topic. The key in my experience for functional trainer programs is to focus on the critical skills of *presentation* for learning, *facilitation* for knowledge building, and effective *system demonstration* with a lot of practice using the digital transformation training materials as part of their own experience as early learners.

- *Assessment Snapshots.* Measure the progress functional trainers make and report the state of the community as a whole and by function two to three times before training starts. Ask the functional trainers and the leads they work with for feedback. Are the processes being learned? Are functional trainers working hands-on in the system? Are they reviewing training materials? Have they observed or carried out any testing activities? Do they join the functional trainer community calls? The IDs may have anecdotal or formal input as well about inputs and reviews of training materials. The same assessment can be used repeatedly; the expectations for scores and engagement change as the start of training and the go live approach. The purpose is to ensure every functional trainer is on track and receives help when needed. In rare cases, the data may reveal a functional trainer who is not well-suited to the role, and this is best known before they interact with end users.

- *Coaches for Each Functional Trainer.* Determine the person who will be available to provide help and ensure appropriate action gets taken when a functional trainer needs assistance. Often this person is a senior SME or workstream lead.

- *A Skill and Knowledge Demonstration.* Before working with any end users, each functional trainer should lead a pilot session to demonstrate their process and system knowledge. Their understanding of the training materials and their ability to facilitate learning with clear communication about today-tomorrow changes also emerge. This demo takes place either in front of a room or virtually, following the same format they will use with learners. Find more detail about skill assessments in chapter 15.

Having functional business trainers is an investment in the overall digital transformation program and, ultimately, the ability to change the business.

Engage with a Strong Program Welcome

A coordinated approach sees the network of cross-team contacts work together to welcome the functional trainers to the digital transformation team and start them on their journeys. Here are some guidelines for coordinating the functional trainer onboarding.

- Send a note from program leaders and sponsors recognizing the employee's manager's or supervisor's willingness to lend their team member's time and expressing gratitude for their support.

- Send a note to each functional trainer congratulating them, recognizing the importance of their role to the business and the project, and emphasizing their manager's or supervisor's support and the project team's commitment to their development and success.

- Hold a formal onboarding session where stakeholders recognize the functional trainers and their selection, express thanks, and commit to supporting each one. Have the relevant team leads use this time to communicate overviews of the program activities, milestones, timelines, expected effort, and what to expect next.

Sponsor a Community of Practice

Provide a regular call where functional trainers from all the business process teams gather to check in about transformation program timelines and their training progress. Create a forum where the functional trainers feel safe asking questions and making requests for support.

Measure Trainer Readiness as It Develops

Periodically, measure the acquisition of functional trainer knowledge, experience, and confidence, and the completion of expected activities, objectives, and expectations that were introduced at the kickoff. As a guideline, I've developed and delivered a self- and workstream-led assessment of functional trainers that can be conducted two to three times (to track progress). The highest-stakes assessment of these is one that sees functional trainers conduct a demonstration for one of their end user sessions. While stressful, this demo is impactful and prepares the functional trainers to lead training. This exercise also generates excitement for the launch among the leaders who may attend.

Mitigate Risk with a Hybrid Trainer Model

At times, you may find it necessary to supplement internal functional trainer resources with external talent with the deep system and broad process knowledge. While these external individuals are not experts in the business, they can help minimize risk when the business process teams are strapped and can't explain the solution. They also offer a backup if unexpected gaps emerge in functional trainer resources. These functional resources need to manage a parking lot of questions they cannot answer during training and have help securing timely, accurate responses.

Ensure Recognition Occurs for the Contributions

Functional trainers, if you have them, support the majority of learning that occurs on the digital transformation, and executives and project leaders do well to recognize them and their work. Stakeholders can attend the demonstrations that functional trainers lead, sit in on a training session, and publicly appreciate the efforts and accomplishments that the functional trainers contribute—along with the commitment, hard work, and hours of preparation needed for them to excel. The training completion and learner feedback data are strong evidence of the positive impact specific functional trainers have. In my experience, exemplary functional trainers often are rewarded monetarily and with promotions, which helps incentivize others to step up the next time.

Despite all the things that help the functional trainers and their development, there are some problems that crop up.

WHAT GETS IN THE WAY

The major gaps in functional business trainer programs come down to poor selection, preparation, and support.

Selecting Unsuitable Candidates

Months of system configuration and testing, instructional design, content reviews, and approvals can be undone by a functional trainer who may have good intentions but fails to appreciate the impact of their work and role. Alternately, overconfident presenters or those in more senior roles may fail to invest the time and effort required to learn the course content, prepare to teach it, and practice system demonstrations. Either way, the learners suffer and post-launch struggles balloon.

Working Smarter: The functional trainers who fall significantly short have issues all along. Their assessment scores are lower than others', and their training demonstration is weak if not ineffective, even after a second demonstration to address specific gaps. I've had the unpleasant task of communicating my professional opinion that certain functional trainers should not work with end users. Sometimes business leaders agree. In other cases, my recommendation is overruled. Business and transformation leaders must support the removal of underperforming functional trainers or accept the consequences indicated by training feedback during training and after the go live, when end users struggle to do their jobs.

Onboarding Trainers Too Late

The later the functional trainers join the program, the more hours they have to spend over fewer weeks getting up to speed. When functional trainers lack time to develop and practice, the learners will suffer from short-changed preparation. If a criterion for the start of training is prepared functional trainers, it's arguable that a go live date may need to get pushed if functional trainers join the program too late.

Working Smarter: Reinforce the importance of functional trainer readiness—having a long enough period to prepare—with program and business leaders when reviewing the training strategy. The approach of having functional trainers may be confirmed and decisions about timing may still be pending at that point. On status calls with business leaders, share the functional trainer assessment results so there's visibility to the situation, whether green and good, yellow, or even red, and how available time has helped or hindered functional trainer preparations.

Not Balancing Conflicting Program Demands

It's unfortunately common, especially on first launches, that user acceptance testing overlaps end user training. When functional trainers who have been selected and prepared to lead training are also expected to carry out testing, the workload often becomes too much. Preparation activities for training get set aside to execute test scripts. Program and business leads realize after the fact what a significant pain point this is and the negative consequences, exclaiming, "Never again!"

Working Smarter: It takes relatively little effort to learn to run test scripts; however, it takes months to become a successful functional trainer who can effectively help end users learn. Communication and coordination among program, testing, and training leads can help ensure that the functional trainers have time for the heavier lift and responsibility of training. Understanding the plans for which functional trainers will lead training and those who will perform testing helps avoid conflict and decrease stress. I've also seen other business employees brought in to carry out testing, which worked very well as a change tactic. Finally, when functional trainers feel over-tasked by the program, they have to be comfortable saying so in their community calls and in conversations with their coach and SME.

Not Managing Work Conflicts for Part-Time Trainers

As noted earlier, expect challenges when functional trainers are partially rather than fully dedicated to their role on the digital transformation program.

Working Smarter: Communicating expectations about the time, effort, and importance of the development will help business leaders and other stakeholders prioritize the digital transformation activities and provide the functional trainers the support they need to succeed. No one wants the people in these key roles to fail.

Missing Support from the Process Teams

Not all transformation process team leads, or SMEs support their functional trainers.

Working Smarter: The self-assessment snapshots should gauge *how* the functional trainers are learning processes and the system in terms of the catalog of activities along with the availability and engagement of those teaching them and coaching them. Report transparency gaps and partner with the workstream lead and program manager to understand and resolve the underlying issues as soon as they emerge. In one case, the functional trainer was ill-suited to the role and unengaged with her team. In another case, the functional transformation team members stepped up and involved the functional trainer in reviews and testing, which closed the gaps. The next assessment should highlight improvements and show the functional trainer is on track to deliver training and support the launch and their learners, as expected.

Skipping Essential Hands-On Practice

Missed hands-on practice happens more than you might expect. "I really don't like the hands-on practice, so I don't do it in training," one functional trainer explained to me when I looked into his learners' inability to use the system after the go live when it emerged as a hypercare issue. This trainer completed the multiday preparatory session and successfully demonstrated his ability to use materials and show people how to perform a task in the system, and he referenced the training materials and exercises, although he failed to guide the learners through their own practice in the system during training.

Working Smarter: After that experience and note, I added a question to post-class feedback asking learners to confirm that hands-on practice occurred to ensure it takes place as expected. Having managers visit in-progress training also drives quality in training delivery and provides the opportunity to recognize and celebrate both the learning and the training. Running reports of user activity in the training environment is another way to validate that the expected hands-on practice is taking place. Finally, any shortcomings in hands-on practice time can be addressed with additional sessions for practice that are more closely monitored.

Backing Out of Their Commitment

Without the time, development, and ongoing support described in the previous section, functional trainers may lack confidence and feel they cannot carry out the planned training. At this point, typically just before end user training starts, they will drop out of the functional trainer program, creating a gap that others have to *try* to fill.

Working Smarter: Functional trainers get asked to commit professionally and personally to support the launch and can follow through with adequate support. Onboard them to the program with plenty of time so they can develop their own skills. Bring together the full group of business trainers, ideally at the same time so they can help one another. Hold an introductory session that welcomes the functional trainers and communicates clear expectations for what they'll be asked to do and a commitment to provide support so they succeed in their role. This strong, structured start helps avoid surprises later on about the responsibilities and time commitment.

Ongoing skill assessments and community calls provide data points about functional trainer progress, needs, and any concerns. Likewise, leaders must follow through to help the functional trainers be ready to carry out training by providing the time, voicing appreciation, and recognizing their dedication and accomplishments.

Final Note

Qualified peers make the best change advocates because they are uniquely positioned to lead, teach, and coach their colleagues through transformational business change. The majority of functional trainers I have had the pleasure and delight of working with over the years bravely stepped out of their day-to-day jobs to take on a key training role. Their efforts accelerated the digital transformation in the business functions where they worked. Their skills and knowledge of the business helped their colleagues adopt new ways of working as the new norm. These outcomes and the less desirable results when things don't go well all showed up in assessments and training reports, the topics of the next two chapters.

18

Progress Updates That Keep Leadership Informed

"Nothing succeeds like success.
Get a little success and then just get a little more."
—Maya Angelou, Poet, Memoirist, and Activist

L ong before anyone starts learning new skills, there's so much that gets planned, started, stalled, and completed along the way. Besides training material development, myriad other activities lead up to training, practice, and certification—notably, work that others must complete. Documenting the full team effort—calling out what's on track and what's not, the handoffs and dependencies—is a necessity. This chapter addresses structured status communication and supplemental reporting that provides a holistic view of the training program. Consistent, credible reporting in a structured format informs the digital transformation project team and business stakeholder community who keep an early eye on training. The best reporting helps ensure everything is in place for learner preparation with measurements about learner readiness in a way that executives and others can see the action they must take.

BASICS

Digital training activities fall into four broad buckets of work: *Planning, Material Development, Preparation*, and *Training Execution*. The training lead plans and tracks progress across all these areas, throughout the stages of a project's timeline. However, these stages overlap one another, and much of the work falls outside the direct control of the training team. Effective reporting keeps everyone informed about progress, needs, and risks so they can pitch in to clear hurdles. A basic status update is the baseline requirement. If you wish to go beyond this, supplemental dashboards and one-page summaries can be helpful subsequent periodic training reporting.

Weekly Updates as a Key Tool

When I began leading digital training initiatives, I saw the value of reporting week over week about accomplishments, planned work, and especially the week-over-week changes. For example, reporting training material completion as 27% (plus 2%) indicated a slight increase over the past week. Combining words, charts, and supplemental visuals effectively told the story about what was on track and what was at risk. What was going well and what was not were evident in these updates. For example, if most process workstreams are in final reviews and starting final approvals except for one, that shines a light and sees program and business leaders ask why.

For weekly status reports, program leadership usually provides a template that all transformation leads use. The format may be text-based, summary on a slide, or a database solution. Whatever the structure and specific inputs, the point is to provide *succinct, specific*, and *traceable* information about transformation training progress, risks, and any needs. Can you make it a one-line statement?

Supplemental Insights About Training Activities

Different stakeholders will appreciate more details than can fit in usual status updates for specific work and stages of training.

- Material development progress, reviews, and approvals by workstream

- Confirmed lists and counts of learners by security role and function

- Training preparation—schedules, logistics, contacts, materials, and supplies

- Training execution—actual to plan, feedback, and readiness

- Functional business trainer program—number of trainers by process or business area and timeline for their preparation and certification

- Summary of preparation and execution for learner readiness

- Training metrics, measures, and trends

If the information you provide is difficult to produce or not valuable to your digital transformation or business leaders, rethink producing it. Besides asking your stakeholders what might be more helpful, these are some ideas that have worked well.

BEST PRACTICES

Status should be a quick update about what's advancing and any risks in a way that helps see problems and needs quickly resolved.

Start Smart with Simple Status Reporting

- A single-line statement works best because detail lives in project plans, work breakdowns, dashboards, and discussions.

- It's usually okay to use acronyms in a status, since the audience is program leadership, project colleagues, and informed business leaders. Acronyms help you report with brevity.

- Use signals to communicate trending changes: up, down, holding: ↑↓←→. Recognize program and business leader expectations for when and how you use these, including the preferred symbols.

- Use charts, data, summaries, and pictures when they make sense and when you have them.

- When you report yellow or red, be sure the status is aligned with project and business expectations and that you note clearly what change will return the status to green.

- Give others time to answer your requests for help before escalating—no longer than two days to two weeks normally, based on the program phase and project work culture.

- When support is lacking, in addition to changing status, document the risk, action, issue, or decision logged and report the risks, actions, issues, and decisions (RAID) item.

Report on What Matters

Include progress and status notes about deliverables others complete when they affect the overall training program. Training relies upon others to complete critical work activities, detailed in chapter 16, "Training Dependencies as Boosters, Not Barriers."

Be Strategic with Details

The job as a training lead is to advance the work, and status reporting should demonstrate that this is occurring and smartly call out needs and risks with respectful professionalism.

- *Accomplishments toward milestones.* Note in one succinct, past-tense verb statement a meaningful progress toward a goal. Also in one line, note any outcomes, decisions, and achievements that came from a working session.

- *Upcoming planned work.* Note any follow-ups and next steps in achieving milestones. Ideally, sequence prior and upcoming work on the same line. For example, an accomplishment could be "Began stakeholder reviews," and the corresponding planned status entry would be "Continue/conclude stakeholder reviews."

- *Progress increments (+/-).* When you report percentages or counts, indicate the change from the last report.

- *Request for support.* Identify who needs to do what, whether these requests are training team–based or involve other workstreams of the business.

- *RAID.* Help the program leadership clear any hurdles the team is facing. When needs and risks remain unanswered after an agreed-upon period of weeks, use the RAID log to document the item in your status if it remains open.

- *Overall status indication.* Use the color and trending indicator aligned with the project standards and signal what's working well or any risks to meeting major milestones and the overall program timeline.

Use Dashboards for Clear Snapshots

Supplement status with data-based snapshots showing progress and status across all the sub-activities for a major deliverable. The samples provided with this book illustrate some possibilities. Full-page, multi-chart, and table summaries, or even simpler tables, serve as effective summaries for business leaders by providing actionable information. The art is finding the most granular level of detail that's both easy to report and capable of driving needed action. Here are some tips:

- *Check that the dashboard is relevant and has meaning.* The "so what" and value of the data need to immediately resonate with leaders. Dashboards should have a clear purpose, be easy to comprehend, and remain consistent. You can check your work with the next step.

- *Prototype.* Share early samples of the dashboard to confirm the information satisfies both the leader and business needs for information. Do all the stakeholders who will use the dashboard agree that it works?

- *Make sure the changes and trends are clear.* Is expected milestone progress across all areas evident? How about the gaps?

- *Check that it's actionable.* Is the information you're sharing associated with specific transformation or business leaders who can take action? Those with responsibility or overall business accountability must help address gaps, reinforce the importance of completing training work, and celebrate their team's successes when called for.

See the sample dashboards provided throughout *Digital Transformation Champions* as samples to get you started. Each dashboard will take more than a few iterations to refine until it suits your needs. If the dashboards prove effective and work well, any material development, training preparation, or training execution issues should be more quickly addressed than they would have been otherwise.

Optimize Time Spent on Reporting

Continuously look for opportunities to streamline the time it takes to produce status. What do the training team members say about providing status inputs? Does it take fewer than five minutes for them to generate inputs? A target time for lead input is five to fifteen minutes weekly and twenty to thirty minutes for a monthly report that includes a thirty-sixty-ninety-day plan.

- *Track the time it takes to produce reports.* In general, the time spent producing the dashboard must be less than the overall value derived from the report. Can automation tools help make production more efficient?

- *Use automation.* It can be helpful once a manual prototype is reviewed and validated. Power BI and some project management platforms may have features that will streamline your dashboard generation.

Finally, I suggest you complete the prior week's status on Friday so you start the week moving forward instead of looking back to continue progress and mitigate any risks.

WHAT GETS IN THE WAY

The challenges that arise with status reporting come down to communication opportunities or gaps in accountability and follow-through.

Skipping Status Updates

Not making updates to your training status sends a red flag signal to program and other workstream leads that there is no work that has been done or needs to be done. This will likely result in a business leader intervention.

Working Smarter: Make regular status updates and ensure there is progress and expected activity against the broader plan, or a request for help. The only exception to weekly updating is when there is no effort or no billed time during the previous period due to holidays, vacations, or paused work.

Neglecting to Use the Risks, Actions, Issues, Decisions (RAID) Log

Some projects move quickly over months while others span years. In both cases, the RAID log serves a database about the transformation program, and as a training lead, you need to use it. You may think you don't have time or you reported what you needed to in status or, worse, you believe others know about an issue, risk, or decision. It needs to be memorialized.

Working Smarter: Always document key decisions, issues that don't get resolved, and the risks that remain because any gaps usually lead to issues over time. Moreover, when a situation isn't fully resolved or is less than ideal for training, constructively record an appropriate RAID item. Provide the options, recommendations, and decision that got made. Note the open training RAID items in weekly status reports and strive to see them closed. Having the documentation records leadership steps taken and provides opportunity for learning when things do not go as planned.

Causing Misalignment or Misinterpretation

Some program teams allow the leads to report exactly what they believe and see, while others choose to control the way status and progress get reported. For example, I reported yellow, given delays and a lack of technical inputs at early stages, on one program. My sense was not aligned with program leadership who struggled with vendor and technology issues on the core system. On another program, we were directed to always report green.

Working Smarter: Speak with stakeholders and program leadership at the outset about status reporting and rules for use of colors and trends. Ideally, this would happen when the transformation program manager holds a session with all leads and introduces the status template for weekly reports. Do listen to needs for communicating risk and how to note trending shifts. Additionally, propose an alternate structure to the leadership for better reporting and communication. On one transformation, all leads used to gather and hear some of the leads talk through their entire status report. There was never enough time for all leads to share, and the reality is that people preferred to read the reports in advance. With feedback from me and others, the program leadership sent the status deck in advance so we could spend in-person time answering questions and getting cross-functional help. Add supplemental dashboards and reports as needed to illustrate training program progress or communicate risk. Always seek feedback about their value.

Missing Clear Get-to-Green Actions

As a training lead reporting yellow or red status, failing to specify the issues and what's needed to resolve them will keep you in a prolonged risk state and leave you without confidence in getting to green.

Working Smarter: If there's a yellow or red status item or for the overall training report, clearly and concisely communicate what must be done or decided to get to green. Does someone else need to take action? Are the action and owner clear? Your goal as a lead is to stay green or identify risks and see them resolved, escalating them when they remain unanswered.

Reporting Inconsistently Across the Teams on the Transformation

In large ERP programs, teams often report status in different formats, using different metrics and timelines. This makes it hard for leaders to get a clear picture of progress, risks, and priorities. However, inconsistent and incomplete status reporting ironically can happen on programs that seek to implement common practices and standardization.

Working Smarter: Status only works when all leads understand the purpose and guidelines, and if they provide timely, accurate updates about their own pillar and read other leads' reports as well. If you're experiencing inconsistencies, seek support from program leaders who have the responsibility for overall reporting.

Final Note

The overarching purpose of reporting about the training program is to provide project and business stakeholders with meaningful updates that inform them and inspire their action when needed. Done well, these reports do two things. First, they communicate problems in a way that others can use to resolve issues. Second, they make evident the value of the partnerships that advance the training work. The purpose and goal of good reporting is to see that people are prepared for the transformation, the topic of the next chapter.

19

Learner Readiness Tracking and Reporting for Day One and Beyond

"Evaluate accurately, not kindly."

—**Ray Dalio,** Finance Executive and Leadership Coach

L*earner success is a sometimes linear series of steps that start long before end user train-ing begins. It's not enough to have a sound strategy, quality training materials, and a great, well-tested digital solution. Rather, success lies in all the ways the pieces come together, across the process areas and business teams, over time. These moving parts all have direct bearing on learner readiness for the go live and ability to realize the trans-formational business vision. Despite the many components, learner success in a digital transformation training initiative is both predictable and measurable. Key measures about training execution and learner readiness can and must be reported.*

BASICS

This section builds upon the previous chapters to demonstrate how the training program deliverables and work help ensure learner readiness or reveal watch areas.

Tracking and reporting about completion of the following applicable elements, by function, process, and/or geographic site, give program and business leaders important insights about the training program so they can take action to quickly address any issues. The idea of accuracy refers to the transparency and accountability that allows learners and transformation teams to receive help when it's needed.

Key Deliverables and Accomplishments to Track

These elements provide key performance indicators about the probability of overall learner readiness.

- Material review, approval, printing, and learning management system (LMS) setup
- Functional trainer preparation and certification
- LMS learning assignments, based on final learner audience or security role-mapping counts
- Training schedules
- Practice schedules
- Actual completion of planned, scheduled training and hands-on practice
- Learner knowledge assessment results and learner feedback
- Certification preparation, completion, and results

Although this sounds like many areas to track, one or two visuals can effectively summarize all of these activities, broken down by business area, geography, and function. In presenting data like this, you can provide a useful snapshot of the work and comparative progress. Ongoing updates to the visuals help ensure the prerequisite activities advance and get completed on time. Samples 6 and 10 are most useful here.

Sample 6, Digital Transformation Training Status at a Glance, is a dashboard of the training program. It highlights key areas for planning, preparation, critical dependencies, and details, including learner readiness by area. Short notes call out successes, gaps, or needs.

The Training Preparation and Learner Readiness Dashboard, sample 10, sequences the preparatory activities for end user training and is meant to be a supplement to status reporting. If the stages are incomplete, training cannot begin. Alone or together, these summaries provide visual indicators about the components required for successful training and positive learner experiences.

The best practices provided throughout *Digital Transformation Champions* seek to ensure learner and transformation success. The following highlight those specific to tracking user readiness and reporting on it.

BEST PRACTICES

Tracking learner readiness for the transformation combines metrics from corporate training, ERP studies, and adult learning fields, along with experience. Additionally, program leaders may add other measures that help ensure business readiness plans are in place so their people are ready to adopt new ways of working.

Track Pre-Training Prep Activities

The preparatory work ahead of training includes final material preparation and the steps to see scheduled time when learners complete their training and hands-on practice. This work must be managed as carefully as training material development. By site or business function, and the total count of learners, track the following against a target complete-by date, pegged to the start of training:

- Final course approvals
- Outstanding process/system decisions
- Functional trainers ready
- Training schedules approved
- Practice schedules approved
- Knowledge checks approved, built, and tested

- Changes in security role assignments

- LMS courses and people "staged" and ready

- Training communications sent to managers and employees

- Training certification needs determined and tests developed

- Training, practice, and certification completed with positive results

The two sample dashboards reviewed above include counts of learners to show the magnitude of the impact and importance of everything staying on track.

Watch Training and Test Completions

A key metric for readiness is whether scheduled training gets carried out as expected. Do the training sessions in the approved training calendar take place as planned? Do the number of people needing training complete it? Is the required re-knowledge check test completed by everyone who needs to take it? Anticipate the situations that can arise and develop contingency plans so the people receive the training in the optimal time frame.

- *Have functional trainer backups.* I've seen the primary trainer become ill and the backup has a family emergency, so the tertiary trainer had to step in and lead training. Broadly communicate the training schedule, invite all trainers, and establish communication plans among those who teach the course about how they'll ensure coverage when someone cannot deliver training as planned.

- *Have a plan to support employees who miss their training.* How will learners make up any training they miss? I've seen learners asked to review materials and attend the next session with questions. Another time, an extra session was added to the schedule for the purpose of makeup or for additional new hires onboarded just before launch.

- *Weather and other incidents require training cancellation.* Snow, hurricanes, electrical outages, or business emergencies may require a decision to cancel scheduled training. Leave time on the training schedule to accommodate additional days if they're needed for rescheduled sessions.

- *People attend training but do not complete or pass their post-training knowledge test.* Ideally, the knowledge check gets completed before learners sign off or leave a room. This may not always be the case. In other instances, employees do not achieve a passing score the first few times and need to wait. Identify the process to follow up with learners who need to complete their training. Often, this is an important responsibility the local training coordinator has.

Leaving time for more training is a smart tactic when building the training schedule. Clearly designating who will follow up on missing training will help ensure all learners complete their training and are prepared.

Monitor Hands-On Practice and Feedback to Identify Support Needs

Provide enough time so learners can work multiple times in the new system and ask questions. Sufficient practice time is an essential component of best learning and sustained adoption in general. After the initial training—whether class-based or self-paced—to gain proficiency, learners need appropriate time to repeat key activities in the system, developing confidence and demonstrating their comprehension of the concepts. In addition, if training ends two or more weeks before the go live date, a window-of-memory period, additional practice and review just before going live using support materials, will help people feel ready to work with new ways of carrying out their day-to-day work. Run system reports about user activity in the practice environment to verify that the expected practice actually occurs or not. Finally, the time during practice is when learners will ask poignant questions. Answers from a functional business trainer who knows the old and new way of completing tasks is essential training that happens in the moment. Getting to practice multiple times, asking questions, and receiving specific answers are core components for both adult learning and digital transformation training. Learner feedback may surface gaps that require intervention.

Plan Certifications for Key Talent

For some learners whose work is high stakes for the business, a formal post-training assessment may take place. This demonstration of process and system knowledge can be specific to those with a job, a security role, or everyone in a department. For example, in one instance at a manufacturing company, all logistics coordinators and material handlers were assessed individually and coached as needed because of the criticality of accurately receiving raw materials and storing and shipping finished goods correctly. In another deployment at a multinational company, all finance team members participated in not just one, but two mock close cycles, coordinated by a key finance executive. In both instances, the outcome was greater confidence among the end users and business leaders. Since it's an additional round of test material development and requires more scheduling and people to administer it, these types of certifications are not always the norm. When business leaders determine the need exists, their target audience should be identified at the start of the project so material development needs can be added to the tracker. This topic is covered in detail in chapter 15, "Metrics for Learner Knowledge and Confidence."

If all the pieces are not in place, training cannot begin; delays and challenges mean other problems may be at play. Despite the obvious value of coordinating and measuring learner readiness because it predicts overall adoption, there are challenges, described in the next section.

WHAT GETS IN THE WAY

The following gaps appear before or during training. Sometimes, the issues relate to the preparatory activities that weren't fully resolved. Sometimes, distinct business challenges exist—some you can anticipate and some you can't, at least not fully. These misses become apparent during end user training and prelaunch. The training lead needs to recognize and monitor these during the training because they indicate issues with learner and ultimately business readiness. These are the most common to anticipate and keep in mind.

Altering Materials or Deviating from Course Design

With good intentions, those in key roles may introduce damaging changes. Examples are re-shared here.

- Business managers not involved in the lengthy review and approval cycles may decide role-based course content is irrelevant and remove it from the training agenda.

- Functional business trainers provided with approved training materials may make changes, add new content, reorder, or remove sections to make it their own or add their own stamp to the content.

- Functional trainers may decide not to deliver the training as designed and omit facilitation, demonstration, hands-on practice, and the discussion that learners need to acquire the new knowledge for their work.

Working Smarter: Make sure that kickoffs with business teams and the functional trainers reinforce the purpose and process of training material creation, review, and approvals. Reiterate who is involved, including functional business leaders, trainers, and the entire project team. Promote the concepts and practice of "deliver as designed" and "do not change materials." These will help see consistent, quality training experiences that benefit all learners. And the most effective step: *Do not provide editable training materials to the business or functional trainers*. Demonstrate and prepare them to teach from un-editable PDF documents or materials in the LMS. "Locked" materials also provide document and version control and make ongoing material updates manageable. Assess the functional trainers with a formal teach-back demonstration to validate their ability to use the materials as expected.

Rushing Training Delivery

In some cases, the training lead may see that an in-person, eight-hour training was completed in three hours, or note that someone completed a self-guided training in thirty minutes that others worked through in several hours. In these situations when training activity reports from the LMS show hours missing from self-paced or in-person delivery, a few things might be happening, and they may warrant investigation. For an instructor-led course, the trainer might have only clicked through slides without providing demonstrations or leading hands-on practice, having no conversations or necessary questioning and thinking about day-to-day work activities that make up effective learning time. In self-paced training, there's an average time all learners take to complete the course. If someone completes the training much faster, they may be skimming and not engaging with the expected content. Also, in some cases, the training may remain open so that the learning time appears unusually large.

Working Smarter: Monitor learning times in the LMS as a check of the learning experience. Sit in on in-person training or have others familiar with the expectations for delivery do so. It's not uncommon or worrisome for in-person training to go over by fifteen minutes or finish around fifteen minutes early. Large class size, many questions, engaged learners, and even system issues can extend the length of training. Small classes with adept learners may see shorter learning times to cover the same material. In my experience, overall ratings are lower when the training time is shorter than needed or expected, notably when the reason is lack of hands-on practice. Besides looking at the LMS data, also review the learner feedback to understand variations in the time spent learning. The feedback statement "I completed hands-on practice in my training" is a clear indicator. If most learners don't work in the system during training, they can't be expected to do so on the job.

Scheduling Training During Busy or Holiday Periods

Remember that holidays and peak business work times are suboptimal for learning. Period. I've seen training need to be repeated because everyone forgot what they learned before the end-of-year holidays. Consider the business's unique calendar, too. Finance has monthly, quarterly, and annual close periods. Logistics has cycle count and peak shipping periods. Training scheduled during these times will limit participation and likely require makeup class dates or other accommodations.

Working Smarter: Mark these busy times as well as spring holidays and other common times off on the training calendar as no-training times in the training Gantt chart. Peak work periods for each function should be identified during the audience analysis. Also, when introducing the digital transformation training strategy or approach, communicate the importance of not training during holidays and other periods as they apply to the project timeline. In the United States, I tend to block off one week for Thanksgiving and one to two weeks at the end of the year when little meaningful training can occur because people are preoccupied, out of office, or covering for those on vacation. In Europe, time off can be three to four weeks in winter and the same during summer months. Creating a training schedule means determining how best to structure the learning time for the learners, their work, the content to learn, the availability of functional trainers and process subject matter experts, and the business calendar. The final training schedule is always a business-based decision and can vary across functions and sites. The training lead provides guidance about options and trade-offs for multiday consecutive training versus "chunked" training over a period of time. Once the training schedule is developed, advance communication about the calendar, smart scheduling, and strong business partnerships helps bridge the challenges that holidays and peak work periods present to digital transformation training when sessions must take place at those times.

Adding Many Unplanned or Small-Size Sessions

The creation and approval of facilitated training schedules is a major milestone. A lot of work and logistics planning goes into them. A few changes in the in-person training or practice schedule are normal. For instance, rescheduling legitimately happens due to weather. Excessive changes to the approved schedule challenge the functional trainers and others. I've seen the number of planned sessions increase fourfold after training is underway, with one- and two-person trainings instead of classes with the planned six to eight people. In one case, the answers pointed to low staffing over the holidays. In another scenario, the business contact who developed the training schedule did not fully vet it with business leaders, a best practice, and managers demanded changes. Finally, in another example, role-mapping updates drove changes—sometimes continually—in the training schedule as counts of people needing different training continued to adjust.

Working Smarter: Initial schedules should factor in the counts of learners by role and course, the length of time learners need to acquire the new knowledge based on the role, and the availability of functional trainers around logistics, and available time away from work for training. By flagging any pending process, system configuration decisions, or role assignment changes, these risks can be factored into the training schedule with more time allowed for the affected learner audiences. Develop and share the confirmed training schedules at least six to eight weeks in advance of the start to help everyone manage work and personal time off to attend training. This is another reason why business teams must be consulted in advance about training and why business leaders need to sign off on the training schedule for their teams. Make sure leaders, functional trainers, and training coordinators recognize how training schedule changes put overall learner and business readiness at risk within a function or site. When there are issues, update the training progress dashboard from complete to show yellow or red when excessive schedule changes occur or training completion remains below the planned levels.

Lacking an Effective Training Point Person

Someone "on the ground" must be identified to act on behalf of transformation training within the business team or a location. Often, this is the person who creates the training schedule—they can help resolve issues with people's schedules, answer training logistics questions, and follow up to see training and practice completed. However, make sure this person isn't overburdened with other work. On one project, the contact for scheduling and training was also backfilling a key leadership position at the site and had conflicting priorities. Digital training was important, but not the priority; the learners and business both suffered.

Working Smarter: During the strategy or approach review, identify the need for on-the-ground contacts as a critical success factor. Assess and validate that those tasked with this responsibility have leadership and manager support to do the work during the key weeks of end user training. If issues arise as time goes on, change the dashboard status. If gaps in resolving these problems occur, call out the need for support. Learner feedback about training in these cases usually corroborates the problems and the need for better support. The needs for this role are detailed in chapter 16, "Training Dependencies as Boosters, Not Barriers."

Changing Role Design and User Assignments

While it's covered in detail as a critical training dependency in chapter 16, excessive changes in security role design and role assignment mean that people are less likely to be ready for the launch. First, the counts of people who need specific training are based on security role assignments. If those numbers are wrong, the training schedules are probably incorrect also. The training materials teach the process and how people, *by role*, carry out the work, including all of the related activities. The business trainers may not understand these changes and may teach the wrong thing because when security roles change, it may mean the process steps are different. When the activities of a role change, the training materials also need updates. The amount of learning time may be less or more. On one program, there were over 1,000 role changes after the go live.

Working Smarter: When instructional designers understand how security roles enable access and data visibility, they can provide early indications about issues in role design and assignment. The training lead needs to partner with those responsible for the work and monitor for changes in counts of learners by role on a weekly basis. In a few of my deployments, I took ownership for role mapping from change management. This required adding one person to coordinate the effort. On another deployment where role mapping was out of scope for training, I nevertheless emphasized it as a key dependency for training success with project leaders. I explained to my transformation colleagues how changes in role design affect training material accuracy and who learns what. Role-mapping counts were kept up to date and the assignments to end users were well-managed, accurate, and maintained up through the go live to support sessions of training and learner tracking. In short, change is a given, and a few security role updates are always going to occur during the first few weeks following a launch. However, hundreds are preventable. Accurate security role design and assignment to users should be a shared goal across all the digital transformation program teams because it's the core of how people use the system and work with data and reports to carry out new business processes.

Seeing Business Exemptions for Who Needs Training

Often the transformation program manager and executive business sponsor determine that *all users* who will be granted access to transact in the system—versus having read-only access—must complete training and pass a post-training knowledge test. But then some other leaders may choose to exempt certain users in their function from completing training, while still approving their access to the production system. They do this despite the risk to accurate and correct use of the system and the upstream and downstream impacts. When asked for the reasons for the exception, I've heard, "The people will complete training later," "They won't really work in the system," and "They don't have time for training."

Working Smarter: Ask about exceptions to training completion as part of the strategy or early conversation with business leaders and reinforce the decisions that transformation leaders made and why. Then, as part of the training closeout task, evaluate security role assignments against training completions. Pass the completion findings on to the program leaders and log a risks, actions, issues, and decisions (RAID) item with the completion rates by function. This documentation supports logical access control auditing conducted by other teams.

Final Note

The callouts in this chapter reinforce how both dependency milestones and preparatory activities determine learner readiness before, during, and after their training. Sample dashboards illustrate how to report these to show readiness or drive action. Ray Dalio's quote at the beginning of this chapter addresses the importance of evaluation and the transparency necessary for both learners and the business to transform successfully. It is unkind to learners to ignore feedback and other data about their needs and gaps in readiness. Any necessary messaging can be delivered with sensitivity to help leaders support site training coordinators and business trainers so learners know how to do their jobs. Remember the theme of getting things right by working together. The next chapter describes the final stage of the digital transformation training program, the closeout, and how to gather data and use the insights to improve training for the next initiative.

---

(20)

Training Closeout for Reflection and Celebration

"Without reflection, I go blindly on the way,
creating more unintended consequences, and failing
to achieve anything useful."
—Margaret J. Wheatley, Organizational Consultant and Author

A t the end of each digital transformation training initiative, the training lead collects, consolidates, and conducts discussions about feedback from the training team and functional trainers about planned and actual achievements. Data about the training program and its execution—along with business KPIs and hypercare metrics—supplement the team's inputs. Together, these spotlight training accomplishments, lessons learned, and opportunities. This summary is an invaluable artifact for the business and becomes an action plan the training team uses for continuous improvement.

BASICS

The training lead has the opportunity and responsibility to provide a post-launch summary for the team and business leaders about the digital training program.

A group-based assessment of each training deliverable affords a simple structure to identify what worked and what could be better. A training closeout is similar to a lean after-action review or a human performance post-job review. It shares the goal of identifying opportunities for continuous improvement and other insights. Additionally, a training closeout captures what went well and what the training team should continue doing to create positive outcomes for learners and, ultimately, the business.

Closeout Structure

The topics and method for capturing inputs and sharing findings must be straightforward and efficient. In my experience, these are six steps for a digital transformation training closeout that work well every time.

1. Use the key deliverables and milestones of the training program.

Consider getting feedback about reviewing training tools and technologies, training material effectiveness, development process, plans, business process documentation, information gathering, training execution, functional trainers, learner readiness, training materials, stakeholder engagement, the training budget, and any others that were added, such as certifications. These deliverables and milestones should mirror the training plan on a page and the training team's key deliverables.

2. Determine the questions and data you need.

Identify the questions you will ask and data points to collect. For each deliverable, decide how to measure, assess, and gather input about the outcome. At a minimum, measure the item quantitatively, then ask, "What worked well?" and "What could be better?"

3. Identify sources for inputs about each area.

Some items get assessed by the training team, such as subject matter expert engagement and reviews. Other data comes from learner feedback, on-time completion of training materials, training execution, and learner accomplishment. Functional trainers can describe their experience facilitating training and using the materials.

Finally, hypercare dashboards and business metrics about operations are useful for training teams to review.

4. Quantitatively assess how well the intended outcomes were achieved for key deliverables.

Add questions that measure the perceived success of each deliverable. For instance, use a five- or six-point scale to measure quality or success. Doing this helps you identify gaps and highlight clear wins. Consider using a qualitative question—"What explains your rating?"—for useful detail, if the two questions above start to feel repetitive. The value of combining qualitative input is getting helpful detail. For example, you might see most ratings average a score of five except for one area. In that case, the open-ended comments should explain the shortcomings.

5. Prepare a draft document of the highlights and review it with the training team.

After structuring the data collection and gathering all the inputs, consolidate the measures and feedback into a summary report. Discuss the findings with the team to confirm and understand the results and to identify the actions needed.

6. Create an action plan and track progress.

For each deliverable or milestone, what actions does the team agree will drive improvement? Who is the owner? What is the time frame for implementing the change or update? A one- to two-page action plan is an important product of the closeout work. It gets used by the training team and can be shared as a status supplement with the program leaders.

Options for Gathering Input

A closeout requires collecting and reviewing structured input. I have experience doing this in three ways. Each method has benefits and trade-offs, summarized in the following table.

Training Closeout for Reflection and Celebration

Option for Gathering Input	Benefits	Drawbacks
1. Group provides input in real time. Have the training team and/or stakeholders gather in person or virtually to provide input during a live session. Provide the topics in advance. A facilitator reviews the inputs with the group to understand the feedback yet does not solve or action any item.	The entire group sees the feedback. Feedback can be collected and shared using physical or digital input options, like sticky notes or chat. The group members bring distinct perspectives about the same information. One person's input may spark a related idea someone else wishes to share.	If participants provide handwritten notes/stickies, these will need to be typed up. In live meetings, it can be difficult for groups of people to avoid solving the problems. Some with introverted traits can find a group input process uncomfortable. Action planning is a follow-on activity requiring additional time and discussion together, which can be hard to schedule. With workers distributed, a blended format with in-person and hybrid participants may be needed, which requires additional consideration and effort.
2. Individuals complete a form or prepare thoughts before a live working session. Each participant receives a document or series of questions to complete on their own, in advance of a live meeting. The discussion with the group involves bringing the documents to the session and sharing the feedback and any recommendations and needs. The training lead consolidates the inputs afterward into a summary report.	Introverts report preferring time and space to reflect on their own first. The conversations are richer when everyone has spent more time reflecting beforehand. Repetitive input is noted, not reviewed, which saves time.	It's time-consuming to rekey or assemble the inputs. The assembled summary may not accurately reflect the group's views because some of the details may not have been shared during the discussion.
★ Preferred Approach **3. Participants complete a digital survey, and the inputs get compiled into a summary, which the group reviews and discusses together to identify the actions to take.** This option achieves the benefits of the previous two models, while overcoming the drawbacks with the greatest efficiency.	The entire group sees the feedback. The group members bring distinct perspectives about the same information. Introverts report preferring time and space to reflect on their own. The conversations are richer when everyone has spent more time reflecting beforehand. Repetitive input is noted, not reviewed, which saves time. There is no rekeying of the inputs and data. Agreeing on the root cause of problems and the actions to take is most productive.	The training lead needs to compile and organize the inputs to ensure a productive discussion focused on alignment about the issues, insights, and needed actions.

For its many benefits, I prefer collecting feedback via survey, consolidating the inputs, and then discussing it as a group after everyone has had time to review the results. Sharing the findings in advance and then meeting as a team to discuss what the data mean and what to recommend or change going forward keeps the conversation focused on actions that will drive improvement.

The tips and pitfalls in the following sections will help training leads master this step of the digital transformation training program.

BEST PRACTICES

The goal of the closeout exercise is consolidating collective insights about what worked and what did not and taking action to continue or improve specific areas.

Encourage Candid Feedback and Ideas

Traditional closeouts do not include recommendations or problem resolution during reviews. However, for training teams whose members frequently move on after the launch, combining discussion and action planning into one step capitalizes insights from members before they get reassigned. It's also an efficient way to work together.

Foster Shared Ownership for Outcomes

Kyle Eliason is a marketing strategist who advocates the use of closeouts for all projects and, in particular, the use of questions about how team members feel (Eliason, 2023). Use specific prompts to elicit responses. He says the following three questions in particular are most valuable:

- Are you proud of our finished deliverables? If yes, what made them great? If not, what was wrong or missing?
- What else could I (the training lead) do better next time? *My add: What else could you do better next time in your role?*
- What was the most gratifying or professionally satisfying part of the project?

The training team and functional trainers have worked hard over the past months, and how they feel at the end is important input. I was surprised and pleased to learn that training team members on one project most appreciated the weekly team gatherings where peer recognition helped everyone feel connected. This was something we continued on subsequent training launches.

Celebrate Training Team Achievements

Organize and share the collected information as part of a post-project team celebration *and* working session. For example, a colleague held an awards show and handed out personalized prizes for each team member based on their personality and instructional design journey. My favorite celebration was a day that combined a hike to the top of a small mountain—a true metaphor for the training work—followed by a lovely lunch, then a working session discussing the team's and others' feedback. The project leaders called in to express their appreciation and gratitude to the training team.

Whatever the format, keep a positive outlook on the training effort, activities, and outcomes. Ensure everyone participates in discussing the meaning of the data and feedback, as well as the action planning. Leave laptops behind if possible. If they're needed during the session, limit their use to the work at hand to avoid distractions.

Share Training Team Insights with Transformation Leaders

Repurpose these collected details and the planned next step to tell business leaders the story about the digital transformation training initiative. If you can, highlight the deltas, positives, and negatives relative to previous projects or deployments to show the effect of changes or ongoing enhancements. Respectfully report problems within and external to the training team. Avoid overly congratulatory highlights about the training effort. Add any pictures—one instructional designer (ID) was gifted a cake from the project business team, and we included a picture of that. Pass along actionable data and feedback to project leaders.

In summary, a good closeout consolidates the training team's wisdom and provides helpful insight. The structured summary also helps business leaders understand how the training activities prepare the learners and the business with measures, concrete examples, and steps to address needs.

WHAT GETS IN THE WAY

There are a few things to watch for that can underserve or overcomplicate a closeout.

Missing the Opportunity to Include Everyone

When your team includes contractors and those who work remotely, planning is key. I've missed taking advantage of the opportunity to collect input, review together, and then share the story. Short deployment cycles or very small initiatives can mean that more formal closeout retrospectives are out of scope. In these cases, business executives and project leaders may use training execution dashboards as "the story."

Working Smarter: Conduct information gathering and compile lessons even for smaller initiatives. Schedule a working session review before team members roll off or get reassigned. A simple structure and summary honor the training team members and help drive small changes to better the next training effort.

Not Following Through on Action Items

Asking a team to dedicate time and provide detailed, thoughtful input, then discuss the actions needed, only to fail to follow through will demoralize the training team and miss an opportunity to improve. Leaders who request input and fail to take action lose credibility among their team members and will not get the input needed after the next launch.

Working Smarter: Convert the actionable items into a table, dashboard, or list no longer than one or two pages long. Monitor the progress implementing each item and share it on team calls. An ID is able to update templates or research a new tool, for instance. Establish the due date and make sure the team knows this is complete and where to find the file. Sometimes, others must action items. For example, on one project the training team's and learners' high regard and appreciation for the functional trainers were offset by the fact that most functional trainers felt unappreciated by their business teams. While this is an important item to action, I had to work with transformation program and business leaders to change the way functional trainers received support. If something cannot be changed immediately, explain why. For instance, the request was made to add licenses for an e-learning authoring tool, which the business did not support.

Overcomplicating the Effort

Different business groups will measure the digital transformation in different ways. It may be tempting to try to group all transformation program assessments into one massive data collection effort. This would see feedback from transformation and business leaders, functional managers, technical team members, system integrators, end users, as well as the training team and functional trainers gathered and summarized about the same things, all at once. The output of this type of assessment is too broad to guide specific training improvements.

Working Smarter: *Training needs to focus on training.* Transformation leaders are responsible for assessing the broader program and post-launch outcomes for the business based on operational KPIs. The training lead must focus on capturing inputs from the training team and functional trainers for insights and perspectives to understand the current digital transformation *training* effort and inform the next ones. The scope of the training closeout is appropriate for the training lead to undertake—potentially in concert with a senior ID—and the effort can be completed in twelve to twenty hours, including a meaningful discussion with the team.

Final Note

The findings from a closeout help improve the overall training program to the benefit of the learners and, ultimately, the business. Highlights about what works well and should continue emerge from a well-conducted closeout, along with plans for impactful changes, as well as any calls to action for transformation leaders or asks of business executives to improve the next digital transformation implementation. Recognizing and celebrating the digital transformation training team members and the accomplishments the team achieved together are final reasons to complete a closeout. The next chapter recaps the topics of a holistic digital transformation training program, which can be used in whole or in parts to recap ways to support your transformation training needs.

(21)

Checklists and Recap of
Digital Transformation Champions

"A champion is defined not by their wins but
how they recover when they fall."

—**Serena Williams,** Tennis Champion and Entrepreneur

A body of research exists about digital transformation training, and yet it's not enough on its own to realize the best outcomes. Success is definable. To what extent do business users feel and show they're prepared for the transformation? Can they demonstrate their desire and ability to work with a new system? Can they describe changed on-the-job processes? Are there effective resources that describe how to correctly carry out role-based work? Designing and implementing a successful digital training program, while challenging, is both achievable and essential for any business to realize its digital transformation goals. Digital training programs fail because there is much that can and does go wrong across all the layers of the transformation program and business functions. The worst outcome sees ill-prepared learners and a painful, extended post–go live hypercare period, even an unsuccessful or failed transformation. Digital Transformation Champions *provides a structured approach, best practices, and course corrections to help training leaders and others achieve the best-case outcomes for learners and, ultimately, the business to achieve the promise of its digital business transformation. This chapter highlights the concepts from the book, starting with a bonus summary from the ERP literature.*

DIGITAL TRANSFORMATION TRAINING ELEMENTS THAT MAXIMIZE ON-THE-JOB TRANSFER

Culled from the existing ERP literature of the time and my own analysis, three factors and ten distinct themes about ERP training emerged for learner success. These callouts for digital transformation training derive from research I conducted comparing the significance of digital transformation training to business system interface design (Parks, 2012). Tactics that maximize on-the-job transfer for digital transformation training are organized below by the training structure, the facilitator, and content.

Structure: How Training Is Organized and Delivered

1. Training occurs in a classroom or other learning setting separate from the usual workplace.

2. Training occurs in multiple learning sessions in manageable time frames.

3. Adequate time is available to learn and practice tasks in advance of needing them for work.

4. A practice instance of the business system is available during training so users can make mistakes while learning and see what happens as they work.

5. Supporting materials such as system and process job aids about how to correctly complete a task are used during training and afterward for reference.

Instructor: The Person Providing Training and Coaching to the Learner

1. Learning facilitators are both knowledgeable about the system and the business processes and also effective teachers of the technology.

2. A coach is available after training to support best use of the system on the job, in the workplace.

Content: Instructional Materials Include Specific Components

1. Communication from a business leader about the importance of the system and the business transformation is a part of the training to build motivation.

2. Information gets communicated about why an activity occurs within the function, pre- and post-step handoffs, and how the data is used elsewhere in the business.

3. Scanning data and selections before clicking "Save" is taught as a final step for every task, and users know what to do when there is a question or problem.

While studies identified these elements leading to the best learner outcomes, they require a broader framework to be truly effective. Providing this structured approach is the purpose of *Digital Transformation Champions*.

A COMPREHENSIVE MODEL

Digital Transformation Champions presents how to design, deliver, and manage a digital transformation training program that bridges the IT project world with traditional learning and development to achieve lasting change. Every digital transformation project and each implementation is unique and therefore requires some tailoring in the approach to upskilling the workforce. Organized around five major milestones, the following pages detail commonsense, proven methods for advancing what matters and enabling training leads to achieve digital transformation training outcomes that benefit learners and the business. With these basic tactics, the probability of digital transformation training success increases. This is the purpose of *Digital Transformation Champions*, summarized with the following five milestones and checklists of the basics, best practices, and relevant samples. Apply these as appropriate for *your* digital transformation training needs.

MILESTONE 1

Project, business, and training leaders align on the digital transformation training strategy, activities, tools, and resources.

Training Strategy for a Winning Digital Transformation—Chapter 1

The training strategy is a shared story about building process, system, data, and reporting knowledge among the different people involved in transforming the business and those who conduct day-to-day work.

- ☐ Founded upon business outcomes and success
- ☐ Built around learner needs
- ☐ Focused on continuous improvement
- ☐ Tailored for specific phases of the transformation

Repeated messaging about the ways people will learn and adopt new ways of working unites the program and business teams for a common cause so the transformation can succeed with learning at the forefront rather than as an afterthought.

Relevant Samples

- Digital Transformation Training Program Checklist—Sample 1
- Milestone Map and Training Timeline—Sample 2
- Vendor Checklist for Training Success—Sample 3

Learning Topics and Audience Insights for a Strong Foundation—Chapter 2

Analyzing and summarizing what will be learned, by whom, and highlighting the training needs ensures the training team starts with and maintains a learner-focused perspective.

☐ Identify the business areas, locations, and processes in scope for the digital transformation program

☐ Identify all learner groups

☐ Identify the key transformation program and business stakeholders

☐ Identify information sources

☐ Determine key training contacts in the business areas

☐ Validate preliminary curricula and audience summaries

☐ Determine preliminary learner counts

☐ Identify the responsible team or person who will coordinate people, counts, and security role work, the basis for training courses and learning assignments

Knowing the business and the learners provides a solid foundation for best training material design and selecting the right tools to build and deliver a digital transformation training program that works for the business.

Relevant Samples

- Learner Audience Snapshot—Sample 4
- Stakeholder Connection Map—Sample 5

Responsibility and Decision-Making Clarity
Drive Success—Chapter 3

Identifying who has responsibility for which training tasks and who has accountability and authority helps the training lead and transformation program teams avoid confusion. This clarity is a necessity if a vendor is coordinating training for the transformation. Once the transformation program is underway, knowing about work ownership avoids delay and minimizes conflict in training work.

☐ Master clarity with the RACI

☐ Decode decision-making dynamics

☐ Use effective approaches for decision-making

☐ Streamline decision-making processes

☐ Balance input from diverse teams

☐ Ensure transparent communication

☐ Make the RACI work well for the digital transformation training program

The art of constructing a responsibility matrix lies in making it as simply useful as it needs to be. It must contain just enough detail, in a format that works for all the people involved and for the situations at hand. The framework should be a useful training artifact that gets kept up to date as work or responsibilities shift and as feedback gets provided.

Relevant Samples

- Responsibility and Decision-Making Matrix—Sample 7
- Vendor Checklist for Training Success—Sample 3

Training Leadership for Lasting Impact—Chapter 4

While all business leadership involves inspiring others and coordinating work that achieves goals, digital transformation training leadership stands out from others. Training leadership is the glue that makes everything else stick for the digital transformation training program. It boils down to strong collaboration and operating with a mindset that everyone's doing their best, all wish to succeed, and others want to step up to help realize shared goals.

☐ Coach and manage the team

☐ Drive for training and transformation success

☐ Lead through self-management

☐ Lead from start to finish

☐ Build connections as a digital transformation leader

☐ Master leadership communication

☐ Balance personal needs and leadership

Leaders who are skilled, inspired, healthy, and grounded are better prepared to lead in general and especially through trying times.

Relevant Samples

- Stakeholder Connection Map—Sample 5
- Digital Transformation Training Status at a Glance—Sample 6

Equipping Project Teams with Core Knowledge—Chapter 5

Project team training sees those businesspeople tasked with driving the digital transformation acquire deep knowledge. They need to learn the system, its configuration options and trade-offs, and also how to complete tasks, structure data, and run reports. The consultant-level understanding enables the transformation business team members to make better decisions about redesigning business processes.

- ☐ Identify the business learners
- ☐ Clarify what they need to know and do
- ☐ Identify and assess the various training options based on the timelines
- ☐ Secure financial backing
- ☐ Determine tracking and reporting needs
- ☐ Communicate expectations for quality training
- ☐ Manage the training delivery

Project team member training is a key investment that the program leaders make to ensure the success of the digital transformation and is a mini project within the larger effort. Because it carries a large cost and has great value to the overall transformation, project team training is an important undertaking.

Relevant Sample

- Learner Audience Snapshot—Sample 4

Funding Support for the Digital Transformation
Training Program—Chapter 6

A digital transformation training budget includes the funding needed to carry out the training strategy. A sound budget ensures that people, tools, and services exist to accomplish the training objectives.

- ☐ Start with the right tool or template
- ☐ Identify your relevant training line items
- ☐ Partner to secure appropriate funding for the training program
- ☐ Calculate the needed number and type of instructional designers (IDs)
- ☐ Know how training costs affect the company's bottom line
- ☐ Add contingency

The training lead must make certain the funding is adequate for the planned and unplanned work to be carried out as part of the transformation training program.

Stakeholder Presentations That Make an Impact—Chapter 7

Digital transformation training presentations can be equal parts opportunity and challenge for training leads. Every presentation—a slide-centered presentation, a one-on-one call, or a meeting—is a chance to re-share the vision, communicate relevant progress, and report gaps and needs, while skillfully gathering feedback and making specific asks of colleagues and stakeholders.

- ☐ Recognize which of three types of presentation you're giving
- ☐ Get in the audience's frame of mind
- ☐ Make the presentation work well
- ☐ Use asks
- ☐ Share relevant visuals and messages
- ☐ Dig into concerns and explore resistance

The real art of a presentation is not in delivery, but in listening and dynamically adjusting to meet the needs of the stakeholder audience.

These first seven chapters help a training lead organize program leaders, business stakeholders, and the training team around the digital transformation training strategy and its key activities.

MILESTONE 2
Learning materials and schedules are approved and ready for end user training.

Tools and Technologies to Power Training—Chapter 8

Identifying the components for training materials, then selecting the best tools to produce them will help learners adopt new technology and carry out redesigned business processes. These steps are an early, important training deliverable.

- ☐ Select the relevant components for your program's digital transformation training materials
- ☐ Identify potential training tools and services
- ☐ Frame a rapid analysis
- ☐ Document existing tools at the company and potential tools needed
- ☐ Conduct trials, note details, and document decisions
- ☐ Look for efficiencies and ratings
- ☐ Assess existing training materials
- ☐ Factor in leading-edge toolsets including AI and also consider sustainability
- ☐ Recognize budget considerations for training tools
- ☐ Hold "show and tell" demos with program and business leaders
- ☐ Make tool selection a team-building and knowledge-sharing exercise

With a planned, straightforward approach to analyze its options, the team also gets a head start on prototypes and begins to create development guidelines. These together increase work velocity and eliminate the potential for costly mistakes and wasteful rework.

Frameworks for Quality Content and Fast-Track Development—Chapter 9

The training team works together to consider options and make decisions about the form and production of each training material component.

- ☐ Recognize the value of style, templates, and standards
- ☐ Start smart with content-boosting templates
- ☐ Leverage company brand and look beyond the transformation
- ☐ Reference free technical writing style guides
- ☐ Secure help with graphic design
- ☐ Hold reviews, gather feedback, then secure and document approvals
- ☐ Develop a process for keeping the tools updated

Together, the style guide, templates, and standards allow the training team to produce quality materials so people can learn new process steps and know how to use the new system to carry out their jobs.

Blueprint for Developing Training Materials—Chapter 10

A plan that details the training materials being developed as part of the digital transformation is a very visible deliverable with multiple uses, including tracking development progress.

- ☐ Determine the best structure for your plan
- ☐ Detail all the training material components
- ☐ Clarify key concepts, including percentage definitions
- ☐ Report consistently

☐ Track changes in the count of items being developed

☐ Plan for modular development, not just courses

☐ Manage control of the tracker and seek opportunities for efficiency

☐ Use the tracker to manage risks and gaps

Address other considerations such as backups and recovery. The training development plan allows for progress reporting toward major training milestones that lead to the start of end user training.

Relevant Sample

- Training Material Development Tracker—Sample 8

Information Gathering with Subject Matter Experts—Chapter 11

The digital transformation program includes business process teams or workstreams, each with one or more designated subject matter experts (SMEs) who help the ID produce training materials. The role of the SME is to answer the ID's questions about new processes. SMEs also show the IDs how the new system gets used to complete the activities that people do for their jobs.

☐ Make a smart start with preparation

☐ Hold an introductory overview session

☐ Send calendar invites

☐ Share the agenda and questions in advance

☐ Send post-call recaps and thanks

☐ Work with consistency to strengthen the relationship

☐ Support IDs in managing their work and the SME relationship, starting with a great kickoff

☐ Articulate what a great SME partnership looks like

SMEs help the ID clarify and describe who does what within the organization, as well as when, why, and how to carry out key tasks using the system. These are necessary inputs to training materials. The strength of the partnership shows in the progress of training material creation and its overall quality.

Relevant Samples

- Digital Transformation Training Status at a Glance—Sample 6
- Training Material Development Tracker—Sample 8

Quality Assurance Through Material Reviews and Approvals—Chapter 12

The best training materials emerge from internal and external benchmarking, reviews, feedback, and validation at different stages of their design and production.

- ☐ Recognize the reviews authorized in the training strategy
- ☐ Establish the process and timing for internal quality reviews
- ☐ Establish the process and timing for material accuracy reviews
- ☐ Validate materials against training standards and learner needs
- ☐ Automate feedback collection
- ☐ Track and document approvals

Reviews—early and ongoing—help win support for the training effort and the business transformation. Finally, material reviews culminate in business sign-off that the course is ready for training delivery to end users—start with this end in mind.

Relevant Samples

- Digital Transformation Training Status at a Glance—Sample 6
- Training Material Development Tracker—Sample 8

Final Material Production with Editing, Translation, and Printing—Chapter 13

Final production of training materials is like the sprint at the end of a race to reach the finish line in best form. Editing, translation, and/or printing may be final treatments required in your digital transformation. The requirements depend on the learners and business demands.

☐ Recognize the relationships between editing, translation, and printing

☐ Assess the options based on learner needs and business requirements

☐ Test everything

☐ Protect the materials

☐ Ensure training material development standards have translation in mind if that's required

In many cases, a single service provider may be the best option, and some may even offer multiservice discounts for the work. If you plan to do it all yourself, be sure to consider volumes, timelines, and backup plans. Whether internal or through a vendor, conduct tests to validate your selected approach for turnaround, quality, and cost.

Relevant Samples

- Training Material Development Tracker—Sample 8
- Training Preparation and Learner Readiness Dashboard—Sample 10

Games to Engage Learners—Chapter 14

While games are not a requirement for digital transformation training, learners generally welcome them. Moreover, games are effective business learning tools.

☐ Consider three game types and formats in a digital transformation

☐ Select the right game for your training

☐ Ensure the learner needs get met

☐ Adapt classic games and make use of online options

During digital transformation training, games can help learners practice their recall of new information and also see them demonstrate their understanding of key concepts. Both recall and demonstration of knowledge are necessary steps in the process of adult learning.

Metrics for Learner Knowledge and Confidence—Chapter 15

Learning a new system to carry out changed business processes is the overarching purpose of a digital transformation training program. An essential training deliverable, then, is the ability to measure end user learning and people readiness.

☐ Appreciate the significance of learning in the context of the digital transformation

☐ Recognize the significance of when to evaluate learning

☐ Identify the types of assessments and distinguish those from feedback surveys

☐ Recognize standard models to measure learning and readiness

☐ Design effective learning checks during training

☐ Design systems practice for multiple stages of learning

☐ Assess how simulations could support the training program

☐ Recognize post-training assessment options

☐ Recognize how to use learner feedback

What happens on the first day of the digital transformation is "live" marks the ultimate test of business user learning: How well can people do their jobs? Before that, however, the goal is to measure *predictably* how learners will perform on that day. It matters. When learners report the training feels relevant for their jobs, that they worked hands-on in the system, and that they feel confident about being able to do their jobs, you'll more likely see rapid, successful adoption of new ways of working in the business functions.

Relevant Samples

• Digital Transformation Training Status at a Glance—Sample 6

• Training Preparation and Learner Readiness Dashboard—Sample 10

These eight chapters help training leads see training materials designed, developed, approved, and produced. The preparatory steps, including schedules completed on time, ready people to begin their learning. Measuring learner readiness and confidence are important training responsibilities.

MILESTONE 3
Risks are anticipated, reported, and managed.

Training Dependencies as Boosters, Not Barriers—Chapter 16

Specific deliverables produced and owned by teams outside training nevertheless directly affect the training team's ability to complete its work. Seven key interdependencies ultimately determine learner readiness, which the training team helps mediate.

1. Functional Trainers—the Critical Dependency
2. Completion of Process Design and System Build
3. End User Security Roles—Design and Mapping to People
4. On-the-Ground Business Contacts for Training Execution
5. A Training and Practice Environment
6. Change Communications
7. Business Requirements for Training

Managing these dependencies comes down to training and transformation program leadership, the strength of cross-functional and business partnerships, and the extent to which there exists a culture of accountability across the transformation program and the business teams.

Relevant Samples

- Digital Transformation Training Program Checklist—Sample 1
- Milestone Map and Training Timeline—Sample 2
- Digital Transformation Training Status at a Glance—Sample 6

Besides all the other issues that can arise, these deliverables from other teams require additional tracking to ensure any risk is mitigated and does not become an issue.

MILESTONE 4

Training facilitators are onboarded and prepared to teach training and lead practice sessions, then support post-launch needs.

Business Trainers as the Essential Factor for Transformation Success—Chapter 17

Functional business trainers are the first early learners of the new system and processes. They are carefully selected then developed to lead training sessions for their colleagues, and they often carry out other transformation tasks as well. During training, they conduct demonstrations and lead hands-on practice, answering questions about new ways of working in relationship to the "current" or old ways. To effectively support this key group, the training team and transformation program leaders must act with intention.

- ☐ Recognize the typical responsibilities of functional business trainers in a digital transformation and decide on how to support training, testing, and other needs
- ☐ Recognize the traits of the best business *trainers* for a digital transformation
- ☐ Decide the term for the transformation business trainers
- ☐ Develop a plan for knowledge building and train the trainer skills, measuring the progress
- ☐ Establish and communicate early with business trainers about expectations for their time commitment, end user training delivery, and the importance of their role for the transformation
- ☐ Consider whether a hybrid approach of internal and external trainers makes sense for your transformation
- ☐ Evaluate functional trainer readiness repeatedly
- ☐ Recognize functional business trainer efforts and achievements

Having the right, well-trained functional trainers enables lasting adoption by seeding knowledgeable resources among business teams, which helps the business transformation become a reality. These coaches convert today's work and bring the vision to life. Business trainers mis-selected or under-skilled will have negative impacts.

Relevant Sample

- Business Trainer Overview at a Glance—Sample 11

MILESTONE 5

Tracking and reporting about training provide useful insights to transformation leaders and others.

Progress Updates That Keep Leadership Informed—Chapter 18

Long before anyone starts learning during training sessions, many things must be planned, coordinated, and completed. It's important to tell an ongoing story about this preparatory work so that training is ready to start on time.

☐ Use status and supplemental reporting effectively

☐ Keep status reporting simple and straightforward; be strategic when appropriate

☐ Report progress about the deliverables training needs and that others complete

☐ Develop and use dashboards for progress snapshots

☐ Be smart about the time spent on reporting

Consistent, credible reporting communicates progress or problems to the broad audience: digital transformation program leads, functional trainers, business stakeholders, and training team members. Done well, these reports allow the right people to take the needed action to resolve issues and celebrate the accomplishments.

Relevant Sample

- Digital Transformation Training Status at a Glance—Sample 6

Learner Readiness Tracking and Reporting for Day One and Beyond—Chapter 19

Learner success in a digital transformation training initiative is both predictable and measurable. It's not enough to have quality training materials and a great, well-tested solution. Rather, success lies in all the ways the pieces come together across the transformation and business teams over time.

- ☐ Identify the deliverables and milestones that matter
- ☐ Recognize the pre-training preparations to track and report
- ☐ Monitor training execution metrics and feedback
- ☐ Report on learner knowledge and readiness risks, calling out any actions others need to take
- ☐ Recognize what gets in the way

Transparency about risks helps others take action before a situation becomes unrecoverable.

Relevant Samples

- Digital Transformation Training Status at a Glance—Sample 6
- Learner Insights Survey—Sample 9

Training Closeout for Reflection and Celebration—Chapter 20

At the end of each digital transformation training cycle, the training lead collects feedback, consolidates it, and coordinates discussion about what to continue, change, or action. Data about the training and its execution—along with business hypercare metrics—supplement the team's quantitative and open-ended commentary.

- ☐ Know easy options for your closeout approach and gathering input
- ☐ Welcome candid comments and solicit recommendations, suggestions, and ideas
- ☐ Make the discussion and action plan session a celebration event

☐ Share the findings with digital transformation leaders and business stakeholders

The closeout report provides a valuable artifact for the business and becomes an action plan the training team uses for continuous improvement.

These three chapters show how the training program tracks and reports on the digital transformation training program, learner progress and readiness, training completions, and learner feedback. Much can emerge from the data: highlights about what works well and should continue, needed changes, calls to action for digital transformation program leaders, and even asks of business executives so that the next digital transformation implementation is even better.

Final Note

Denis Waitley noted, "Mistakes are painful when they happen, but years later a collection of mistakes is what is called experience." *Digital Transformation Champions* organizes years of experience and learnings to help see more success in digital transformations through training programs that achieve their purpose. The framework, samples, best practices, and ways to navigate the challenges intend to help training leads and others prepare their business users for new ways of working, regardless of the size of the digital transformation. Done well, the training program prepares a company's business teams to readily adopt new processes and confidently use new technology, the finish line of every successful digital transformation.

Samples

1: Digital Transformation Training Program Checklist

Planning

- ☐ Strategy business- and learner-based, broadly reviewed and approved
- ☐ Approach prepared or strategy updated as needed
- ☐ Learner audiences described and needs documented
- ☐ Course curricula reflect the scope and audience
- ☐ Training team staffed to create needed content in time needed
- ☐ Key tools and technologies for creating and presenting content tested with proof of concept and budgeted
- ☐ Material development plan created

- ☐ Stakeholders identified and collaboration plans exist
- ☐ Content and user-facing tech designs created, documented, and business approved for engaging, effective learning
- ☐ Development scope created
- ☐ Functional trainer development shared with process teams
- ☐ Functional trainers named and have business support for their time and commitment
- ☐ Dashboards created and ongoing reporting begins

Key Dependencies for Training

- ☐ Security role owner designated for creation and management
- ☐ People-to-security role mapping conducted early
- ☐ On-time input provided by material reviewers
- ☐ Single material approver designated for each process area
- ☐ Business trainer resources and the preparation timeline established
- ☐ Local business contacts identified to maintain training scheduling and problem-solving during training/practice
- ☐ On the ground training coordination liaisons arranged
- ☐ Process team partnership with training and proactive inclusion evidenced

- ☐ Project leaders ensure training's seat at the project table early on and respond to data, risks, and requests provided
- ☐ Training lead is focused on management with only material review (not development) responsibility
- ☐ Gaps, opportunities, and lessons learned get identified early on and addressed as part of continuous improvement
- ☐ Senior business leaders promote training within their teams and provide direct feedback about concerns
- ☐ Business leaders provide input, ongoing feedback, and support and make decisions about logistics, reporting, and training expectations

Training Execution

- ☐ Training completion actual to plan rates
- ☐ Training windows appropriate and managed
- ☐ Training technologies function as planned
- ☐ Feedback data and requests addressed
- ☐ Business assessments pre- and post-launch

Learner Readiness

- ☐ Learners confirm today-tomorrow awareness
- ☐ Learners report high confidence
- ☐ Learners report quality learning experience
- ☐ Learners confirm hands-on practice
- ☐ Learners confirm recognition of support options
- ☐ Knowledge check pass average => target %

Training Materials/Content

- ☐ Content development aligned with audience needs and best practices for adult learning, role- and process-based training, and modular development
- ☐ Content style, design, and development standards documented and their use is verified across IDs

- ☐ SME info gathering
- ☐ Content refinement strategy in place around project schedule and training start
- ☐ Effective, value-add meeting time and outcomes
- ☐ Quality standards

Preparation

People, Security Roles, and Counts

- ☐ Preliminary list of learners mapped to roles received to aid in logistics and content creation planning
- ☐ Security role design well-managed and stable with push reports of changes

Logistics

- ☐ Training and practice schedules set, approved, and shared, factoring in holidays, trainer schedules, and makeup needs
- ☐ Courses loaded to the LMS
- ☐ Pre-training communications prepared and sent

Functional Trainers

- ☐ Identified
- ☐ Onboarded
- ☐ Participate in train the trainer
- ☐ Complete demonstration certification

Tracking and Reports

- ☐ Reports and training dashboard drafted and approved
- ☐ Reports developed and tested

2: Milestone Map and Training Timeline

Legend: ■ Analysis | ■ Design | ■ Development | Implementation | ☐ Evaluation
◇☐ Dependencies from Others | ◆ Training Milestone

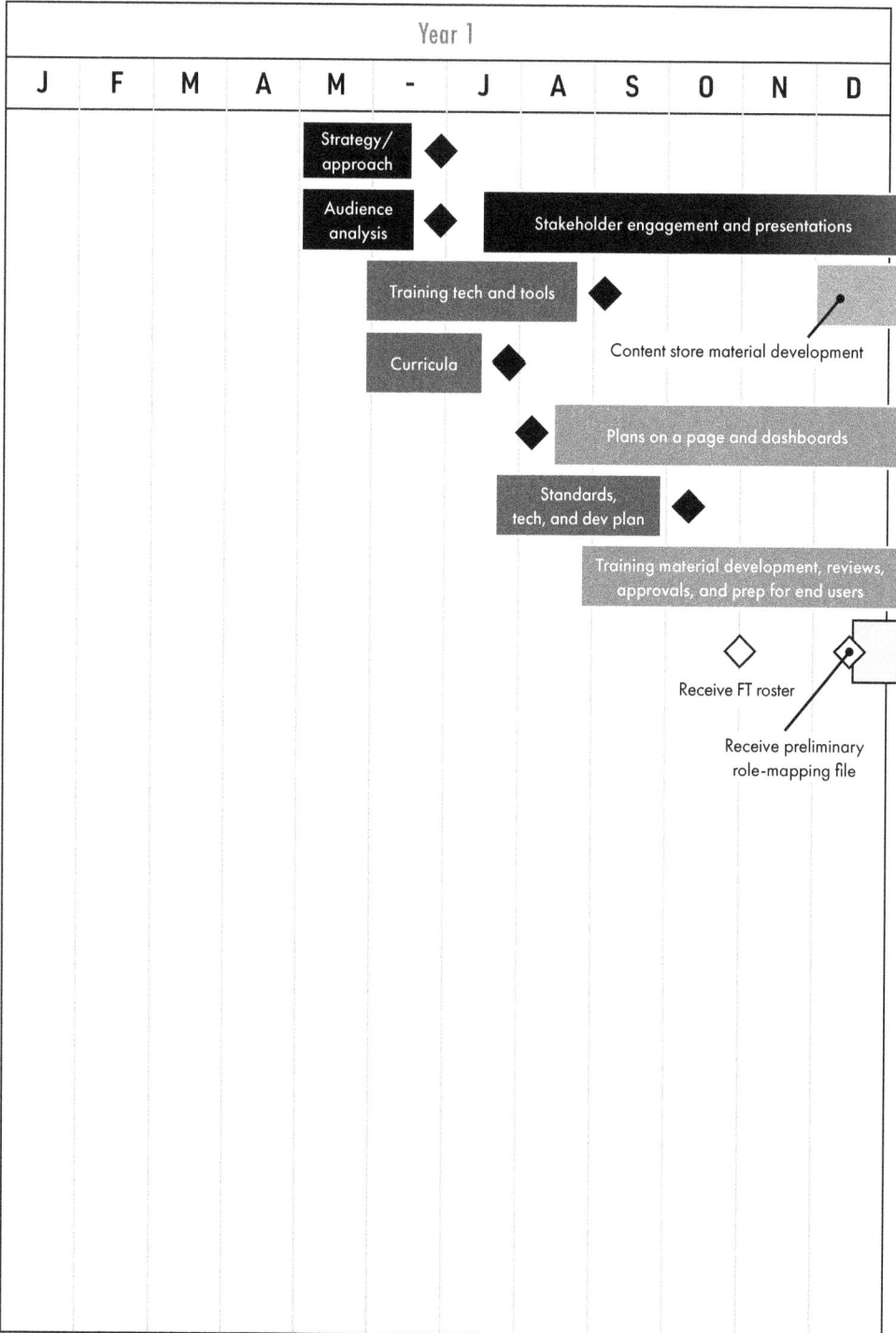

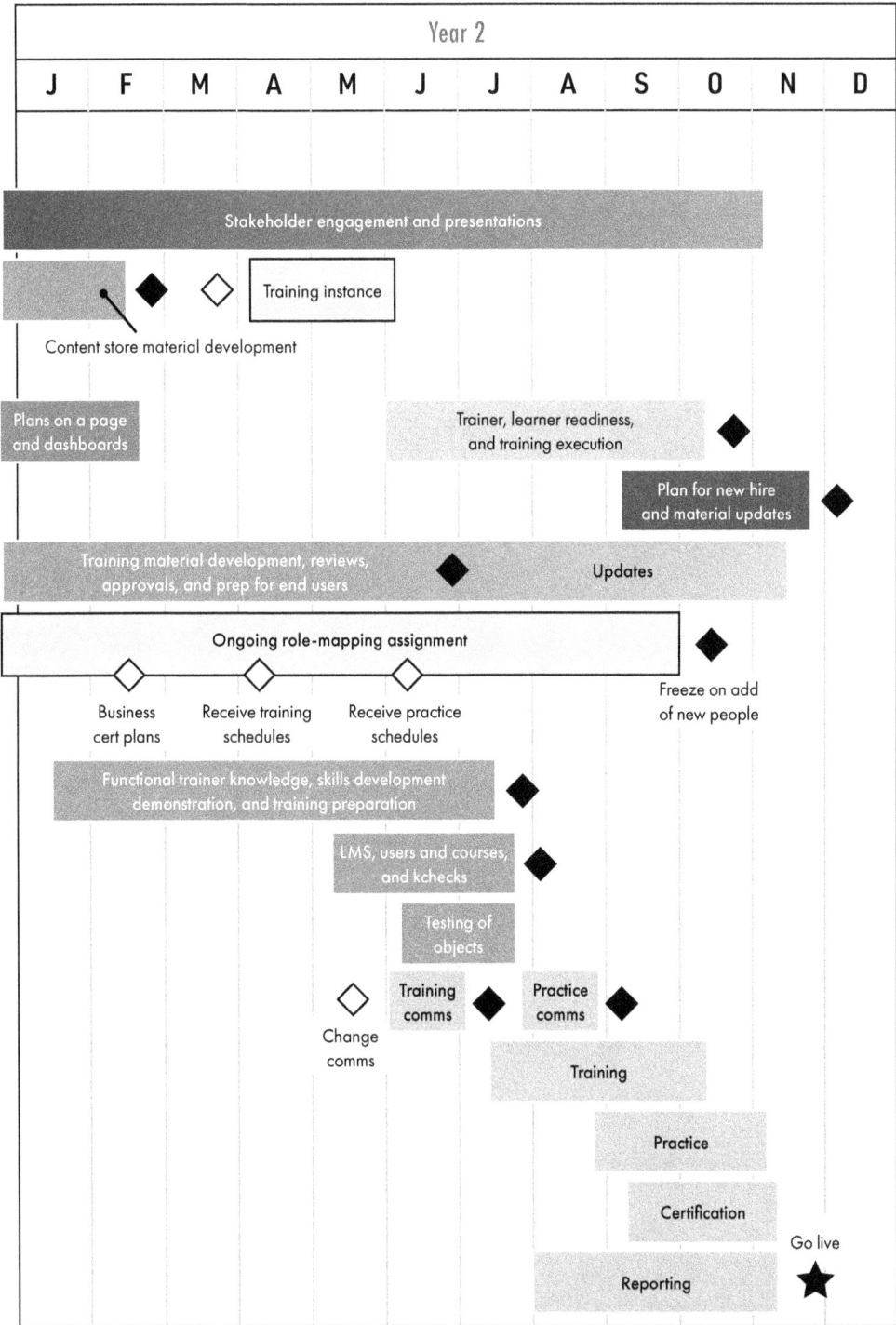

Notes Page

3: Vendor Checklist for Training Success

Ownership of Training Responsibilities			
Legend: B=Business V=Vendor NA=Not Applicable	B	V	NA
Define training scope			
Define key outcomes for the business and learners			
Set training program phases, timelines, and critical path milestones			
Detail activities and deliverables			
Detail all activity for training program, including key interdependencies			
Create the RACI-D for the major deliverables and key aspects of training			
Manage, track, and report on the training plan			
Audience analysis: learner and stakeholder			
Explain foundational philosophy and models for adult learning, training, and materials related to deployment			
Training delivery decisions			
Make-buy decision and material ownership			
Training material development and/or customizing			
Material reviews and approvals			
Learning maps by user role			
Server/site designated for material storage			
Training assignments, scheduling, and logistics			
LMS administration			
Trainer/coach identification (vendor and business)			
Trainer/coach preparation			
Provision and support of training and practice instance			
Create knowledge checks			
Create certification assessments			
Build training schedules			
Prepare and send today-tomorrow change summaries			
Create and send training comms			
Set metrics for training delivery and people readiness			
Log risks, actions, issues, and decision items			
Coordinate, monitor, support training/practice completion			
Track k-transfer to IT and support resources			
Prepare and send training/practice reporting			
Develop material/training sustainability post-launch plans			

Contacts

Vendor
Name/Title/Role/Contact Info
Name/Title/Role/Contact Info
Name/Title/Role/Contact Info

Business
Name/Title/Role/Contact Info
Name/Title/Role/Contact Info
Name/Title/Role/Contact Info

Costs

Breakout
Oversight/management
$_____
Material development
$_____
Ownership $_____
Delivery total* $_____
   Cost per session $_____
   Cost per pupil $_____
Knowledge transfer $_____
Post-launch material edits
$_____
Post-launch delivery/support
$_____

* Note service level agreement for learner feedback and test performance

Date of last update

4: Learner Audience Snapshot

Legend:

Work Hours: ● 24x7 Shifts | ◉ 8–5

Delivery: 🖥️ In-person instructor-led | 🖥️ Virtual instructor-led | 🧍 Individual learning

Business and Processes	# People	# People Managers	Training Delivery	Work Hours	No-Train Periods
Location or Business Unit 1	213				
Process Area List Item 3	120	8	🧍🖥️ In-person	● 24x7	
Process Area List Item 4	80	3	🧍🖥️ In-person	● 24x7	✓
Process Area List Item 5	13	4	🧍🖥️ Virtual	◉ 8–5	✓
Location or Business Unit 2	123				
Process Area List Item 3	75	4	🧍🖥️ In-person	● 24x7	
Process Area List Item 4	40	3	🧍🖥️ In-person	● 24x7	✓
Process Area List Item 5	8	3	🧍🖥️ Virtual	◉ 8–5	✓
Location or Business Unit 3	50				✓
Process Area List Item 4	40	3	🖥️ In-person		✓
Process Area List Item 5	10	3	🧍🖥️ Virtual		✓
Location or Business Unit 4	85				
Process Area List Item 1	18	4	🧍🖥️ Virtual	◉ 8–5	
Process Area List Item 2	15	4	🧍🖥️ Virtual	◉ 8–5	
Process Area List Item 3	20	3	🧍🖥️ In-person	● 24x7	✓
Process Area List Item 6	32	5	🧍🖥️ Virtual	◉ 8–5	
Location or Business Unit 5	123				
Process Area List Item 3	75	4	🧍🖥️ In-person	● 24x7	✓
Process Area List Item 4	40	3	🧍🖥️ In-person	● 24x7	✓
Process Area List Item 5	8	3	🧍🖥️ Virtual	◉ 8–5	✓

Approved-Updated Date

Training Rooms	After-Training Practice	Readiness Certification	Training Contact	Notes About Learning Needs
✓			F. Lastname	
	✓			Instructor fluent in 2nd language
	✓			Instructor fluent in 2nd language
	✓	✓		
✓				
	✓	✓	F. Lastname	
			F. Lastname	
	✓	✓	F. Lastname	
✓				
			F. Lastname	
	✓	✓	F. Lastname	
✗			F. Lastname	Conference room and small class size
	✓	✓		Prefer training Thursday/Friday
	✓	✓		Prefer training Thursday/Friday
	✓	✓		Consideration for vision and hearing needs
	✓	✓		Prefer training Thursday/Friday
✓				
	✓	✓	F. Lastname	Instructor fluent in 2nd language
	✓	✓	F. Lastname	Instructor fluent in 3rd language
	✓	✓	F. Lastname	

5: Stakeholder Connection Map

Business and processes	Impact the project has on person's team (L, M, H)	Influence over the project (L, M, H)	What fears or frustrations exist about training?	What are the wants, needs, and success metrics for training?
Core Team				
Stakeholder 1 Name	L	H		
Stakeholder 2 Name	L	H		
Location or Business Unit 1				
Stakeholder 1 Name	M	L		
Stakeholder 2 Name	L	M		
Stakeholder 3 Name	H	H		
Location or Business Unit 2				
Stakeholder 1 Name	L	H		
Stakeholder 2 Name	M	M		
Stakeholder 3 Name	H	M		
Location or Business Unit 3				
Stakeholder 1 Name	H	M		
Stakeholder 2 Name	H	M		
Location or Business Unit 4				
Stakeholder 1 Name	M	M		
Stakeholder 2 Name	M	H		
Stakeholder 3 Name	M	M		
Stakeholder 4 Name	M	M		
Location or Business Unit 5				
Stakeholder 1 Name	L	H		
Stakeholder 2 Name	M	H		
Stakeholder 3 Name	H	M		
Stakeholder 4 Name	M	L		
Stakeholder 5 Name	H	L		

Samples

Awareness of business need for the project?	What is said and done in public about training—attitude, behavior?	What is visible about training—information, feedback, etc.?	What others in the function say about training?	Plans to engage, inform, and collaborate with the stakeholder

6: Digital Transformation Training Status at a Glance

Commentary

Planning
Recognition/appreciation 1
Recognition/appreciation 2

Preparation
Support-risk-need ask 1
Support-risk-need ask 2
Change note

Critical Dependencies
Support-risk-need ask 1
Support-risk-need ask 2
Recognition/appreciation 1

Material Development
Next milestone
Support-risk-need ask 1
Support-risk-need ask 2
Change note

Learner Readiness
Support-risk-need ask 1
Support-risk-need ask 2
Change note

Key Counts
Support-risk-need ask 1
Support-risk-need ask 2
Change note

RAID items logged indicated by (#) added to the above.

● Planning

Strategy	●
Tools and technology	●
Audience analysis	●
Development scope/curricula	●
Functional trainer approach	●

● Preparation

Material development	●
People, security roles, and counts	●
Schedules	●
Logistics	●
LMS loads	●
Functional trainers prepared	●
Communications	○
Reports and training dashboard	○

● Critical Dependencies

Security role design and mapping	●
Material reviewers and approvers	●
Functional trainer resources	●
On-the-ground liaisons	●
Program prioritization and support	●

○ Learner Readiness

Preparations	○
Training completion	○
Knowledge check pass %	○
Learner feedback	○
Certification	○

Updated Date

Material Development Detail

Status	Process Area	# Roles	# Objects	% Complete	Development Status	Reviewers Approved
●	Process area item 1	5	111		●	●
●	Process area item 2	4	97 (+3)		●	○
●	Process area item 3	6	240 (-60)		●	○
●	Process area item 4	2	TBD		●	○
●	Process area item 5	3	195		●	●

Learner Readiness Highlights

Status	Process Area	Approved Materials	Schedules	Functional Trainer Status	LMS Loads	Knowledge Checks
●	Process area	●	●	●	○	○
●	Process area	●	●	○	○	○
●	Process area	●	●	○	○	○
●	Process area	●	●	○	○	○
●	Process area	●	●	●	○	○

Training by Business/Geography

Status	Business/Geography	# People	# Roles	# Courses	Functional Trainers	SME Support	Training Completion	Practice Cert.
●	Business team/geo 1	#	#	#	●	●	●	●
●	Business team/geo 2	#	#	#	●	●	●	●
●	Business team/geo 3	#	#	#	●	●	●	●
●	Business team/geo 4	#	#	#	●	●	●	●
●	Business team/geo 5	#	#	#	●	●	●	●
●	Business team/geo 6	#	#	#	●	●	●	●

7: Responsibility and Decision-Making Matrix
Option A

Date of Last Update

Work and deliverables that benefit from role and responsibility clarification	Responsible	Accountable (decision-maker if different)
Develop the training strategy and define scope	Name 1, Name 2, Name 3, Name 4	Name 1
Define key outcomes for the business and learners	Name 1, Name 2, Name 3, Name 4	Name 1
Set training program phases, timelines, and critical path milestones	Name 1, Name 4, Name 5	Name 1, Decision-maker 1
Detail activities and deliverables		
Detail all activities for training program, including key interdependencies		
Manage, track, and report on the training plan		
Audience analysis		
Explain foundational philosophy and models for adult learning, training, and materials		
Training delivery decisions		
Make-buy decision and material ownership		
Training material development and/or customizing		
Material reviews and approvals		
Learning maps by user role		
Material storage solution—whose server/site		
Training assignments, scheduling, and logistics		
LMS administration		
Trainer identification (vendor and business)		
Trainer preparation		
Provision and support of training and practice instance		
Create knowledge checks		
Create certification assessments		
Build training schedules		
Set metrics for training delivery and people readiness		
Log risks, actions, issues, and decision items		
Lead training and/or practice sessions		
Knowledge transfer to IT and support resources		
Training preparation and execution reporting		
Sustainability plans and post-launch training admin		

Samples

Option B

Legend: A= Accountable for Completion | R=Responsible for Doing Work | D=Decision-Maker/Approver
C=Consulted for Input | I=Informed About Work

Date of Last Update

Work and deliverables that benefit from role and responsibility clarification	Trng Lead	Inst Dsgnr	Wrkstrm Leads	Process SME	Prgrm Mgr	Bus Ldr Stkhldr	Bus Trn Stkhldr
Develop the training strategy and define scope	A/R	I	C	I	C/P	C/I	C/I
Define key outcomes for the business and learners	R	R	C	C/I	C/I	D	C/I
Set training program phases, timelines, and critical path milestones	A/R	I	I	I	C	I	I
Detail activities and deliverables	A/R	R	C	I	I	C/I	C/I
Detail all activities for training program, including key interdependencies							
Manage, track, and report on the training plan							
Audience analysis							
Explain foundational philosophy and models for adult learning, training, and materials							
Training delivery decisions							
Make-buy decision and material ownership							
Training material development and/or customizing							
Material reviews and approvals							
Learning maps by user role							
Material storage solution—whose server/site							
Training assignments, scheduling, and logistics							
LMS administration							
Trainer identification (vendor and business)							
Trainer preparation							
Provision and support of training and practice instance							
Create knowledge checks							
Create certification assessments							
Build training schedules							
Set metrics for training delivery and people readiness							
Log risks, actions, issues, and decision items							
Lead training and/or practice sessions							
Knowledge transfer to IT and support resources							
Training preparation and execution reporting							
Sustainability plans and post launch training admin							

8: Training Material Development Tracker

Should align with program, workstream, and process areas with accountable project and business leaders. Can also be "Training" or "Program" when cross-area.

Should reflect digital transformation process and subprocesses.

This list includes the components, training material components, and final learning objects.

Combining the labels enables more detailed reporting.

Process Area	Subprocess	Asset Type	Description
Process Area 1	Subprocess A	Module	Title
Process Area 1	Subprocess A	Lesson	Title-Audience
Process Area 1	Subprocess A	Kcheck	Title-Audience
Process Area 1	Subprocess B	Process Module	Title
Process Area 1	Subprocess B	Lesson	Title-Audience
Process Area 1	Subprocess B	Kcheck	Title-Audience
Process Area 2	Subprocess A	Title	Title

The detail feeds the training program snapshot sections about materials development.

Matching security role "audiences" to the components is necessary to determine the amount of learning people will have.

Associate the count of activity tasks to one object—avoid double-counting them.

Update the object completion based on pre-set criteria where X%=a specific development state, review, component, completion, etc. for each asset type.

Audiences	Number of Activities (by Module and/or Lesson)	Percent Complete (Based on Criteria)
A1	0	25%
A1	#	25%
A1	-	0%
A1, A2, A3	0	50%
A1, A2, A3	#	50%
A1, A2, A3	-	15%
A5	0	75%

The detail feeds the training program snapshot sections about materials development.

9: Learner Insights Survey

Option A: Assessing the Training Experience and Learner Needs

Based on *ATD Infoline* survey instruments, ERP training research, and my own experiences.

Learners provide feedback by scoring questions using a six-point Likert scale.

The six high-stakes questions whose data are significant for learning outcomes in my experience, have an asterisk (*).

Stars (★) indicate the three questions whose data business leaders valued as indicators of learner readiness and post-launch support.

1. **How likely is it that you would recommend this course to a work colleague?** *
    Measures the quality of the training experience based on a person's willingness to suggest someone else repeat it.

2. **I worked hands-on in the system during my training.** ★
    Confirms that the expected systems practice took place.

3. **I learned how to solve problems during my training.**
    Confirms that dealing with and learning to solve problems was part of the course content.

4. **The amount of time for training was appropriate.**
    Checks on the perceived effort spent learning and can hint at delivery or design issues.

5. **The classroom facilities were adequate and comfortable.**
    Learning new processes and tools should not be uncomfortable. On multiple deployments I've been shocked that businesses ask people to attend training in conditions that are not conducive to learning: loud noises, no water allowed, and over-heated as well.

6. **The course materials were effective and helped my learning.** *
    The business invests in material creation, and many were involved in developing the materials. Feedback about whether or not they helped learners is warranted. Also, low scores here mean that the materials may not have been used as designed.

7. **The exercises completed during class supported my learning.** *
    Measures that hands-on practice occurred. This can be verified with reports about end user log-ons and system activity during training.

8. **The instructor was effective in delivering the training content.**
    Intends to measure facilitator ability to teach the material. Typically, this score is a bit inflated because the person is someone known from the business and a learner appreciates someone helping them, without perhaps knowing what effective means.

9. **The instructor was knowledgeable about the course topics, processes, and system.** * ★
    Measures the facilitator's preparation and knowledge of the content, processes, and system.

10. **What I learned will help me perform my job.** * ★
    Assesses the relevance of the course to on-the-job work, a key tenet of digital transformation training.

11. **When I need help, I know where to get assistance and find support materials.** *
    Confidence and the willingness to use new systems require support, and this feedback ensures the learner knows where to find a person and information resources.

12. **Please add any other comments that explain your answers above, or let us know any specific needs/requests you have to support your success.** An optional text box for open-ended comments from a learner. These should always be reviewed and acted upon.

Option B: Feedback Using Performance-Focused Outcomes

In the course of developing *Digital Transformation Champions*, I recognized an opportunity to rewrite questions to potentially collect better data. During a talk about our brain's difficulty in staying focused to learn and recall new information, Will Thalheimer famously simplified learning as a formula: Remembering – Forgetting. His passion for measuring learning evolved, and his book *Performance-Focused Learner Surveys* challenges the value of net promoter-score and Likert scale–based measures. He and others prefer a performance-focused framework for more meaningful data, illustrated below. My critical question about applying what's learned on the job, #10 in Option A, is substituted with Will Thalheimer's question #101. The questions are similar. A set of detailed response options replaces my 6-point numeric scale and there are notes for how the results should be interpreted (Thalheimer 2022, 83).

	How able are you to put what you've learned into practice in your work? Choose the ONE option that best describes your current readiness. (Used to determine how prepared learners feel about being able to take what they've learned and use it in their work.)	Standards. (Not shown to learners.)
A	My current role does not enable me to use what I learned.	Alarming
B	I am still unclear about what to do, and/or why to do it.	Alarming
C	I need more guidance before I know how to use what I learned.	Unacceptable
D	I need more experience to be good at using what I learned.	Acceptable
E	I can be successful now in using what I learned (even without more guidance or experience).	Superior
F	I can perform now at an expert level.	Superior/overconfident

I have used performance-focused questions for assessing functional trainers and found that the cautionary notes applied: It takes more time to develop, more time for learners to complete, and more time to evaluate the results. Option A remains highly valid for measuring and tracking learner readiness, and I continue to recommend and use it for measuring workforce upskilling as part of a digital transformation.

10: Training Preparation and Learner Readiness Dashboard

Option A: Preparation and Learner Readiness Tracking

Legend: ☒ NA | ☐ Not Started | ▨ WIP, On Track
▨ Delayed | ▪ Risk-Escalated | ☑ Complete

Business and Processes*	Number of People*	Final Course Approvals	Outstanding Process Design Decisions	Functional Trainers Ready	Training Schedules	Practice Schedules
Process Area 1	3,000	▨ (Delayed)	X			
Process Area 2	800	▪ (Risk-Escalated)	▨ (Delayed)			
Process Area 3	500		X			
Process Area 4	250		X			
Process Area 5	100	✓	X			
Process Area 6	2,000		X			
Department, Location, or BU1	2,100	X				
Department, Location, or BU2	1,200	X				
Department, Location, or BU3	750	X				
Department, Location, or BU4	400	X				
Department, Location, or BU5	100	X				
Department, Location, or BU6	300	X		▨ (Delayed)		
Department, Location, or BU7	200	X				
Department, Location, or BU8	100	X				

*People can be assigned multiple roles in more than one process area

** Business leaders determine that training and practice mitigate the need for certification

Samples

Knowledge Checks Approved and Tested	Change Role Map, Comms	LMS Course and People Staged	Training Comms Sent	Training Execution	Hands-On Practice Execution	Certification	Comments
						* *	Process owner delayed
✓						* *	

DIGITAL TRANSFORMATION CHAMPIONS

Option B: Training Preparation by Business Area and Process

Legend: 🖥️ In-person instructor-led | 🖥️ Virtual instructor-led
🧍 Individual learning | 🕐 Overtime

Business and Processes	# Learners	# Roles	First Training Date	Training Delivery	Logistics	Training Schedule Set
Location or BU1						
Process Area List Item 3	120	4	TBD	[in-person]	✓	✓
Process Area List Item 4	80	5	May 1	[overtime + in-person]	✓	✓
Process Area List Item 5	13	3	TBD	[individual + virtual]	✓	✓
Location or BU2						
Process Area List Item 3	75	4	May 4	[in-person]	✓	✓
Process Area List Item 4	40	3	May 6	[in-person]	✓	✓
Process Area List Item 5	8	3	May 12	[individual + virtual]	✓	✓
Location or BU3						✓
Process Area List Item 4	40	5	TBD	[overtime + in-person]	✓	✓
Process Area List Item 5	10	3	May 12	[individual + virtual]	✓	✓
Location or BU4						
Process Area List Item 1	18	2	April 30	[individual + virtual]	✓	✓
Process Area List Item 2	15	3	May 4	[individual + virtual]	✓	✓
Process Area List Item 3	20	4	TBD	[in-person]	✓	WIP
Process Area List Item 6	32	3	May 10	[individual + virtual]	✓	✓
Location or BU5						
Process Area List Item 3	75	4	TBD	[in-person]	WIP	WIP
Process Area List Item 4	40	5	TBD	[overtime + in-person]	WIP	WIP
Process Area List Item 5	8	3	TBD	[individual + virtual]	WIP	WIP

Samples

Approved-Updated Date

Practice Cert Scheduled	Manager Comms Sent	LMS Setup Done	Functional Trainers Prepared	Training Comms Sent	Notes, Needs, and Risks
✓			F. Lastname		
WIP	WIP	WIP	WIP		Delay in final schedule drives risk
✓	✓	✓	✓	✓	
WIP	WIP	WIP	WIP		Delay in final schedule drives risk
✓	✓	✓	✓		
✓	✓	✓	✓		
✓	✓	✓	✓		
WIP	WIP	WIP	WIP		Delay in final schedule drives risk
✓	✓	✓	✓		
✓	✓	✓	✓	✓	
✓	✓	✓	✓		
WIP	WIP	WIP	WIP		Delay in final schedule drives risk
✓	✓	✓	✓		
WIP	WIP	WIP	WIP		Delay in final schedule drives risk
WIP	WIP	WIP	WIP		Delay in final schedule drives risk
WIP	WIP	WIP	WIP		Delay in final schedule drives risk

11: Business Trainer Overview at a Glance

Purpose of the Functional Trainer Program

Ensure end users have skilled, knowledgeable support.

Ensure functional trainers have time to learn and demonstrate abilities.

Have early learners validate the materials, training, processes, and tools.

Build a bridge between the program and the business—a key change role.

Criteria for Selection

Personable, respected, professional.

Technically proficient and business knowledgeable.

Positive outlook, can-do attitude.

Comfortable with ambiguity, change, and continuous improvement.

Seeks solutions.

Able to say, "I don't know."

Comfortable speaking with confidence to groups.

Selected for skills and ability to have a positive impact, not because they're available. (Phelan, 2012b)

Success

Facilitate
Engage learners about context and content.

Demonstrate
Show mastery of system and data, integrations, metrics, and problem handling.

Leverage
Apply best practice, training materials, and other resources.

Teach and Coach
Prepare for and deliver excellent training and measurably affect end user training.

Functional Trainer Responsibilities

Facilitate training sessions and hands-on practice sessions; in-person or virtual.

Learn new processes and the new tool(s).

Review draft training materials.

Prepare practice scenarios, reviews, questions, and data for training and practice sessions.

May conduct testing.

May provide demonstrations to stakeholders.

Deliver a facilitation demonstration to a small group of other functional trainers and stakeholders to be certified.

Stakeholder Supporters

Workstream Leads/SMEs
Primary points of contact.
Teach process and system and answer questions.

Managers/Supervisors
Free up time when needed.

Business and Training Leaders
Appreciate the role's importance and recognize success.

Program Leaders
Ensure program support.

Program Training Team
Coordinates development, train the trainer, certification, and community calls.

Functional Trainer Milestones and Effort

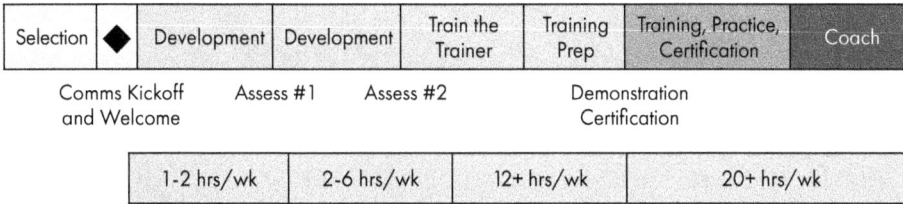

Learners and Trainers		
Processes	# People	# Functional Trainers*
Process Area 1	3,000	50
Process Area 2	800	30
Process Area 3	500	20
Process Area 4	250	12
Process Area 5	100	4
Process Area 6	2,000	45
Process Area 7	75	3
Process Area 8	100	5

* Ratio reflects the degree of change, complexity of tasks, and a model of 1:25–40. (Phelan, 2012b)

Acknowledgments

Recognizing the wealth of opportunity and good fortune in my career, I also appreciate the mentors and teachers who generously influenced me, my work, and my thinking. My long-term coaches, Dianne Percy and Mike Williams, modeled leading-edge thinking and people-centered leadership and encouraged me to write this book. I am so grateful to them and to colleagues and friends who were beta readers of early chapter drafts: Poonacha Mandeda, Jennifer Stanley, Alexis Nelson, Claire Belisle, Rick Daniel, and Lillian Miller. Each reviewer contributed their own experiences with digital transformation training leadership, instructional design, and learning management system administration. They shared hours of time and provided insightful comments, suggestions, and stories that helped enhance the overall quality of the chapters. Cindy Spreiter, Jean Muller, and Tina Bissonnette also provided helpful input.

My editor Kristen Havens had the Herculean task of reviewing the early chapter drafts for a business topic new to her. Like a personal trainer, she worked with me to add shape, definition, and strength with continuous prompts for examples and specifics about who, what, when, and why. The result of her guidance is more relatable information and a clarity that was lacking.

The team at Greenleaf shepherded the final manuscript and polished it into the book you have in hand. Thank you, Steve Elizalde, Leah Pierre, and Claudia Volkman, for your guidance, talent, and support throughout the process. Laurie MacQueen skillfully created a beautiful cover and inside design that invites a reader in and makes it easy to browse and find a topic. Tess Newton stepped in and up to carry me and the book through to the end, for which I'm so appreciative and grateful.

Finally, to the reader, may the content prove helpful and benefit your own digital transformation training work—thank you for reading *Digital Transformation Champions*.

—Missy Parks

April 2024

Bibliography

Aldrich, C. (1999). Best practices in end-user training. *Research Note*, TU-09-4549. Gartner.

Allen, L.E. (2008). Where good ERP implementations go bad: A case for continuity. *Business Process Management Journal*, 14(3), 327–337.

Anderson, D. (2022). How to create a style guide for E-Learning. Webinar.

Appleton, E.L. (1997). How to survive ERP. *Datamation*, March, 50–53.

APQC. (2024, October 10). Process classification framework (PCF) version 7.4. https://www.apqc.org/pcf-excel.

Ashley, J. (2024, February 17). Why multidimensional self-care is essential to better leadership. *Forbes*. https://www.forbes.com/sites/forbescoachescouncil/2021/06/28/why-multidimensional-self-care-is-essential-to-better-leadership/?sh=2103eed65d56.

ATD. (2024, February 18). Train the trainer courses. ATD. Train the Trainer Courses | ATD.

ASTD (n.d.). "Taking the Pulse Survey: Change Readiness." Infoline Job Aid.

Baton Simulations. (2011). SAP introductory game. Training handout. Baton Simulations.

Belhassen, D. (2022, October 15). Know your eLearning goals and audience before choosing tools. Learning Guild. https://www.learningguild.com/articles/know-your-elearning-goals-and-audience-before-choosing-tools/.

Biech, E. (2010). *The ASTD Handbook for Workplace Learning Professionals*. American Society for Training & Development (ASTD).

Blanchard, K. (2024, October 21). No one of us is as smart as all of us. Ken Blanchard. https://www.kenblanchardbooks.com/no-one-of-us-is-as-smart-as-all-of-us/.

Bowman, S. (2011). *The Ten-Minute Trainer: 150 Ways to Teach It Quick & Make It Stick!* Pfeiffer.

Boykin, R.F., and Martz, W.B. (2004). The integration of ERP into a logistics curriculum: applying a systems approach. *Journal of Enterprise Information Management*, 17(1), 45–55.

Bradley, J., and Lee, C.C. (2007). ERP Training and user satisfaction: A case study. *International Journal of Enterprise Information systems*, 3(4), 33–50.

Brandon, B. (2023, November 12). Learning games meant for adults. The Learning Guild. Learning Games Meant for Adults : Articles | The Learning Guild.

Brandon Hall Research Group. (2007). LMS selection guide: LMS and LCMS demystified. *Elearning!*, Spring, 25–28.

Bunker, K. (2008). Responses to change: Helping people manage transition. *Ideas Into Action Guidebooks*. Center for Creative Leadership.

Bushman, S. (2013). Creating an internal certificate program. *Infoline*, 1302: February. ASTD.

Calisir, F., and Calisir, F. (2004). The relation of interface usability characteristics, perceived usefulness, and perceived ease of use to end-user satisfaction with enterprise resource planning (ERP). *Computers in Human Behavior*, 20(4), 505–515.

Cameron, M. (2009). *Oracle General Ledger Guide: Implement a Highly Automated Financial Processing System*. Oracle Press.

Clark, R.C. (1999). *Developing technical training: A structural approach for the development of classroom and computer-based instructional materials*. International Society for Performance Improvement.

Clark, R.C., and Mayer, R.E. (2003). *E-Learning and the Science of Instruction*. John Wiley & Sons, Inc.

Clark, R.C., and Lyons, C. (2004). *Graphics for Learning: Proven Guidelines for Planning, Designing and Evaluating Visuals in Training Materials*. Pfeiffer.

Clark, R.C. (2010). *Evidence-based training methods: A guide for training professionals*. ASTD Press.

Communication briefings. (1993a). Get your idea accepted. *Communication briefings*, January, 6.

Communication briefings. (1993b). The power of just one word. *Communication briefings*, January, 6.

Connellan, T.K., and Zemke, R. (1993). *Sustaining Knock Your Socks Off Service*. American Management Association.

Coscarelli, W., and Shrock, S. (2008). Level 2: Learning—five essential steps for creating your tests and two cautionary tales. *Four Levels of Training Evaluation: Reaction, Learning, Behavior, and Results*, Chapter 29, 511–521.

Creasey, T.J., and Stise, R. (2016). Best practices in change management 2016: 1120 participants share lessons and best practices in change management. Prosci.

Cuevas, R.F. (2019). *Course Design Formula: How to Teach Anything to Anyone Online*. Learn and Get Smarter.

Davenport, T.H. (1998). Putting the enterprise back into the enterprise system. *Harvard Business Review*, 76(4), 121–132.

Davis, F. D. (1989). Perceived usefulness, perceived ease of use, and user acceptance of information technology. *MIS Quarterly*, 13(3), 319–340.

DeLone, W.H., and McLean, E.R. (1992). Information system success: The quest for the dependent variable. *Information Systems Research*, 3(1), 60–95.

DeTuncq, D. (2012). Demystifying measurement and evaluation. *Infoline*, 1211: November, 20-22. ASTD.

Detz, J. (1993). Proven ways to prevent and deal with speech nerves. *Communication briefings*, 12(10), 8a–b.

Domenick, K., Gallup, D., and Gillis, M. (2007). Build credibility for the training function. *Infoline*, 0709: September. ASTD.

Duarte, N. (2008a). Seven questions to knowing your audience. Slide:ology course handout. Duarte.

Duarte, N. (2008b). *Slide:ology: The Art and Science of Creating Great Presentations*. O'Reilly.

Duarte. (2024, October 11). Want more influence at work? Try these simple vocal techniques. https://www.duarte.com/blog/want-more-influence-at-work-try-these-simple-vocal-techniques/.

Duplaga, E.A., and Astani, M. (2003). Implementing ERP in manufacturing. *Information Systems Management*, 20(3), 68–75.

Eliason, K. (2023, December 11). Tips for a successful post-mortem. https://www.portent.com/blog/marketing-strategy/tips-for-a-successful-post-mortem.htm.

Emelo, R. (2012). Mentoring: Bridging the competency divide. *Chief Learning Officer*, September, 26–27.

Esteves, J., and Bohórquez, V.W. (2007). An updated ERP systems annotated bibliography: 2001–2005. Instituto de Empresa Business School Working Paper No. WP 07-04.

Fletcher, A. (2023, December 11). A better approach to after-action reviews. *Harvard Business Review*. https://hbr.org/2023/01/a-better-approach-to-after-action-reviews.

Fred, C. (2001). *Breakaway: Deliver Value to Your Customers—Fast!* Grand River Press.

Friedman, P.G., and Yarbrough, E.A. (1985). *Training Strategies from Start to Finish*. Prentice Hall.

Galbraith, M.W. (2004). *Adult Learning Methods: A Guide for Effective Instruction*. Krieger Publishing Company.

Gerard, A., and Goldstein, B. (2005). *Going visual: Using Images to Enhance Productivity, Decision-making and Profits*. John Wiley & Sons, Inc.

Google. (2024, February 22). Developers style guide. https://developers.google.com/style.

Grosnick, P. (2001). Dealing with resistance. In Peter Block, *The Flawless Consulting Fieldbook and Companion* (pp. 91–94). Pfeiffer.

Grossman, T., and Walsh, J. (2004). Avoiding the pitfalls of ERP system implementation. *Information Systems Management*, 21(2), 38–42.

Gottfredson, C., and Mosher, B. (2010). *Innovative Performance Support: Strategies and Practices for Learning in the Workflow*. McGraw Hill.

Gottfredson, C., and Mosher, B. (2012). *The learner's five moments of need*. Conference handout.

Gupta, A. (2000). Enterprise resource planning: the emerging organizational valuesystems. *Industrial Management & Data Systems*, 100(3), 114–118.

Hamerman, P.D. (2007). ERP applications 2007: Innovation rekindles among the ashes of consolidation. Forrester Research. June 8, 2007 (updated June 19, 2007). Id 41883.

Harvey, E.L., and Lucia, A.D. (2012). *144 ways to walk the talk*. The WALK THE TALK Company.

Haugen, H., and Woodside, J. (2010). *Beyond Implementation: A Prescription for Lasting EMR Adoption*. Magnusson Skor Publishing.

Hertzum, M., Hansen, K.D., and Andersen, H.H.K. (2009). Scrutinising usability evaluation: does thinking aloud affect behaviour and mental workload? *Behaviour & Information Technology*, 28(2), 165–181.

Jarvis, P., Holford, J., and Griffin, C. (2003). *The Theory & Practice of Learning*. Kogan Page.

Kadakia, C., and Owens, L.M.D. (2020). *Designing for Modern Learning: Beyond ADDIE and SAM*. ATD Press.

Kapp, K.M., Latham, W.F., and Ford-Latham, H.N. (2001). *Integrated Learning for ERP Success: A Learning Requirements Planning Approach*. St. Lucie Press/APICS The Educational Society for Resource Management.

Kelley, H. (2001). Attributional analysis of computer self-efficacy. Dissertation. School of Business Administration, University of Western Ontario.

Kirkpatrick, D.L., and Kirkpatrick, J.D. (2006). *Evaluating Training Programs: The Four Levels (3rd Edition)*. Berrett-Koehler Publishers.

Knowles, M. (1996). *The Adult Learner: A Neglected Species*. Gulf Publishing Company.

Kouzes, J., and Posner, B. (2006). Values cards: A leadership challenge resource. Kouzes-Posner.

Landry, L. (2019, April 3). Why emotional intelligence is important in leadership. Harvard Business School Online. https://online.hbs.edu/blog/post/emotional-intelligence-in-leadership.

Lyman, F.T. (2022). *100 Teaching Ideas That Transfer and Transform Learning: Expanding Your Repertoire*. Routledge Taylor & Francis Group.

Masie Center. (2004). *701 eLearning Tips*. Masie, E. (Ed). The Masie Center.

Masie Learning Consortium. (2012). Project report: A fresh look at the classroom. O'Brien, C. (Project lead). The Masie Center.

Matey, B. (2002). Training and system implementation impact study: 'But we just got used to the old system.' Dissertation. College of Human Resources and Education at West Virginia University.

McChesney, C., Covey, S., and Huling, J. (2012). *The 4 Disciplines of Execution: Make Your Most Wildly Important Goals Happen*. Free Press.

Medved, M.B. (2022). *The Guide to Working with Subject Matter Experts (SMEs): Key Strategies to Bring Expert Knowledge to Workplace Learning*. Gopublished.

Microsoft. (2023, January 16). Microsoft Writing Style Guide. https://learn.microsoft.com/en-us/style-guide/welcome/.

MIT. (2022). The five building blocks for digital transformation. *Digital Transformation Design*, MIT Sloan Business School Management Executive Education course.

Morgan, R. (2022, November 21). How to do RACI charting and analysis: A practical guide. IOSH. https://www.iosh.co.uk/~/media/Documents/Networks/Branch/Humber/Branch%20Presentations/how-to-do-raci-charting-and-analysis.pdf?la=en.

Nah, F.F., Tan, X., and Teh, S.H. (2004). An empirical investigation on end-users' acceptance of enterprise systems. *Information Resources Management Journal*, 17(3), 32–53.

Bibliography

Neal, A., and Sonsino, D. (2012). Developing a leadership strategy. *Infoline*, 1209: September. ASTD.

Paine, N. (Ed). (2011). Learning strategies. New York: The Maise Center, 2011.

Paloff, R.M., and Pratt, K. (2003). *The Virtual Student: A Profile and Guide to Working with Online Learners*. John Wiley & Sons, Inc.

Paradigm Learning. (2023, March 26). How to communicate corporate vision and strategy to employees. Discovery Map Client Story. https://www2.paradigmlearning.com/hubfs/Resources/CS%20Courier.pdf.

Parks, N.E. (2011). Assessing ERP usability: A user-centered and business-focused approach. Thesis. McCallum School of Business Human Factors in Information Design at Bentley University.

Parks, N.E. (2012). Testing and quantifying ERP usability. *RIIT'12—Proceedings of the ACM Research in Information Technology*, 31–36.

PeopleSoft. (2002). Corporate backgrounder. Accessed September 4, 2011. http://web.archive.org/web/20020103053327/http://www.peoplesoft.com/corp/en/about/overview/corp_back.asp.

Phelan, P. (2010). ERP support: Organizational frameworks for ERP/Business application training. *Gartner Research Note*, G00208123: November 9.

Phelan, P. (2012a). ERP training best practices. *Gartner Research Note*, G00238656: September 12.

Phelan, P. (2012b). Methods for delivering ERP/business application training. *Gartner Research Note*, G00239116: September 28.

Pike, B. (2008). *Creative Training Techniques Newsletter*, 21(7): July.

Pike, B., and Pluth, B. (2008). Creative Training Techniques™ for Webinars. The Bob Pike Group.

Pike, R.W. (1994). *Creative Training Techniques: Tips, Tactics and How-To's for Delivering Effective Training*. Lakewood Books.

Reynolds, G. (2008). *Presentation Zen*. New Riders.

Reynolds, G. (2023, September 27). Delivery tips. https://www.garrreynolds.com/delivery-tips.

Rosenberg, M. (2022, January 15). Marc my words: Testing your eLearning strategy. Learning Guild. https://www.learningguild.com/articles/1063/marc-my-words-testing-your-elearning-strategy/.

Rossett, A., and Gautier-Downes, J. (1991). *A Handbook of Job Aids*. Pfeiffer & Company.

Saldanha, T. (2019). *Why Digital Transformations Fail: The surprising disciplines of how to take off and stay ahead*. Berrett-Koehler Publishers, Incorporated.

Salvatore, P. (2015). *Working with SMEs*. Balboa Press.

SAP. (2011). Gulfstream. Education Best Practice Awards Presentation.

Scherer, E. (2005). Results of the ERP user satisfaction survey: Conclusion for the real-world scheduling. i2s GmbH, Zurich. www.hops-research.org/.../M10_62_108200521387xzhhtjyqncedrxz.pdf .

Scott, J.E. (2005). Post-implementation usability of ERP training manuals: The user's perspective. *Information Systems Management*, 22(2), 67-76.

Shank, P. (2021). *Write Better Multiple-Choice Questions to Assess Learning*. Learning Peaks.

Spring Laurel, D. (2007). Conducting a Classroom Audit. *Infoline*, 0707: July. ASTD.

Stolovitch, H.D., and Keeps, E.J. (2002). *Telling Ain't Training*. American Society for Training and Development.

Sumathi, P. (2014). What's your learning brand? *Chief Learning Officer*, June, 12.

Thalheimer, W. (1996). Talk in Providence, Rhode Island.

Thalheimer, W. (2022). *Performance-focused Learner Surveys: Using Distinctive Questioning to Get Actionable Data and Guide Learning Effectiveness*. Work-Learning Press.

Toenniges, L., and Patterson, K. (2008). Managing training projects. *Infoline*. ASTD.

Transperfect. (2013). Localization best practices. Transperfect.

Velada, R., Caetano, A., Michel, J.W., Lyons, B.D., and Kavanagh, M.J. (2007). The effects of training design, individual characteristics and work environment on transfer of training. *International Journal of Training and Development*, 11(4), 282–294.

Whaley, R.L. (2005). *Training End Users to Use ERP Software*. Accolade Publications.

Whatfix. (2022, July 2025). What is digital adoption? https://whatfix.com/digital-adoption/.

Wheatley, M. (2007). ERP training stinks. *CIO*, June 11, 86–96.

White, J. (1988). *Graphic Design for the Electronic Age*. Watson-Guptil Publications.

Wick, C.W., Jefferson, A.M., and Pollock, R.V. (2008). Learning transfer: The next frontier. *The ASTD handbook for workplace learning professionals*. Biech, E. (Ed). ASTD, 271–281.

Williams, M. (2022). *Doing to Done: Productivity Made Simple*. Doing to Done, LLC.

Wood, S.D., and Kieras, D.E. (2002). Modeling human error for experimentation, training, and error-tolerant design. The Interservice/Industry Training, Simulation & Education Conference (I/ITSEC). https://web.eecs.umich.edu/~kieras/docs/GOMS/Wood_IITSEC2002.pdf.

Wu, J.H., and Wang, Y.M. (2007). Measuring ERP success: The key-users' viewpoint of the ERP to produce a viable IS in the organization. *Computers in Human Behavior*, 23(3), 1582-1596.

Yeh, J.Y. (2006). Evaluating ERP performance from the user perspective. *IEEE Asia-Pacific Conference on Services Computing (APSCC'06)*.

Index

About the Author

MISSY PARKS has spent her career empowering people to navigate the digital age with confidence. Her journey began in Washington, DC, where she introduced professionals across industries to the world of personal computers and software, with a focus on revolutionizing page layout, printing, and business operations. After moving to Vermont, Missy brought her expertise to noted ice cream maker Ben & Jerry's, teaching everyone—yes, even Jerry and Ben—the ins and outs of new technology. She then joined Green Mountain Coffee Roasters, which later became Keurig, where her role evolved into leading technical training teams driving large-scale digital transformations. Along the way, Missy earned a master's degree in human factors and usability. She published research measuring the impact of interface design and digital learning on people's ability to complete a standard task. Over the years, she has spearheaded digital transformation training programs and led remarkable teams that have prepared tens of thousands of learners to thrive during times of business change. After relocating to Minnesota, her training work expanded in size and scope and broadened into business transformation leadership roles, building upon technical expertise, human learning, and business change. Missy believes wholeheartedly in the power of digital transformation training to not only deliver measurable business success but also create an engaging and enjoyable experience for learners.

An avid learner, Missy attends classes and events weekly, tends a community garden plot in summer, and travels as often as she can. She volunteers with and supports organizations promoting community, education, women, children, and the arts.

www.ingramcontent.com/pod-product-compliance
Lightning Source LLC
Chambersburg PA
CBHW051751200326
41597CB00025B/4511